THE SANDS OF TAMANRASSET

T0165966

THE SANDS OF TAMANRASSET

The Story of Charles de Foucauld

BY

MARION MILL PREMINGER

CRAVEN STREET BOOKS
FRESNO, CALIFORNIA

124689753
The Sands of Tamanrasset
by
Marion Mill Preminger

© Hawthorn Books, Inc. 1961.
Published by arrangement with Dutton, a division of Penguin Putnam Inc.

Cover art and map by James Goold
First Craven Street edition 2002

ISBN: 0-941936-75-9

Library of Congress Cataloging-in-Publication Data
Preminger, Marion Mill.
  The Sands of Tamanrasset : the story of Charles de Foucauld / by Marion Mill Preminger.-- 1st Craven Street ed.
    p. cm.
Originally published: New York : Hawthorn Books, 1961.
Includes bibliographical references (p.   ).
  ISBN 0-941936-75-9
  1. Foucauld, Charles de, 1858-1916. 2. Hermits--Algeria--Biography.
I. Title.
  BX4705.F65 P7 2002
  271'.97--dc21

A Craven Street Book

Linden Publishing Inc.
2006 South Mary
Fresno CA 93721
800-345-4447
www.lindenpub.com

Scripture quotations in this book are from
The Catholic Bible, St. Peter's Edition, Hawthorn Books, Inc. NY

To His Excellency the Cardinal,
the Eminent Archbishop of New York,
and Vicar of the Armed Forces of the United States
FRANCIS SPELLMAN
whose great heart and simple human qualities
are even more memorable than the titles
of his high office are impressive—
as a sign of my deep gratitude
for his personal friendship,
and his tolerance and patience with me—
this book is most humbly dedicated.

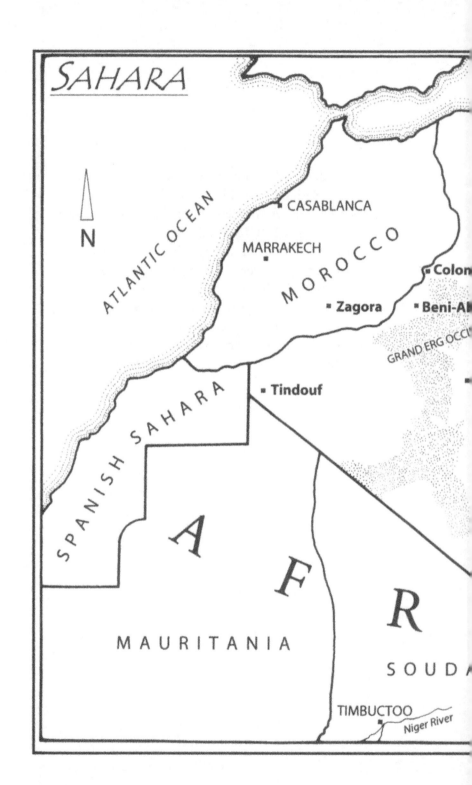

FOREWORD

Charles de Foucauld is undoubtedly one of the most fascinating religious figures of the last century. Part of his enduring appeal reflects the great drama of his personal story, so well recounted in this excellent biography.

He began his life as a spoiled aristocrat. He pursued a career as a military officer, but showed no evidence of special gifts or abilities beyond the satisfaction of his considerable appetite. It is clear, however, that beneath this appearance of indolence, there was all the while an appetite for something deeper. It was awakened, curiously, by his exposure to Muslim piety during a military engagement in Algeria. There followed a dramatic conversion and return to the Catholic faith of his childhood, after which he left his old life behind, determined to walk in the footsteps of Christ.

Foucauld pursued his calling quite literally. He moved to the Holy Land and lived in Nazareth for some years, walking in the actual village streets where Jesus had lived. It was from this experience that he achieved his essential insight: that Christ, though Son of God, had spent most of his life as a humble carpenter in an obscure village in Galilee. He had embodied the Gospel in its entirety before he ever embarked on his public ministry of teaching and healing.

This became the foundation for Foucauld's unique vocation. First in Nazareth and then among the Muslim nomads in North Africa, he set out to emulate the "hidden life" of Jesus, proclaiming the Gospel not simply by words but by his life of prayer and humble service. He conceived of a new religious order, the Little Brothers of Jesus, who would live out this vision. But at the time of his death in 1916 he had not attracted a single follower. His life was apparently a complete failure.

And yet Foucauld's story is more than a fascinating tale of spiritual adventure. Many regard him as one of the most important Christian witnesses of our time—a true prophet, who speaks to our own age even more urgently than he did to his own. For one thing he anticipated a new model of contemplative life, not in a cloistered monastery, but in the midst of the world. Thus he overcame the artificial divide between "religious" and "secular" worlds, pointing to a way of holiness that is accessible to everyone, in whatever "desert" we may find ourselves.

Foucauld's approach to mission is particularly significant. In contrast to the triumphalistic models of his day, Foucauld exemplified an evangelism of "presence," a willingness to encounter people of other faiths on a basis of equality and mutual respect. Although his asceticism was extreme by the standards of most missionaries or even of the Trappist monks with whom he lived for a time in Syria, he essentially embraced the poverty of his neighbors. He wanted to bear witness to the Gospel by living it, by being a friend and brother to all. He knew how much the church undermines the credibility of its witness when its representatives enjoy a status and comfort far above the level of the poor.

Today as never before we are realizing the crucial need of improved understanding between Christians and Muslims. Foucauld was himself killed by members of a Muslim sect whose fundamentalist zeal has obvious contemporary counterparts. And yet if Foucauld's path had been more characteristic of the encounter between Christians and Muslims in the past, who can say whether history might be different. In an age when Christianity is no longer synonymous with the outreach of Western civilization and colonial power, the witness of Foucauld—poor, unarmed, stripped of everything, relying on no greater authority than the power of Love—may well represent the face of the future church, a church rooted in the holy memory of its origins and its poor Founder.

After a century exhausted by grand projects, world wars, and ostentatious display, Foucauld's appreciation for the value of inconspicuous means, modest goals, and the hidden life of faith and charity, exerts a powerful and subversive challenge. It reminds us, among other things, that Christ himself pursued the path of apparent failure, choosing "what is low and despised in the world, even things that are not, to bring to nothing things that are" (1 Cor 1:28).

One final note: At the end of this biography, the author speculates about the prospects of Foucauld's eventual canonization. In April 2001, eighty-five years after his death, the Vatican issued an official "decree on the virtues" of the Servant of God Charles de Foucauld. This marked the final step, pending a miracle, to his eventual beatification. After remarking on the many levels of resemblance between Foucauld and Jesus, the decree takes note of the many men and women who have followed his example and teachings: "Thus came true once more the word of Jesus when he said, 'Unless a wheat grain falls on the ground and dies, it remains only a single grain; but if it dies, it yields a rich harvest.' (Jn 12:24)."

Robert Ellsberg
June, 2002

Robert Ellsberg is Editor in Chief of Orbis Books. He has written and edited a number of books including *Charles de Foucauld: Essential Writings.*

PREFACE

When I first spoke of the idea of writing this book about Père Charles de Foucauld, the reaction of my friends could be sharply divided into two kinds.

The Americans said: "Who is Père de Foucauld?"

The French asked: "Why another Foucauld biography?"

The first question convinced me that the project was a sound one. If, despite the fact that thirty-odd books have already been written about Charles de Foucauld, a half-dozen or so available in English, there are still intelligent, well-read people who have not heard about this remarkable man, then surely his life story needs retelling.

The same answer might, in a measure, be given to the second question. Why, in fact, have so many books been written about this roistering cavalry officer who became a Christlike figure? Each succeeding author, I am convinced, has felt that his predecessors have in some manner failed to present a true and complete portrait, or that their examination of Foucauld's conversion and intense religiosity has been inadequate or badly interpreted. In other words, each author's approach to this amazing life has been subjective.

My own approach is likewise personal, and I suppose somewhat emotional. I first learned to know and admire Father de Foucauld on my first visit to Africa ten years ago. That trip ended by my flying to Tamanrasset in the Hoggar highlands of the Sahara on my first pilgrimage to the spot where Père de Foucauld lived and died in the spirit of Christ.

I was so moved by his life story that during the succeeding years I made other pilgrimages to the chief points of three continents which figured prominently in Charles de Foucauld's existence: from Strasbourg where he was born (in a house once occupied by Rouget de Lisle, composer of *La Marseillaise,* now torn down to make way for a branch of the Bank of France), to Beni Abbès, site of his first African hermitage, and El Goléa, the oasis where his bones now lie. I spent many days in the library in Algiers where he prepared for his history-making Moroccan exploration, and in the Archives Nationales in Paris where much of the Foucauld documentation is housed.

At this point I knew why I had to write about Charles de Foucauld: I didn't only admire him; I loved him. However, I wanted objective confirmation of my inner convictions, so I consulted four eminent men of widely divergent backgrounds: Thornton Wilder, French scholar and Pulitzer-prize-winning author, whose knowledge of France and the French and whose judgment in literary matters I had regarded as infallible for twenty years; Dr. Albert Schweitzer, conservative, erudite theologian and Nobel prize winner who has been the authoritative voice of Africa for forty-seven years; His Excellency, Jacques Maritain, former French Ambassador to the Vatican, the great Catholic philosopher and now professor emeritus at Princeton; and Professor Louis Massignon, one of the most outstanding living authorities on Arabic culture, disciple of Father de Foucauld, and his last surviving friend.

Mr. Wilder not only encouraged me, but wrote me a long and considered letter in long-hand which I still cherish. He is one of the great letter writers, and in a few lines he pictured a whole era more vividly than it has been done in many a book. He wrote:

> I think you can usefully explore the Vicomte de Foucauld's identification with the cult of *Dandyisme* which had many followers in the 1860's, 70's, and I think up to the 80's. There were groups of exquisites who carried the *raffinements* of dress and manners to the point of decadence. To us now they would seem to be mere tiresome *poseurs.* Barbey d'Aubervilly led a lobster on a string through the Palais Royale! But Baudelaire, a powerful but tormented intelligence, wrote the defense of *Dandyisme* and raised it to a demonstration of a state of mind that strains toward an extreme—partly repudiation of the mere

conformity of society at that time; and partly in an effort to create a *Lebensstil* that was, in its way, perfect. They had courage in that they braved ridicule, and they had intensity.

Since they believed in no values of the spiritual tradition, they sought to create an art of living as beautifully as it can be done in this world. Often absurd, it was nevertheless an effort to achieve a difficult and extreme perfection. The same writers and *viveurs* in Paris borrowed another word from the English language: Spleen, which they interpreted as boredom, black, menacing boredom. *Dandyisme* was their attempt to find a mode of living that would rescue them from *Spleen*.

That movement has left an important mark on French literature: Baudelaire's prose pages in defense of *Dandyisme* and a notable poem called *Spleen*. Joris-Karl Huysmans wrote a novel, *À Rebours*, which contains a portrait of a hero, Des Esseints, who is the complete exemplification of the Dandy—almost unreadable now in its lush emphasis on luxury and exotic bric-a-brac. Mallarmé wrote a poem inscribed to Des Esseints. The last Dandy was Proust's friend, a Comte de Montesquieu-Fezansac, a little-read author now.

The important thing for your book is that both Baudelaire and Huysmans became intensely religious. Baudelaire's last poems and last journals are of a terrible penitence and religious earnestness. Huysmans wrote the outstanding Catholic novels of the time and not surpassed by Mauriac—*l'Oblat* and *La Cathédrale*. In other words, the same inner drive which as worldings pushed them to the extremes of *Dandyisme*, drove them later to the extremes of religious abnegation. The Vicomte de Foucauld eating pâté de foie with a small golden spoon undoubtedly came under the influence of that *époque;* and he has himself left us powerful statements of the extent to which, even as a Dandy, he was obsessed by an overwhelming boredom, a *spleen,* from which he sought relief by joining the army, then by the admirable map-making trip through Africa. . . .

Somewhere you can very fruitfully draw up a comparison between St. Francis and Le Père Foucauld. Le Père Foucauld seems to have fixed his gaze so completely on Christ that he did not find any help or consolation in the figure of St. Francis. Yet both started out in search of a total *depouillement*. Francis achieved it also. But Francis was a great preacher. Foucauld was not . . .

Much as I respect and admire Thornton Wilder, for the first time in my life I must disagree with him. I do not believe that Charles de Foucauld was influenced by *Dandyisme,* or made a sort of religion of extreme sophistication. While he may have shared something of their exhibitionism, he was not a true sophisticate. He was a simple creature at heart. I doubt very much that he ever heard of *Dandyisme* or its prophets. Certainly there is no evidence in the archives that he did.

Dr. Schweitzer, although he approved of my writing this book, was also at variance with my appraisal of Father de Foucauld. For Dr. Schweitzer, world authority on St. Paul the Apostle, Foucauld was an important personality but not a saint—a great African figure, yes, but even as a missionary and a priest, a crusader for the French spirit and, wittingly or unwittingly, an agent of French civilization and political aims. Dr. Schweitzer considered him as a great patriot rather than as a great martyr who died for his religious beliefs.

With these two distinguished gentlemen disagreeing not only with me but with each other, no one could have been more surprised than I to find that Professor Jacques Maritain disagreed with both Thornton Wilder and Dr. Schweitzer and agreed with me. He believes that Father de Foucauld was indeed worthy to follow in the footsteps of the Apostles. "According to the dictionary and Catholic tradition," he said, "an Apostle is an ardent propagator of the Faith who has renounced all well-being and all satisfactions of life. Charles de Foucauld was certainly such a man."

As for Louis Massignon, he has long considered himself as one of the spiritual heirs of Father de Foucauld. It is not surprising, therefore, when I asked him to appraise Foucauld's life, that he should tell me: "As a matter of fact, there was not a single thing that he did, said, chose, used, or even thought that does not exactly follow the rule of Christ."

But my reason for writing this book remains the same: I not only admire and revere Charles de Foucauld; I love him.

MARION MILL PREMINGER

Tamanrasset, 1958
New York, 1961

CONTENTS

LIST OF ILLUSTRATIONS

ONE

THE GALLANT FOREBEARS

I

The fantastic life story of Viscount Charles Eugène de Foucauld began some nine hundred years before he was born.

The earliest date which genealogists connect with the name of Foucauld is 970 A.D. In this year the Sire Hugues de Foucauld, a plump and pious landholder of Périgord, a region of southwesterly France already famous for its fat geese and succulent truffles, decided that he had had his share—or perhaps somewhat more than his share—of material success and the good things of life. The time had come, said the Sire de Foucauld, when a man should turn his back on the sweet white wines of Monbazillac and Montravel, on the chicken pies with salsify, on the pink-cheeked girls of Sarlat and Périgueux, and give heed to matters of the spirit.

Some of his sharp-tongued neighbors declared that the sudden awakening of Sieur de Foucauld's interest in things spiritual was due to a decline in his bodily functions, notably his digestion, and the onset of gout, rheumatism, and the vapors. However the gossips very probably did not believe their own malicious talk, for they came eagerly to the great feast the Sire de Foucauld gave for his friends, serfs, and tenant farmers upon his retirement from the world. A dozen cattle were barbecued, a hundred jars of preserved goose were opened, and scores of *ballottines* of hare, stuffed with brandy-soaked truffles and goose-livers, were consumed by the merry-makers. Thereafter Hugues de Foucauld presented his worldly goods to the neighboring abbeys of Chancelade and St. Pierre d'Uzerches and withdrew to a monastery to end his days in the worship of God and the adoration of Jesus Christ.

The Sire's descendant of some ten generations later was less contemplative in his devotion to God and Christianity. Bertrand de Foucauld was a man of action as well as of piety. In 1248 he kissed his wife and children goodbye, bade farewell to hearth, home, and France, and joined King Louis IX—later to become St. Louis—in the sixth Crusade to rescue the holy places of the Middle East from Moslem domain.

Bertrand de Foucauld and his king sailed from the walled port city of Aigues-Mortes. The expedition stopped at the island of Cyprus, then governed by the French feudal family of Lusignan, for supplies and consultation. It was here that St. Louis decided against a frontal attack on the Palestinian coast. Since the Holy Land had been overrun by the Egyptians, the Crusaders would accomplish a double purpose by attacking Egypt first. Thus they would not only destroy the Moslem overlords of Palestine but they would protect their own flank before swinging north to Jerusalem.

A brave man, this de Foucauld was in the forefront of the lancers who established a beachhead on the Nile delta. The Egyptian sun flashed on lances, armor, and suits of mail as the men and panoplied horses landed from the offshore galleys. In a matter of days Damietta fell and the cross was planted on Mohammedan soil. With the colorful flutter of the Crusaders' pennants all about him, sweating like a horse inside his armor, Bertrand de Foucauld fell to his knees and thanked God.

It took the Crusaders many months to consolidate their positions at Damietta in preparation of moving south across the Nile delta to attack Cairo. Meanwhile the Moslem troops were not idle. Under Ayubite Sultan Turanshah they were preparing a warm welcome for the Christian forces at El Mansurah, fifty miles up the river and one-third of the distance to Cairo.

While the Christian fervor of St. Louis, Bertrand de Foucauld, and the French Crusaders was certainly equal if not superior to the fanatic zeal of the Infidels, the Sultan's men had the advantage of terrain and surprise. In April, 1250, the Crusaders attacked. They marched straight into an ambush.

The magnificently bedecked horses were panicked by the smell and squealing of camels. Scores of the animals stampeded into the Nile and floundered helplessly while their riders were cut down. Arab foot soldiers darted among the Crusaders to hamstring their horses from the rear. The French forces were cut to pieces at Mansurah. King Louis and the survivors were taken prisoner.

Bertrand de Foucauld was not a survivor. When his horse was killed beneath him, he continued fighting on foot. When his lance was broken, he slashed at his attackers with his saber. When cut down at last by an Arab scimitar, he died with the praise of God on his lips, a valiant example of an upholder of the de Foucauld device *"Jamais Arrière!"*

St. Louis was soon ransomed, but spent some years in Palestine, visiting the holy places he had been unable to liberate from the Infidel's domination. In 1254 he returned to France and his throne. Five years later he yielded Périgord (and the remaining Foucauld estates) to Henry III of England in return for English recognition of French claims to Normandy and the North.

The Foucaulds, however, remained faithful to the French throne. Two more centuries passed. Louis IX had long since been canonized St. Louis. The dynasty had deteriorated. Charles VI had lost his mind and most of France when Jean de Foucauld became chamberlain to the Dauphin. And when the Dauphin became King Charles VII in 1422, Jean de Foucauld was one of his trusted counsellors. He was one of those who advised the King (almost without a kingdom) to listen to Joan of Arc. When the Maid of Orleans had thrown the English out of much of France and decreed that the timorous, vacillating King Charles should have a proper coronation at Rheims like every French monarch worth the name since the first Clovis, Jean de Foucauld approved. And when the future St. Joan placed the crown on Charles' head with her own hands, Jean de Foucauld stood at her side in the nave of the great Rheims cathedral on that momentous July 17 of 1429.

The Foucaulds continued to be courtiers for the succeeding several generations, but they did not interest the historians much until great-grandson Gabriel figured prominently in the short life of another Dauphin, the son of Henri II and Catherine de Medicis, who was to become King François II. The Dukes of Guise were considerably more influential at the French court than the Foucaulds at this time, but when the contemporary Duke de Guise decided that his little niece Mary Stuart would make an excellent future Queen of France (as well of the Scots), he sent Gabriel de Foucauld to Scotland to arrange the marriage. Henry II blessed his mission. The Dauphin (who at that time was four years old) was not consulted.

Gabriel de Foucauld sailed for Scotland in July, 1548, when the Straits of Dover and the North Sea should have been fairly comfortable for a landlubber. However, he is reported to have thanked God devoutly when the royal sloop at last beat its way into the Firth of Forth to land the matrimonial mission at Leith. A carriage was waiting to bear Monsieur de Foucauld toward the first scenic foothills of the Highlands and Stirling Castle to be presented to Mary Stuart, Queen of Scots.

Her Majesty had been queen for nearly five years when Gabriel de Foucauld presented his credentials from the French court. Her father James V of Scotland had died just a week after her birth, and when she was crowned queen at Stirling Castle the following year, she was not quite a year old. She was six when Gabriel de Foucauld came to ask her hand for the Dauphin.

The marriage agreement was signed by the Scottish regency, and Matrimonial Envoy de Foucauld returned to France with Her Majesty the Queen, her dolls, and her governess.

In October of that year Mary Queen of Scots was sent to Saint-Germain-en-Laye to be educated with the royal children of France. On April 24, 1558, she married the Dauphin in Notre Dame cathedral in Paris. She was not quite sixteen, her husband was fourteen. The following year the teen-agers were crowned king and queen of France—and Gabriel de Foucauld's mission was accomplished.

It was not his fault that the teen-age King François II was to die tragically seventeen months later or that Mary would ultimately lose her own life to the headsman.

Two more generations of Foucaulds lived and died before we find the name spread again on the pages of history. This time it was another Jean de Foucauld—Jean III.

Jean de Foucauld III seemed to have inherited all the characteristics of his earliest forebears—a devotion to France and his native soil of Périgord, a great liking for the good things of life (of which Périgord produced a bountiful supply), a brotherly regard for his fellow men, and a devout love of God. It was only natural that he should have hit it off well with a king like Henri IV who is reputed to have been weaned on Jurançon wine and a clove of garlic and who proclaimed his wish that each worker in his kingdom should have a chicken in the pot every Sunday.

There is some evidence that Jean de Foucauld may have helped influence the Huguenot monarch's decision to embrace the Roman Catholic faith. There is also good reason to believe that he was in some measure responsible for the restitution of Périgord to the French crown. When Henri IV brought this ancient province back into the fold after more than three centuries, he wrote a letter to his "good and trusted friend," expressing his esteem "of you and your virtues," and naming him Count of Périgord, Viscount of Limoges, and Governor of both.

The fortunes of the Foucauld family had come a full cycle. They were home again in Périgord—and in France.

II

As they walked in the garden of the monastery that September day of 1792, the two men knew they were going to die—they had more or less come to Paris under the shadow of death. Both knew that they could save their lives by a single stroke of the quill pen, and each knew that neither would sell his soul by such a betrayal of principle. But their features showed no fear, no sign of distress. They were at peace with themselves and with their God.

The tall, white-haired ecclesiastic was Jean-Marie du Lau, Prince-Archbishop of Arles. The younger priest with the greying temples was his cousin and grand-vicar, Armand de Foucauld de Pontbriand.

As Armand de Foucauld was the fifth of eleven children, his

older brothers had inherited the Périgord estates retrieved by his great-great-grandfather. Armand himself, however, was a poor man by choice. His piety and charity, after his ordination as Canon of Meaux, had attracted the attention of ill-starred King Louis XVI who gave him the commendam of the Abbey of Solignac near Limoges, not far from the Abbey of St. Pierre-d'Uzerches which had been endowed by his ancestor Hugues de Foucauld eight centuries earlier. Armand de Foucauld gave most of the revenue from his commendam to the needy.

At the outset of the French Revolution, one of the first acts of the National Assembly in 1790 was to equalize clerical salaries and the extent of bishoprics; and to decree the election of the higher clerical officials who would thus become civil servants and be required to swear allegiance to the new revolutionary constitution. The Archbishop of Arles immediately wrote a tract condemning the law as an attempt by anti-clericals to usurp episcopal rights and to split the church. Although addressed primarily to the clergy of his archdiocese, the Archbishops' remonstration was circulated throughout France and endorsed by hundreds of churchmen, among them his grand-vicar, Armand de Foucauld.

On May 26, 1792, the Assembly decreed that clerics refusing to take the civil oath were to be deported. The Archbishop of Arles left for Paris to protest. Grand-vicar de Foucauld joined him there in time for both to be arrested on August 11.

The two men were imprisoned in the old Carmelite monastery on the Rue de Vaugirard which had been confiscated by the Revolutionaries.

Nothing could be more peaceful than the monastery garden as the afternoon shadows lengthened on September 2, 1792. The weeping willow beside the door leading from the cloistered hall was still green, but the long straight hedges of hornbeam were beginning to yellow with the signs of an early autumn, and the berries of the Japanese ivy that clothed the walls were turning red. It was indeed a quiet Sunday, yet the air of revolutionary Paris was redolent with death and rumors of death. Word had spread along the grapevine that the mobs were slaughtering priests at the Abbey of Saint-Germain-des-Prés not far away and that the gutters were running blood.

It was no surprise to Armand de Foucauld, therefore, when heads wearing red liberty caps appeared suddenly at the grilled windows, and the cloisters rang with shouts and profanity. The door beside the weeping willow opened and the bleeding body of a young priest tumbled down the six stairs to the garden. Instantly the doorway was blocked by the silhouette of Stanislas Maillard, the most militant and blood-thirsty of the anti-clerical revolutionists.

"Don't kill them so quickly," cried Maillard. "Let's try them first."

Maillard's ruffians swarmed into the garden—howling, drunken, sneering, with sleeves rolled up, their forearms bloody, their faces streaked with red from having mopped their brows with bloody hands. With pikes and sabers they awaited their victims.

Maillard's idea of a trial was simple enough. It consisted of one question addressed to each of the trembling priests: "Have you taken the civil oath?"

Then the priests were pushed down the stone steps where the butchers fought for the privilege of striking the first blow. Their cassocks were torn from them, they were slaughtered like sheep, and their nude and bleeding bodies stacked like cord-wood in the garden. A few of them, terrified by the smell of blood and the imminence of death, ran across the garden where by climbing on the stone statue of a monk they could scale the ten-foot wall. Four or five actually escaped. Most of those who fled, however, were shot down as their fingers clung to the top of the wall. Or they were cornered like animals before they could reach the wall, cut off by a dozen howling ruffians who pursued the black cassocks through the trees and shrubbery.

Sickened, the Archbishop of Arles and his cousin Armand de Foucauld walked slowly to the little oratory, dedicated to the Virgin Mary, at the other end of the garden. Their backs to the slaughter, they knelt to pray.

"Let us thank God," said the Archbishop, "that we have been called to seal our faith with our own blood."

"God grant," said Armand de Foucauld, who had just turned forty-one, "that I not be the last Foucauld to die for the glory of our Lord."

They did not hear the swish of the saber nor see the gleam of late sunlight on the pikes. They were on their knees when they fell—the one hundred nineteenth and one hundred twentieth martyrs to die that Sunday afternoon.

It would be more than a century before Armand de Foucauld's last wish would be fulfilled.

TWO

THE MAKING OF A HUSSAR

Between man's purposes in time and God's purposes in eternity there is an infinite qualitative difference.

—Kierkegaard

I

Charles Eugène de Foucauld, great-grand-nephew of the martyred Armand de Foucauld, gave no sign, in his early years, of great piety or dedication to the cause of the Lord. In fact, he was considered rather a nasty little boy, fat, headstrong, and stubbornly self-centered. By general concensus, he was one of the most perverse foot-stampers and blue-murder screamers in Strasbourg, where he was born on September 15, 1858.

The martyred Armand's older brother's direct line produced only army officers before it produced Charles' father, François-Edouard de Foucauld, a civil servant. François-Edouard did not appear to have inherited either the outstanding courage or sanctity which distinguished so many of his ancestors. He was a deputy inspector of Forests and Waterways for the Department of the Lower Rhine of which Strasbourg was the prefecture. A nervous, high-strung man, frequently in ill health, he was so often away from home that Charles remembered him only vaguely. Whatever piety Charles absorbed in his childhood he got from his mother.

Elisabeth de Morlet de Foucauld was indeed a pious bourgeoise who came not from a family of churchmen but of professional soldiers. How often had she told her son Charles about his great-grandfather Morlet who had fought with Napoleon. (There was only one Napoleon then, the great Napoleon.) Great-grandfather Louis de Morlet had been a major in command of artillery when the sun broke through the morning mists at Austerlitz, the battle field of the three emperors. During that day of December 2, 1805, the tide of battle had changed several times before the Russians and Austrians were finally thrown back. At one point a whole battery of great-grandfather's command had been silenced because shrapnel had killed or wounded the gun crews. Major de Morlet had shanghaied enough sound artillerymen from more fortunate batteries to form skeleton crews for his own guns, then, although wounded himself, he pitched in to swab, load, and fire so that none of his pieces was actually out of action for long. As a result the Emperor himself had given Great-grandfather de Morlet a battlefield promotion to colonel.

Maternal Grandfather Charles Gabriel de Morlet was also a colonel. A distinguished officer of engineers, he had just retired from active service when Charles de Foucauld was born. And Charles heard from his own lips the stories of his exploits under the last three Bourbon kings of France, as well as Napoleon III, which won him two promotions in the Legion of Honor—the red ribbon of Chevalier and the rosette of Commander. And when little Charles graduated from toddling to walking, silver-haired old Colonel de Morlet took him by the hand to show him the fortifications he had built in the Strasbourg region to keep the Germans on their own side of the Rhine.

Elisabeth de Morlet was born in 1830, of Colonel de Morlet's first wife who died soon afterward. She became the Vicomtesse de Foucauld at the age of twenty-four; her husband was ten years her senior. In their second year of marriage, she presented her husband with a son, christened Charles, who died in infancy —two years before the birth of the Charles who is the subject of this biography. A sister, Marie Inès Rodolphine, came along in 1861.

Mme. de Foucauld had Charles christened in St. Peter's Cathedral in Strasbourg on St. Charles' Day (Nov. 4) of 1858. She gave Charles a tiny altar for his room and always had a *crèche* in the house every Christmas. Unfortunately there were only six of them, for Mme. de Foucauld died in 1864 at the age of thirty-four. "May God's will be done," she murmured on her death bed, "not mine."

There is some indication that Mme. de Foucauld died of grief over her husband, who had developed deep melancholia, given up his job, and gone to Paris to consult physicians for symptoms which were never clearly defined. He lived with his beautiful and distinguished sister Inès de Foucauld Moitessier in Paris until he died—by his own hand, according to some—a few months after the death of his wife, bequeathing to his young son Charles the title of Viscount de Foucauld de Pontbriand.

II

The boy viscount and his sister Marie were adopted by his maternal grandfather, Colonel de Morlet, and his second wife, née Mlle. de Latouche. The indulgent old gentleman, like most doting grandfathers, spoiled his charges, particularly Charles whose tantrums he considered a sign of character. He paid no attention to sister Marie's complaints that Charles pulled her hair and otherwise tormented her. After all, a girl could not learn too early that in this world man is master.

Grandfather de Morlet first put the boy into the diocesan school of Saint-Arbogast and later into the Strasbourg Lycée. He himself gave the boy a taste for reading, particularly the classics, but although he exposed the lad to all the outer forms, he did not seem to arouse much interest in religion.

When the Franco-German War broke out in 1870, and the Prussian Legions goose-stepped into Alsace despite Grandfather Morlet's fortifications, the old colonel fled to Switzerland with his family. After the peace of Frankfort which gave Alsace to Germany, no patriotic Frenchman could return to Strasbourg, so Colonel de Morlet, now well past seventy, settled in Nancy, across the Vosges mountains from his beloved city, and about as close as he could get and still be in France.

Viscount Charles de Foucauld, now fourteen, received his first communion at Nancy Cathedral, a family event for which his Aunt Inès and his favorite cousin Marie Moitessier came all the way from their Château de Louye not far from Chartres. Cousin Marie brought him a present: a copy of Bossuet's *Exaltation of the Mysteries.*

At fourteen Charles also entered the Nancy Lycée which was already shaping more future illustrious men than most provincial French schools—men like Louis Lyautey who was to become Marshal of France and architect of French influence in Africa; Maurice Barrès, destined to become a noted author; and the two great mathematicians, Paul Appel and Henri Poincaré. In honor of the latter the school was later rechristened the Lycée Poincaré.

Young Foucauld was an average student at first, getting above-average grades in history and geography. However, he soon showed tendencies to prefer leisure to Latin, the erotic to the erudite, reason to religion. In spite of everything, he nevertheless managed to graduate at the age of sixteen and was summoned by his grandfather for a decisive conference.

"Charles, my boy," said the old man, twisting his snowy mustaches and stroking his white goatee, "you have reached a cross-roads. You must make up your mind what you wish to become as a man. There are many distinguished soldiers in your mother's family as well as among the Foucauld de Pontbriands. I can think of no more honorable career than the profession of arms. As an old engineer, I should of course like to see you enter the École Polytechnique. It is a proud and distinguished school, but I must warn you that it is a strict and difficult school. There is no toying with its academic standards."

"That's what I'm afraid of," said the young viscount. "I can't make head nor tail of logarithms. I am sure I could never manage the mathematics."

"My boy, I am sure that if you apply yourself—."

"What's wrong with Saint-Cyr, *mon grandpère?* I would just as soon be an infantry officer. Or cavalry. I much prefer horses to howitzers and bayonets to ballistics."

"Charles, you are growing lazy."

"Perhaps. If you would rather, I won't enter the army at all. There are so many roads to follow. And after all, we are rich, aren't we, grandfather?"

Colonel de Morlet shook his silvery head. He sighed.

"Very well," he said. "Saint-Cyr it shall be. But you will have to prepare. I will send you to Paris. You have the honor of two distinguished families to uphold."

"Don't worry, grandfather." Charles de Foucauld's smile had the peculiar quality of being at once cynical and engaging. "I won't let you down."

So everything was settled. The young viscount would become an army officer like so many of his forebears. In 1874 he left for Paris to enroll in the Jesuit school of Sainte-Geneviève in the Rue des Postes, a street which no longer exists. He was to prepare for his entrance to Saint-Cyr, the storied "West Point of France."

III

Viscount Charles de Foucauld hated school. First of all he was homesick. Even Paris was strange and unattractive—except for its fleshpots which he had tasted surreptitiously and found good. He admired the erudition of the Jesuits and respected their teaching skills, but he was bored by their school and skeptical of their faith. He no longer believed in God. He was drunk with youth and the heady sense of freedom. As he was to write later:

"At seventeen I began my second year in the Rue des Postes. I was all selfishness, all vanity, all irreverence, consumed by desire for evil. I was completely disoriented. . . ."

He wrote to his grandfather every other day, incredibly long letters, some of them thirty or forty pages long, all of them begging the old colonel to let him come home to Nancy. Colonel de Morlet was heart-broken but adamant. No Foucauld could back away from an entrance examination to Saint-Cyr. He might fail miserably but honorably, yes, but back away— never! He must remember the motto on the Foucauld coat-of-arms—*Jamais Arrière!* Never to the rear!

The young viscount did not have the courage to tell the old gentleman that he could never get geometry through his head and would probably be bounced at midterm. When the time came, however, and he learned that he was to be bounced not only because of his lack of familiarity with Euclid but because of his overfamiliarity with certain addresses in the Rue des

Moulins and the Rue Joubert, he begged the good Jesuit fathers to spare Colonel de Morlet's sensibilities. If he were allowed to continue his studies as an extern, he argued, his evil influence on his fellow students would be reduced to a minimum if not eliminated entirely. The Jesuits relented and reinstated him as a day student. Charles went to live with his Aunt Inès—always a stuffy household, in his opinion, and now a sad one because his favorite cousin Marie had recently married the Viscount Olivier de Bondy—although in his letters to his grandfather he complained that Aunt Inès too frequently served no wine but Tokay, which was corked.

In the Spring of 1876, however, the Jesuits sent him back to Nancy for good—theoretically for reasons of health. Grandfather Morlet engaged a tutor named Dumont, whom Charles upbraided for preferring Racine to Corneille and George Sand to Prosper Mérimée. Professor Dumont seems to have done a fair job, however, for in August of that year Charles squeaked through the entrance examinations for Saint-Cyr, somewhat to his own surprise. To his grandfather who deplored the fact that a Viscount de Foucauld should be admitted so near the foot of his class, Charles replied consolingly (if not very convincingly) that, on the contrary, his low standing would be an inspiration for him to reach the top during the following two years.

When Charles applied to the military academy in person, he was rejected for failure to pass the physical. He was overweight.

Perhaps by the grace of God (whose existence he doubted), perhaps by the grace of a telegram from Colonel de Morlet detailing the illustrious military names in the Foucauld ancestry, the medical examining board reversed its decision. And the plump Viscount Charles de Foucauld was accorded the right to wear the red-plumed kepi, the gold-fringed epaulets, and the white gloves of a cadet of Saint-Cyr.

He could not immediately exercise the right, however. In all the cadet quartermaster stores there was not one uniform sufficiently spacious of seat, wide of girth, or ample of collar to fit the Viscount. For several days, therefore, until a rush tailoring job could be completed, he drilled in civilian clothes and a kepi.

He was not a very prepossessing cadet. He bulged. His neck was too short and too thick. His flabby face was too round and without character, unless you accepted as a sign of character the red blob of sensuous upper lip that bisected his small black mustache. His hair was parted in the middle and plastered flat. His small, deep-set eyes were almost invisible between folds of fat, but at times they gleamed with the curious inner light of a dreamer.

Cadet de Foucauld, since he could not escape drill, went through the movements of the infantry manual like a sleep-walker. He rarely opened a book on military theory or history. Instead he read the ribald comedies of Aristophanes in Greek (although his Greek was far from thorough) and Plautus and Terence in Latin (which was not very good either), trusting to luck that he would somehow muddle through at examination time. When he felt particularly energetic and was not confined to quarters, he would walk the three miles to Versailles with pencil in hand and sketch pad under his arm. He got his highest marks in geography and topographical drawing.

His fellow cadets liked him. They called him "Piggy" but it was a term of affection, for he shared his debaucheries and his gourmandizing with them all. He spent money like a wind-jammer sailor just ashore from an eight-months run around the Cape.

He was graduated from Saint-Cyr in 1878, No. 333 in a class of 386, far below such classmates as Henri Philippe Pétain, future Marshal of France. His grandfather was spared from hearing this disappointing bit of news, for the old colonel had died earlier that year, leaving to the twenty-year-old Viscount de Foucauld 840,000 gold francs!

IV

Ordered to Saumur in the lovely Loire valley for a year's specialized training at the Cavalry School, Second-lieutenant de Foucauld devoted himself assiduously to transmuting his inheritance into pleasure.

His roommate was another shavetail of sufficiently aristocratic background to share his exquisite tastes: Second-lieutenant Antonio-Amadeo-Maria-Vincenzo Manca, son of the Duke of

Vallombrosa, who had Gallicized his name to Antoine de Val-
lombrosa. Young Vallombrosa came from an old and noble
Tuscan family, was born in Paris and was the same age as
Foucauld. Until he inherited his father's title, he was only the
Marquis de Morès.

The room which Foucauld and Vallombrosa occupied was
always well-stocked with the finest wines of France. Foucauld
experimented, of course, with the local vintages. He found
Rabelais' favorite Château Chinon to be too sweet, although the
rosé d'Anjou was quite pleasant. The sparkling white of
Saumur was also a charming little wine but not serious enough
to accompany caviar or his native Strasbourg foie gras studded
with the truffles of his ancestral Périgord. Only champagne was
worthy of that honor.

When he entertained in town, he took his guests to what
he had decided after preliminary but expert research to be the
best restaurant in Saumur—a place in the Hotel Budan operated
by a *fin-bec* named Martin who made a specialty of cold roast
partridge on toast, washed down with the best Alicante the
young viscount had ever tasted.

When he gave a dinner party in his quarters, he served the
choicest Corton that Burgundy could produce, and the great
château clarets of Bordeaux. He had bought all the Pontet-
Canet in the Budan cellars.

He would not smoke if he happened to be out of the cigars
made especially to his order. He never set foot inside a barber-
shop. The barber always came to his room to shave him, cut his
hair, and trim his mustache, an arrangement dictated as much
by necessity as by swagger. For hardly a week passed without
the wealthy second-lieutenant being confined to his luxuriously-
furnished quarters for some breach of discipline: shoes not
shined, bed improperly made, failure to observe lights-out,
reporting on sick call when in perfect health. . . .

There is no record of which military sin Viscount de
Foucauld was expiating that afternoon in early Spring which
found him stretched cozily upon his Louis XV divan, sipping
champagne and eating pâté de foie gras with a golden spoon,
when three fellow subalterns made a ceremonious entrance,
saluting gravely. As Foucauld eyed the black mourning bands

pinned to their sleeves, Lieuts. Vallombrosa, Maumené and Laperrine recited in unison: "We offer our condolence. The Commandant won't budge a centimeter."

"I didn't think he would," said Foucauld.

"He says he was being very lenient when he gave you only one week's confinement to quarters," said Henri Laperrine, "and that under no circumstances would he lift the quarantine before next Wednesday."

"Which means," added Maumené, "that you will miss the gala ball at Tours tonight. Our deepest sympathy."

"Mademoiselle Mimi must have been very disappointed when you wrote her not to come down from Paris for the ball," Vallombrosa added.

"I wrote her nothing of the kind." The Viscount was annoyed. "She's probably on her way now."

"That makes it doubly sad," said Maumené. "A beautiful girl like that alone in Tours. But count on our friendship. We'll take care of your sweetheart—very good care."

"You'll do no such thing!" Viscount de Foucauld banged down his empty champagne goblet with such force that it splintered into a thousand glittering shards. "I'll take care of Mimi myself. I'm meeting her in Tours this evening as prearranged."

There was a moment of awed silence. Then:

"You're crazy, Charles."

"I must be. My lovely cousin Marie de Bondy tells me so in every letter."

"Listen, *mon vieux*." Maumené put his hand on Foucauld's shoulder with genuine concern. "That lone stripe of yours isn't sewed very securely to your sleeve. Do you realize how little it would take for the Commandant to rip it off—gleefully?"

"I do," said the Viscount. "And do I have to tell you I'm a gambler. How much have you won from me these past two weeks? Three hundred louis? Four hundred? Anyhow, you know that a gambler can't win without taking chances. My luck is bound to turn tonight."

There was a knock at the door.

"That must be my barber," said the Viscount. "Would you

gentlemen like to pour yourselves a small libation while I'm being made beautiful for Mimi?"

He opened the door, and the most fashionable barber of Saumur made an obsequious entrance. As the barber unpacked his case and set out his instruments, towels, soaps, a pewter jug of hot water, and various nards and unguents, the visiting shavetails tried to slip past him to escape.

"Do not let me disturb you, messieurs," said the bush-bearded barber. "I have just come to shave the lieutenant. Perhaps my services would also—."

But the visitors were already well down the hall.

An hour later the sentry at the exit gate of the Saumur Cavalry School stopped a plump, bearded man in civilian clothes, carrying what was obviously a barber's home-service kit.

"Don't you remember me, *nom d'un nom?*" exclaimed the civilian with a beard. "I have been shaving Lieutenant Charles, Viscount de Foucauld."

The sentry waved him on.

At the same moment Monsieur Polycarp Plon, master barber of Saumur, was reclining on Viscount de Foucauld's Louis XV sofa, grimacing as he spat out a mouthful of Beluga caviar, and rinsing the fishy taste from his mouth with vintage champagne.

V

The blonde stood in the doorway of La Belle Tourangelle, her blue eyes anxiously scanning the brightly gas-lighted hall of the restaurant. Her perfect poise and the touch of makeup on her lips and cheeks idicated that she was not a daughter of the bourgeoisie; rather a girl of the theatre or the half-world of Paris. Her hour-glass figure was perfectly groomed, her long full skirt the last word of fashion, with just the proper amount of bustle. Her right hand sparkled expensively as she raised her fingers to appraise the angle at which her ultra chic hat was set upon her wheat-colored coiffure.

She had taken only a dozen exploratory steps into the restaurant when a plump, bearded civilian arose from his table and threw his arms around her.

She retreated two steps, her blue eyes round with indignation.

Two cavalry officers arose from adjoining tables, ready to spring to her defense.

The bearded one renewed his bear hug and kissed her.

She drew back her arm, preparing to slap him soundly, when he murmured: "Come now, Mimi chérie, why so belligerent?"

The girl shook herself free. She stared. "Charles!" she gasped. She kissed him at last. "You idiot!" she laughed. "You didn't tell me this was to be a masquerade ball."

"It isn't, my little cream puff."

"But you are out of uniform. . . . And the beard?"

"Come sit down. I will tell you all about it. I have already ordered dinner. We will start with *rillettes de Tours,* of course. Then some pike *au beurre blanc,* and a *tournedos flambé.* . . . What are you laughing at, my pretty one?"

"Your beard. I just can't resist pulling it." Still giggling, Mimi leaned across the table and tugged at her plump companion's chin whiskers. They came off in her hand, dropped from her surprised fingers, and splashed into the champagne which the waiter was at that moment pouring into Viscount de Foucauld's goblet.

The waiter backed away quickly, dropped the bottle into the ice bucket, napkin and all, and scuttled off to notify the maître d'hôtel of the suspicious-looking gentleman who was dining in disguise. The maître d'hôtel called a conference of his captains and after much whispering, nodding, and glancing at Foucauld, sent a chasseur for the police.

To the two local policemen who responded, the Viscount cheerfully displayed his identity papers and laughingly explained the situation. But the policemen were neither laughing nor cheerful. The matter was not one for the police of Tours. The military police function was in the province of the Gendarmerie Nationale. . . .

The two gendarmes and the brigadier who responded to the call had no better sense of humor than the Tours police. They were sorry but there was no alternative. The lieutenant must be escorted to Cavalry School at Saumur to face charges of being absent without leave, of conduct unbecoming an officer and a gentleman, of being out of uniform without authorization, and of violation of house arrest.

The departure from the restaurant was a tragi-comedy of confusion. In her moistly tearful adieus to her beloved, Mimi's golden locks got stuck to the Viscount de Foucauld's chin with the same traitorous spirit gum which had failed in its original purpose of anchoring the chin whiskers. Mimi's oath of eternal love and fidelity to her nonchalant cavalier was interrupted by the maître d'hôtel presenting a bill for the uneaten dinner and untouched wines. And Lieutenant de Foucauld's rigidly military bearing as he started for the door with his escort of gendarmes was somewhat disturbed by the appearance from nowhere of Lieutenants Laperrine and Vallombrosa, both in dress uniform, both ceremoniously solicitous.

"What filthy luck, Lieutenant," said Laperrine.

"But don't worry about Mimi, Lieutenant," Vallombrosa added. "As we told you before, we'll take good care of her."

"Very good care," said Laperrine.

Mimi sobbed.

Lieutenant de Foucauld's one-word reply will not be reproduced here, even though characterized by Victor Hugo, when attributed to General Cambronne in reply to a demand to surrender the Old Guard at Waterloo, to be among the most eloquent words in the French language.

VI

Colonel Jacquemin, Commandant of the Saumur Cavalry School, let the wayward viscount stew in his own Sauce Veloutée for several days before summoning him to account.

The Commandant's waxed cavalry mustache bristled as his titled culprit stood before him at last.

"What have you to say in your own defense, Lieutenant?" he growled.

"Nothing, sir." Foucauld's face was expressionless.

"Do you realize the seriousness of the charges against you?"

"Yes, mon Colonel."

"You know, then, that you have given me grounds to expel you from Saumur?"

"Yes, mon Colonel."

"And that expulsion means the loss of your commission and the end of your military career?"

The lieutenant nodded, seemingly unperturbed.

"And knowing the consequences of your ridiculous perform-ance, you risked your career for—for what, Lieutenant?"

"I had a rendezvous of long standing with a lady who was coming from Paris to meet me, *mon Commandant*. I simply had to keep the engagement. My personal honor was involved."

"You place your personal pleasure—honor, if you wish—above your honor as an army officer?"

"In this case, *mon Commandant,* the answer is yes. I know you do not understand, sir, because you refused my request to add an extra week to my confinement to quarters in return for one free evening in Tours. The matter happened to be very important to me, so I had to keep the engagement by whatever means available."

Viscount Charles de Foucauld was still standing at attention in front of the Commandant's desk. The Colonel now arose so that he might look at the culprit's face on the same level. Fou-cauld's plump features were still impassive, yet his eyes seemed to burn with a strange, unwavering, ethereal light.

The Commandant sat down again. He frowned, as he absently touched the ends of his mustache.

"I will take your case under advisement, Lieutenant," he said. "You may return to your quarters. You will be notified of my decision. Dismissed."

On the long walk back from the Commandant's office, Fou-cauld was stopped every few steps by a chorus of inquiries.

"How did you make out, Charles? . . . Did he cashier you, Piggy? . . . When do they tear off your insignia?"

He did not reply until he had reached the entrance to his quarters. Pausing on the door sill, he turned to announce:

"I am being guillotined at dawn tomorrow. You are all in-vited. The rum and cigarettes will be on me."

Solemnly he saluted. Then, breaking into a broad grin, he thumbed his nose at his fellow subalterns.

The woman had been announced to Colonel Jacquemin as Madame the Viscountess Marie de Bondy. She was tall and slim, dark of hair, and noble of bearing. She was young but she was poised. Her sensitive features exuded great charm as she explained the purpose of her visit, watching the Commandant's gray eyebrows rise in astonished arches. She sat quietly, her hands folded demurely in her lap, waiting for the grizzled colonel to speak.

"So you are a cousin of Lieutenant de Foucauld's," he said.

The Viscountess nodded. "I have heard he is in serious trouble," she said.

"That is a frequent occurrence, Madame."

"I know my young cousin is too proud to plead for leniency, so I have come myself to ask you, Colonel, that when you deal with my cousin's fate and future, you consider the distinguished service to France and the army rendered by so many of his ancestors."

"You are too late, Madame."

"Too late?" Mme. de Bondy half rose from her chair. Her face was ashen.

"I have already made my decision regarding your cousin," said the Commandant sternly.

"Is he—?" Mme. de Bondy swallowed audibly. "Are you dismissing him from the service?"

"I am giving him more time to ponder his sins." The Commandant chuckled. "I am extending his confinement to quarters from one week to four."

"You are very good, *Monsieur le Commandant*." Mme. de Bondy leaned back in obvious relief. "What kind angel prompted you to clemency?"

"No angel," said the Commandant gruffly. "I want to keep him in the army. The lad will make a good soldier. He has character. He has the stubborn courage of his principles, even if they are often distorted principles. When he learns discipline, he will be a first-class officer. Strong. His strength burns in his eyes. Have you ever noticed his eyes?"

"I have seen his eyes." Marie de Bondy looked at the floor. "May I visit the prisoner, *Monsieur le Commandant?*"

The colonel nodded and rang for his orderly.

Marie de Bondy paused outside the door of her young cousin's quarters and drew a deep breath. Why did she hesitate to knock after having come all the way from Paris on his account? She herself did not know exactly. There was a curious, undefinable quality about her relationship with Charles de Foucauld. There had always been a great affection on her part, but she had never been able to make it a maternal affection—her eight years' seniority was not quite enough for that—and Charles had always rejected the sisterly pose she had tried to assume.

She and Charles had met for the first time on August 9, 1869. She remembered because it was her nineteenth birthday and Colonel de Morlet had brought his grandson Charles to the celebration at Château de Louye, the summer home of Aunt Inès de Foucauld Moitessier and her husband, an elderly tobacco millionaire. At the birthday party, eleven-year-old Charles had danced with his Cousin Marie. The younger assorted relatives laughed and jeered at the sight of plump little Charles solemnly waltzing the svelte, lovely Marie, almost a head taller than he. And although their elders merely smiled tolerantly, Charles was stung with humiliation. With his usual contrariness, he had taken Cousin Marie into the garden where he had declared:

"Let them laugh. You are the most beautiful girl in the world and I love you. As soon as I come into my inheritance, I intend to marry you."

Even though she knew it was puppy love, Marie had been strangely flattered. And she did not laugh, because there was something terribly sincere about the boy's declaration.

Three years later, when Marie and her parents came to Nancy for Charles' first communion, he had declared to her:

"I hope you haven't forgotten what I told you on your nineteenth birthday. We won't have long to wait now."

He was fourteen then—old enough to know that he was talking nonsense. And he was not quite sixteen and preparing for Saint-Cyr when Marie had married Viscount Olivier de Bondy.

It was no secret that the marriage had been arranged by Aunt Inès. With characteristic Foucauld stubborn contrariness, Aunt Inès was determined that both her daughters should marry blue-bloods to compensate for her own union with a plebeian tobacco importer from a small town in the Vosges. Monsieur Moitessier (who was some twenty years older than

Aunt Inès) was a very wealthy and greatly traveled man, but he embarrassed his wife even more by his lack of the aristocratic *de* before his name than by his Munchausenesque stories of Mexico and New Orleans which he insisted on injecting into his wife's fashionable dinner parties.

So Marie had married the Viscount *de* Bondy and her sister Catherine had married a retired diplomat named Count *de* Flavigny.

Of course, Charles had always pretended—and she was sure it was just a joking pretense—that his old puppy love was not puppy love at all, but the great, enduring passion of his life. But he had not been bitter over her marriage. How could he be? Moreover, she had not come to Saumur to discuss adolescent nonsense.

Marie de Bondy's well-gloved right hand struck three light but resolute taps at the door of Second-lieutenant Charles de Foucauld's quarters.

A torrent of profanity burst forth behind the closed door.

"Ghouls! False mourners! Hypocrites! All right, come in and gobble the funeral meats, you bunch of cretins! Come in and drink the condemned man's wine!"

The door handle turned softly, the door opened timidly.

Foucauld was reclining on his favorite Louis XV divan, one hand clutching a half-empty goblet of Baccarat crystal, the other a small volume of Aristophanes exquisitely bound in hand-tooled Morocco. His round face was flushed with wine as he addressed his visitor without turning around.

"Why so quiet, conspirators? Who needs money now? How much this time?"

"Charles . . . ?"

At the sound of the familiar voice, Foucauld sat up suddenly. He turned. His whole manner changed. He smiled sheepishly. He exuded tenderness. His voice was gently solicitous as he said:

"My sweet cousin! I have been thinking of you constantly, hoping you might be moved to come and relieve the suffering of my cruel punishment."

"Cruel?" Marie smiled sadly. "You are very lucky, Charles. I fully expected to see you drummed out of the army."

"But four whole weeks!"

"Do you realize, Charles, that this is your forty-fifth breach of discipline? And for what? You must really love this woman to risk your whole career to see her."

"You know very well that there is only one woman in my life whom I have ever loved and will ever love." He heaved an exaggerated sigh. "But she betrayed me. She married another."

"Stop making calf's-eyes, Charles. I've come to talk seriously."

"But I am serious, Marie chérie. Always. Do you remember that I once told you I would marry you when I came into my inheritance? Well, for nearly a year I have been a man of independent means."

"And for five years I have been married, Charles."

"Then we will run away together. How many children have you now? Four? Then we will take the children along. We will go to Africa. I hear Africa is very good for children. Warm climate. Lots of fresh fruits. . . ."

"Charles, listen to me. You talk about your inheritance. Do you realize what you are doing to it? Have you any idea of the money you have been spending? Your tailor bills? Your boot-maker? Your tobacconist and wine merchants?"

"Not the slightest," said the Viscount de Foucauld.

"Do you think it was reasonable to spend 18,000 gold francs for I don't know how many bottles of Pontet-Canet?"

"I do indeed. It was a bargain. If there had been more of that wine in the Budan cellars I should have bought that, too. You, my dear, could never appreciate the value of a good Bordeaux because you have been brought up on that frightful Tokay your mother serves."

"And your huge gambling debts, Charles? And all the money you have been throwing away on—on this Mimi?"

"Look, my beloved cousin, have you come all the way to Saumur just to preach to me?"

"No, Charles. I've come to talk sense to you."

"Too late," said the Viscount. "Too late—by five years."

"Idiot! Charles, you really must get rid of this girl."

"Why? She fills a great need. She is as sweet as she is pretty. She loves me in her own way without making a fuss about it. She doesn't bother me when I'm thinking of other things. And she makes a highly-ornamental focus for an otherwise empty and aimless life."

There was a moment's pause. Marie de Bondy's lips parted, but she said nothing, apparently surprised by her cousin's sudden and unexpected instant of self-appraisal. At last she said:

"Charles, I came to Saumur because I wanted to warn you that my father and mother are outraged by your reckless spending. My father is going to ask the appointment of a trustee to manage your finances."

"I can't believe it!" Charles was on his feet. "Dear Uncle Moitessier can't do that to me."

"You underestimate my father when my mother makes up his mind. And you are, after all, still a minor—until September. Under the law he can have you declared in a 'state of prodigality.' And he will—unless you convince him that you can live reasonably and economically. Please try, Charles dear—for my sake as well as your own."

The young viscount's clenched jaws gradually relaxed. He smiled a little. He held out his arms, but dropped them limply when Marie de Bondy stepped back.

"How could any man help loving you, *ma chère cousine*," he said. "You are as kind and good as you are beautiful."

Marie colored slightly. Then she moved forward quickly and kissed Lieutenant de Foucauld on both cheeks.

"Au revoir, Charles," she said. "I will write to you. Remember what I have been saying."

The door closed behind her.

A few months later the class of 1879 was graduated from Saumur Cavalry School. Eighty-eight second lieutenants received their spurs and sabers as full-fledged cavalry officers. Lieutenant Charles de Foucauld was No. 87.

THREE

THE AMORIST AND THE ARMY

It is part of probability that many improbable things will happen.

—Agathon, 445–401 B.C.

I

With his fledgling fellow subalterns Foucauld was assigned to the Fourth Hussars, garrisoned in Lorraine. The little town of Pont-à-Mousson, on the Moselle, not far from his boyhood home of Nancy, was host to the Hussars for only a few months, but for years afterward Pont-à-Mousson was not quite the same.

The colorful, not to say gaudy, uniform of an officer of Hussars seemed to bring out the last extravagant ounce of all that was rebellious and licentious in the character of young Viscount Charles de Foucauld. The splendid plumed shako, the flowing cloak of the dress uniform, the magnificent gridiron of silken brandenburgs that covered the front of the sky-blue dolman, the scarlet trousers and the high, burnished boots—all seemed to proclaim that the French cavalry officer was the most glamorous creature on earth.

The revels which had won Foucauld so many demerits at Saumur were mere apprenticeship to his performance at Pont-à-Mousson. His cousin Marie de Bondy's warning of financial brakes about to be applied by her father seemed no more than a challenge to the wealthy lieutenant to increase his "state of prodigality." Instead of merely his roommate and a few select friends, all the junior officers of the Fourth Hussars were invited to partake of the fine wines and choice viands, the music and the feminine laughter that were the mark of a riotous Foucauld party—with the result that often the Viscount was asked to seek new lodgings.

Foucauld delighted in giving one of his parties on an evening when Colonel du Pont, commander of the Fourth Hussars, was entertaining the senior officers. Foucauld would then hire every fiacre in town so that the Colonel's guests were without transportation. In fact, he seemed to need an extra fillip to make any of his parties as satisfying as they used to be. On one occasion when he was confined to quarters and forbidden to receive visitors, he again hired the fiacre drivers, had them line up outside his quarters, turned on all his lights, and played the piano like mad, occasionally shrieking with laughter. When the officer of the day arrived with instructions from the Colonel to arrest all the roistering officers who were helping the profligate viscount while away the boring hours of his punishment in violation of orders, they found only Lieutenant de Foucauld, sitting alone at the piano, wide-eyed with innocent surprise.

On another occasion he stepped up the pace of a happy evening by having the coffee made with boiling *quetsch,* a spirit distilled from the small purple plum of Alsace-Lorraine, instead of boiling water.

And of course there was Mimi.

During Foucauld's tour of duty at Pont-à-Mousson, Mimi was promoted from a part-time caprice to a full-time girl-friend. Mimi was a dancer of small talent but great physical appeal. A girl of humble origin, she was quite willing to forego critical acclaim in favor of sympathetic notice from gentlemen in a proscenium box or the first three rows of the orchestra, particularly gentlemen who sent flowers to a girl's dressing room. Mimi —Marie Cardinale, as she was billed in rather small type—was obviously not first attracted to Charles de Foucauld because he was the most handsome cadet at Saint-Cyr. It is quite probable that she more impressed by his credit with Rue de la Paix jewelers and Rue du Faubourg Saint-Honoré fashion houses, than by his plump silhouette or even his title of viscount, which did not buy many sables under the republic.

Although the beginning of their affair was certainly mercenary on her part, there is no doubt that once the liaison was

established, Mimi was loyal to her lieutenant in the best tradi-
tions of the code of the Paris demi-monde, which in that period
was almost as rigid, although admittedly less permanent, than
the bonds of matrimony. She grew sincerely fond of Foucauld,
was tenderly responsive to all his moods, and always tried to
please him in the most delicate manner.

In return, of course, she had the best Paris couturiers at her
service and in Pont-à-Mousson a suite at the best hotel and a
yellow-wheeled dogcart in which she could follow the Fourth
Hussars on parade.

From one part of Foucauld's life, however, Mimi was strictly
barred: that of his family. The viscount had inherited Grandfather Morlet's apartment in Nancy, just an hour's train ride
from Pont-à-Mousson. He frequently organized a week-end
binge for his fellow officers at his boyhood home, but Mimi
never came along.

One subaltern of the Fourth Hussars who often came was
the Duc de FitzJames, who was to become one of Foucauld's
lifelong friends. Despite his name, FitzJames' family had been
French for generations. The first Duke of FitzJames was (as
the name indicates) an illegitimate son of James II. When his
royal natural father was forced from the throne of England in
1688, the first FitzJames crossed the Channel, became a naturalized Frenchman, and served in the French army as Marshal
de Berwick. There had been a FitzJames in the French army
ever since.

It is from the memoirs of Lieutenant de FitzJames of the
Fourth Hussars that many details of Foucauld's life at Pont-à-
Mousson have come to light. In particular FitzJames remem-
bers having been provoked into a duel by some hot-head in
the regiment, and that his friend Foucauld had wanted to take
his place on the field of honor.

As Viscount de Foucauld became progressively more and
more bored by his own parties, he increased his efforts to outdo
himself. Why was he bored? If he was not titillated by his own
revels, his guests must also be bored. He would remedy this
sad state of affairs.

In December 1880, the River Moselle was frozen over at
Pont-à-Mousson—the ideal setting for a winter carnival. Fou-

cauld had a safe sector of the ice roped off and swept clear of drifted snow. He obtained from the regimental *maréchal des logis* the shoe sizes of all his guests, then bought ice skates for them all. He had a sleigh built in the shape of a swan in which Mimi would ride as he introduced her as "honorary colonel." He brought an orchestra and entertainers from Paris and hired caterers from Nancy. He himself selected the wines—enough champagne to float away the cares of a regiment, or at least of its junior officers.

On the afternoon of the winter gala, just as Charles de Foucauld was about to leave his quarters to supervise the caterers who were unloading their tables and provisions on the snowy banks of the Moselle, FitzJames rushed in with a breath-taking piece of news.

"The Fourth Hussars have been ordered to North Africa!" he announced. "We leave within the week."

"Good," said the viscount. "I need a change of scene."

"But what about Mimi?"

"Well, what about her?"

"I hope she doesn't take it too hard. She's awfully attached to you, you know. Would you like me to break the news?"

"Certainly not. Don't even mention it to her. Let her enjoy the party."

"Very well. But afterward, don't forget, I'd be glad to smooth the way."

"Stop worrying about Mimi," Foucauld said. "I haven't made up my mind about her yet. Come along and sample the champagne and pâté de foie they've brought over from Nancy."

By nightfall, buffet tables laden with mouth-watering delicacies lined the river bank, and torch-bearers lined the roped-off area of the ice. The frosty breath of the skaters made little clouds in the wavering torchlight. A great bowl of hot Martinican rum punch flanked each end of the buffet and at regular intervals the torches were put out while more steaming rum was floated on the punch and set afire. What went on in the flickering half-light of the blue flames could only be guessed from the feminine squeals.

The host watched glumly as the torches were lighted again and his fellow officers, with swoops, curlicues and figure-eights, propelled Mimi around the ice in her swan sleigh. Mimi was having the time of her life. She was radiant, wrapped in furs, her hands hidden in a muff. Her cheeks glowed with the cold. A few blonde ringlets escaping from her mink toque gleamed copper in the torchlight. Her laughter was a silvery trill above the baritone chorus of tipsy Hussar officers.

Yes, they were all enjoying the party except the host. Why, the Viscount mused, couldn't he share their fun? Everything had been perfect, and he had the prettiest girl of the lot. Why? It was certainly not because of the news that the Fourth Hussars had been ordered to Algeria. That, in fact, was rather exciting news. . . .

"Did you have a good time?" he asked Mimi as she snuggled against him in the carriage going home.

"Yes—and no, *mon chéri.* Of course it was a magnificent evening. . . ."

"Then why the 'no'?"

"Because you were not enjoying it, *mon chéri.* I was watching you, and you were sad. And so I was sad, too, because I know why."

"Why?"

"Several of your comrades said that the Fourth Hussars are going to Africa. Is it true, *mon chéri?*"

"Yes, we have been ordered to Sétif."

"That makes it more beautiful than ever. I am going to cry, *mon gros chéri.*"

"Don't talk nonsense."

"It is not nonsense that you should give such a beautiful farewell party for me. What a lovely way to say goodbye."

"Who's saying goodbye?" demanded the Viscount.

"But aren't you going to Africa with your Hussars?"

"Of course I am. And so are you, my little Mimi."

"I? But is it permitted for an officer to—?"

"Leave everything to me," said Charles de Foucauld.

He was suddenly overwhelmed in a flurry of fur while warm lips were pressed against his.

II

Mimi Cardinale crossed the Mediterranean in the style to which she had been accustomed by Viscount de Foucauld. The Viscount had engaged a deluxe cabin for her on a ship sailing from Marseilles several days ahead of the transport bearing the Fourth Hussars, a regiment which would be rechristened the Fourth Chasseurs d'Afrique upon reaching Bône. Her name appeared on the passenger list as Mme. la Vicomtesse de Foucauld.

Mimi carried off the role of Viscountess with great charm. She was certainly dressed for the part, and she knew how to achieve a balance between aristocratic aloofness and gracious condescension. She fascinated the captain, at whose table she was of course seated. And she could relax and laugh with the other ship's officers without in the least compromising her blonde dignity.

While port formalities were being satisfied at Bône, word of the lovely "Viscountess'" presence aboard ship was officially conveyed ashore, and the highest representative of the French Republic at Bône, the sub-prefect of the Department of Constantine, hurriedly donned his gold-braided ceremonial uniform to greet the distinguished visitor. The sub-prefect, too, was charmed, and was pleased to install the lovely "Viscountess" in a suite in the best hotel of Bône, atop the red cliffs, where, half smothered in sub-tropical greenery, she could look out over the blue Mediterranean.

Mimi was shrewd enough to get out of Bône before the arrival of the Fourth African Chasseurs and the wives of their senior officers. She was going on to Sétif, she explained to Monsieur le Sous-Préfet, to prepare quarters for Monsieur le Vicomte de Foucauld. She was infinitely regretful . . .

III

When Monsieur le Vicomte de Foucauld came ashore at Bône, he was the first Foucauld to set foot on African soil in more than six hundred years. He seemed to sense that he was going through some sort of historic experience. He could appreciate the beauty of the little port, of course, but it was the strangeness of the land and of the people that fascinated him. It was strange and yet it was somehow familiar, exactly why he could not tell. The swarm of ragged, grimy Arabs who were doing the physical labor of disembarkation, were more interesting than they were repulsive—particularly when they dropped all work, sank to their knees in unison, faced Mecca in the East, and touched their foreheads to the ground in prayer. It was only afterward that the Viscount could hear the stimulus which had set them off—the falsetto drone of a muezzin from the minaret of some unseen mosque, calling upon the faithful to bear witness to the fact that Allah is great and that there is no other god but Allah.

Charles de Foucauld was greatly impressed.

He was not impressed by Sétif which he reached after a dreary journey by rail some hundred miles inland. Surrounded by farm lands on a half-mile-high plateau, Sétif was a dismal bit of provincial France transplanted to Africa. It was provincial in every sense of the word. It had only one redeeming feature—Mimi, who had transformed a hotel suite into a homey, attractive nest. With rugs, brasses, tooled leather, and other products of Arab handicrafts, she had surprised and delighted her lover on his arrival.

Lieutenant de Foucauld was neither surprised nor delighted by the storm that was obviously gathering about Mimi's pretty blonde head. Although Mr. Kipling insists that the Colonel's Lady and Judy O'Grady are sisters under the skin, Mme. la Colonelle du Pont repudiated any relationship with Mimi Cardinale. In fact, Mme. la Colonelle was carrying on an active campaign to get Mimi out of Sétif and out of Africa. She began by upbraiding the poor Sub-prefect of Bône for not knowing that Viscount de Foucauld was a bachelor and for showering honors upon a woman who was so obviously a strumpet that she could not possibly have been a Viscountess. And in Sétif, she enlisted the willing help of shocked army wives not only to snub Mimi in shops, hotels, and in the street, but to bring organized pressure on the colonel to get rid of the false Viscountess.

At first Colonel du Pont passed on the pressure through channels, and it reached the Viscount only as a friendly admonition by his troop captain to be discreet and keep Mimi out of sight of Pecksniffian wives. The Viscount laughed.

When the colonel ordered his adjutant to repeat the admonition in stronger terms, the old Foucauld family stubbornness was aroused. The Viscount now made a point of appearing with Mimi in cafes and other public places where he was sure he would meet army wives.

Finally he was called to the carpet by the colonel himself. Colonel du Pont began with the paternalistic I-was-young-once-myself approach.

"Of course we can't expect you to lead a celibate life, my lad," he said. "A red-blooded young fellow like you is certainly not cut out to be a monk. But be discreet, Foucauld. Be discreet."

"Yes, *mon Colonel*."

"You say 'yes, *mon Colonel*,' but that's not enough. You know how army wives are, Foucauld. All wives, in fact. So promise me to keep her out of sight, will you? Or better yet, send her home."

"I'm afraid I can't send her anywhere, *mon Colonel*. She's here of her own free will and accord."

"Come now, Foucauld. She uses your name. Flaunts it, in fact. Registers as Mme. la Vicomtesse de Foucauld. Isn't that a bit steep?"

"She does it with my full permission, *mon Colonel*."

"But it infuriates the wives, Foucauld. Do me a favor, Lieutenant. Send her home. You'll find the local talent more than satisfactory, I'm sure."

"You are very kind, *mon Colonel*, but I'm afraid that I can give no orders to Mlle. Cardinale. She is a free agent. She came here freely. She likes it here, in spite of everything. She wants to be near me. How can I force her to return to France?"

"That is your problem, Lieutenant," the colonel said, "but fortunately it is not mine. I *can* give *you* orders. You are under my command. I command you to send this woman home."

"May I suggest, *mon Colonel*, that this order is hardly a matter of military import?"

Colonel du Pont sprang up behind his desk, his lips tight, his gray mustache bristling.

"I see," he said. "You choose to disobey my order?"

Lieutenant Charles de Foucauld did not reply. He was thinking not of Mimi but of the motto on the family coat of arms. *Jamais Arrière!* Why should he retreat now? He had taken an oath to defend the French Republic, not the wives of French army officers.

"Very well," said the colonel. "Either you will send this woman back to France, or I shall arrange to have you detached from my command and sent back to France yourself. I will give you twenty-four hours to decide."

The Viscount de Foucauld moistened his sullen lips. He had no desire to go back to France after only three months of Africa. He was intrigued by the new world opening up before him. He was touched by the loyalty of his Arab orderly and stable boy. He was amazed by the blind religious faith of both Arabs and Berbers he met in his trips into the field. And he had even started to learn both languages. Still, he was not going to be browbeaten by an aging army officer too uxorious to stand up against organized wifehood.

"Let's not waste time, *mon Colonel,*" he said at last. "I have already decided."

"You realize the consequences of whatever decision you may have made?"

"I do, sir."

"Then you agree to send this woman back to France?"

"No, sir. I refuse."

"Very well." The colonel sat down. His frown was puzzled. "I will refer your case to the War Ministry in Paris. You will be apprised of the outcome. I am sincerely sorry."

"I'm sure you are, sir."

Ten minutes later, over an excellent bottle of Algerian wine from Mascara, the Viscount re-enacted the scene for Mimi, with gestures and roars of laughter. Mimi did not laugh very much.

On March 20, 1881, Second-lieutenant Charles de Foucauld, by order of the Minister of War, was placed on inactive service by reason of insubordination and conduct unbecoming an officer and a gentleman.

IV

When Charles de Foucauld returned to France that Spring, he brought with him not only his lovely blonde Mimi but something of Africa as well. The Dark Continent, long reputed to be a seducer of men's souls, had apparently already cast her notorious spell upon the viscount. His three months in Sétif and particularly his patrols into the surrounding Kabyle country had given him a taste for more, and he had actually regretted having to leave the country. And he took along textbooks of the Arabic and Berber languages and copies of the Koran both in Arabic and in French translation.

The former cavalry officer and his Mimi went directly to Evian, a fashionable watering place at the foot of the French Alps where a man and his sweetheart could sit on the broad veranda of an expensive hotel and look out across the blue waters of Lake Geneva into Switzerland. He was not interested in the mineral springs; the hotel had a good cellar and an excellent chef.

Mimi was a joy, as ever, always eager to share his gregarious moods, ever ready to go into eclipse when he was deep in his books. The fact that they could now live together openly without fear of being ostracized or called to military account may have removed some of the spice from the situation as far as Foucauld was concerned, but Mimi liked it. Nobody in Evian cared whether she was Vicomtesse with or without benefit of clergy, and her lover, needless to say, did not show her the letters from his family.

The family letters were of course disapproving. Sister Marie was bewildered and questioningly reproachful. Cousin Marie de Bondy was sadly reproving. Aunt Inès and Uncle Moitessier were shocked, scandalized and furious that a Foucauld could wreck his career and disgrace his name over a demimondaine.

The young viscount shrugged, tore up the letters, and buried his nose in his books, looking for some key to the mysterious appeal of Africa and its Moslems.

He also pored over the newspapers—the *Journal de Genève*, because it arrived first; the *Echo de Paris*, because Grandfather Morlet always said it was an army officer's paper; and

Le Figaro because Aunt Inès and Cousin Marie de Bondy
looked upon it as required reading—for news of Africa. He
found plenty. The debacle of the Flatters expedition was still
causing resounding echoes in the French press. A few weeks
before Foucauld and Mimi had left Sétif, an expedition led by
Lieutenant-colonel Paul Flatters set out to explore the possibilities of a trans-Saharan railroad. The mission was ambushed
and cut to pieces in the Sahara nearly a thousand miles south
of Wargla. Many of the survivors were poisoned by Tuareg
tribesmen. The whole disaster, the question as to whether the
Flatters expedition had been ill-conceived and under-manned,
and whether the desert wastes of Africa were worth the ex-
penditure of French lives and treasure in the first place, raised
arguments throughout France. With Tunisia newly attached
to France by treaty and with Algeria finally pacified after fifty
years, why seek new trouble? The age of colonialism was at its
peak, however, and with French pride still smarting ten years
after defeat by the Prussians, the march of empire in Africa
had wide appeal.

The political aspects of the African situation bored Viscount
de Foucauld even more than did lovely Mimi, now that there
was no immediate and violent objection to the liaison. The
military angles, however, intrigued him. When a marabout
named Bou Amama took French indecision for weakness and
raised, in southern Algeria, the cry of *jihad*—holy Moslem war
against the unbelievers—Foucauld was doubly intrigued. When
a cavalry patrol from the Fourth Chasseurs d'Afrique was cut
to pieces by Bou Amama's men, his interest became personal,
and when early in May all four troops of the Fourth Chasseurs
(which barely six weeks earlier had been *his* regiment) were
despatched to the mile-high plateau south of Oran with orders
to kill or capture Bou Amama, his interest rose to fever heat.

For a whole day he alternately paced the veranda of the
fashionable hotel or sat brooding as he stared at the sullen
gray lake, cheerless under leaden skies. He thought of his soldier
ancestors: of Bertrand de Foucauld who had fought with Saint
Louis and died for God and King in Africa; of Great-Grandfather Louis de Morlet who had been promoted by Napoleon
on the battlefield of Austerlitz; of Grandfather Gabriel de

Morlet, Commander of the Legion of Honor, colonel of engineers, whose heart was broken when his fortifications failed to keep the Prussians from crossing the Rhine into Alsace, and who had suggested the Army as a fitting career for Viscount Charles de Foucauld. For the first time in his life Charles de Foucauld was aware of the warrior blood running in his veins.

As he thought of his comrades riding into combat, he realized that the army was more than merely the boring routine of barracks life, of discipline to be thwarted if possible and fought against always. The army was really a means of expression for a man who loved France, and who could push his love to the point of supreme sacrifice. The army was the place where a man could find out whether or not he was meant to be a soldier in the highest sense of the word.

Charles de Foucauld, when he had read for the twentieth time the account of his old regiment entraining for Saïda, decided that he was a soldier and the descendant of soldiers; that the family motto *"Jamais Arrière"* meant more than stubborn resistance to a colonel's order to send his mistress back to France; and that he must at all costs return to Africa.

Mimi, who had crept up behind her lover to kiss the nape of his neck, knew when the third caress brought no reaction that a radical change was going on within him. She silently withdrew to their room, leaving him still sitting in his chair, apparently unaware of her presence. She was not surprised, therefore, when he announced that night that they were leaving immediately for Paris.

In Paris Foucauld went at once to the War Ministry to ask for return to active duty. If his past conduct would not permit his resumption of duties as an officer of the Fourth Chasseurs d'Afrique, he offered to enlist as a private in the Spahis or as a trooper in a cavalry regiment. Inasmuch as graduates of Saint-Cyr and the Saumur cavalry school did not grow on trees, his proffered sacrifice was rejected.

On June 3, 1881, he was restored to his rank as second-lieutenant of cavalry and ordered to rejoin his old regiment in Africa.

That same night he took the train for Marseilles. His blonde, blue-eyed Mimi went to the Gare de Lyon to see him off. The

girl for whom he had so readily given up his military career
knew that she had lost on the second and final round. She had
won against the colonel's lady, but when the stakes were raised,
and a soldier had to decide between his girl and his country,
she had no chance.

She cried a little. She thanked him for the money he had
given her to live on until—. Until what? She hugged him
desperately, and kissed him as though she would never see him
again. When the station master shouted *"En voiture"* and the
shrill whistle piped the signal for departure, she ran alongside
the moving train, waving a little lace handkerchief until she
could no longer see his head at the window.

Second-lieutenant Charles de Foucauld had been on inactive
service exactly seventy-five days.

V

The domes and minarets of the mosques of Oran gave
Lieutenant Charles de Foucauld a queer feeling of home-
coming as he set foot on African soil for the second time. He
paused only long enough to check with military authorities and
pick up his transportation to Mascara, rear headquarters of
the Fourth Chasseurs d'Afrique.

From Mascara, a veritable metropolis of some thirty thousand
in the heart of the northern Atlas ranges, he went south to the
railhead where the supplies of the Chasseurs were trans-shipped
from freight cars to camel-back, then by horse with the supply
caravan over the high plateau to Géryville, where his regiment
was bivouacked at the foot of the Amour mountains.

The Fourth Chasseurs in the field bore little resemblance to
the Fourth Hussars of Pont-à-Mousson, or even to the Chasseurs of Sétif. First of all, the regiment had been strengthened
by a contingent of old campaigners, officers and men, who had
served with Louis-Napoleon's ill-fated expedition to keep
Maximilian on the throne of Mexico and who consequently
gloried in the nickname of "Mexicans." The Mexicans were
without doubt the toughest, most slipshod soldiers who ever
wore a French uniform, if it could be called a uniform after
the slovenly individualistic treatment they accorded it. And
they looked with something less than admiration upon an

elegant, well-fed, well-tailored garrison-type of officer such as
Lieutenant Charles de Foucauld. Even his fellow subalterns
from Pont-à-Mousson and Sétif had changed. They were lean
and brown from their service in the field, and they had shed
blood in combat.

The married officers were still resentful of the domestic
trouble Foucauld had caused them by flaunting his paramour
at Sétif, and greeted him coldly at mess. One old friend of
cadet days who welcomed him with open arms, however, was
Lieutenant Henri Laperrine, now bronzed and bearded, wedded to the profession of arms, and wildly in love with Africa.

At Géryville Foucauld also made two new friends who were
to become an integral part of his life: Captain Henry de Castries,
his troop commander, and Lieutenant Calassanti-Motylinski,
language officer, interpreter, and Arab expert.

It was from Motylinski that Foucauld learned the back-
ground of Bou Amama and his fanatic Senusi followers, the
raison d'être for his return to the army. Bou Amama—né
Mohammed ben El Arbi ben Bou Hafç—was a product of the
Ksour mountains, in the southern Oran province near the
Moroccan border. The country had long been controlled by the
Uled Sidi Sheikh—Sons of the Master Patriarch—who were in
almost constant revolt against French penetration, and who
were ripe for Bou Amama's organization of a Senusi zawia.
Although the Senusi sect, when founded in Mecca in the early
part of the nineteenth century was a puritanical and religious
fraternity of Moslems, it developed in North Africa as rabidly
nationalistic and anti-European, or merely as an outlet for
Arabs of homicidal and larcenous tendencies.

With Motylinski also Foucauld advanced his study of Arabic
and began his study of Berber. But his soldiering was by no
means confined to academic matters. The desultory horsemanship of the fat, fun-loving cadet was miraculously transformed
into the expert equitation of the seasoned cavalryman used to
spending all day in the saddle. The undisciplined subaltern, the
rebel against military authority, became a bold leader of men.

Riding at the head of his patrol, the young lieutenant ran
down every scent that might lead to the trail of Bou Amama.
He galloped rashly into ravines where more experienced

soldiers might have feared an ambush, trusting not only his instinct but the Arabs he had questioned as his own intelligence officer.

Foucauld was undoubtedly a fearless leader in his first brush with actual combat, but he was not quite as reckless and foolhardy as the "Mexicans" believed. The old campaigners of Puebla were convinced that no "native" could be trusted; that all non-Frenchmen were liars, cheats and thieves. Foucauld, however, was impressed by the great God-fearing qualities of the Moslems.

While returning from a reconnaissance mission one day, his patrol was jumped by a band of Uled Sidi Sheikh snipers hidden in the scrub growth of a hillside. The Chasseurs of course returned the fire. The skirmish continued for a good half-hour, with Foucauld calling at last for fresh ammunition supplies. There was no response from his own Arabs who had taken cover with the pack animals. Furious, Foucauld galloped back to read the riot act to his men—only to find them prostrating themselves in prayer. The sun had just set behind the hills and it was time for the faithful to turn their faces toward Mecca and proclaim the greatness and oneness of Allah.

On the opposite hillside too, the firing had stopped. At the risk of being shot like sitting ducks, the Uled Sidi Sheikh had emerged from cover, turned their backs to the sunset, and bowed down to the East in acknowledgment of the fact that there is no other god but Allah and Mohammed is his prophet.

Allah akhbar!

A strange silence filled the little wadi, a stillness that reminded Foucauld of the awesome quiet of Nancy Cathedral in his boyhood days when he still believed in God. That silence, in fact, had meant to the boy that he was indeed in the presence of God. He had laughed at himself since for such mawkish credulity, but he did not laugh now. These Arabs took God seriously. They had stopped fighting because it was time to pray to Allah. They had exposed themselves to possible massacre to prostrate themselves before their god, refused to neglect prayer even in the face of the enemy. How could such intensity of faith not be taken seriously? Curiously enough, even the hard-bitten cavalrymen of the patrol must have felt this, too, for not one shot was fired at the Moslems during the moment of prayer.

Ever since that evening in the foothills of the Djebel Amour, Foucauld would believe an Arab if he swore to Allah that he was telling the truth.

To most of his fellow officers who did not share his trust, Lieutenant Charles de Foucauld was nevertheless courageous beyond the call of duty. Even "the Mexicans" grudgingly admired him.

His men not only admired the lieutenant; they liked him. He was a blue-blood, but he was human. He knew the words to all the ribald marching songs. After a hard day under the blazing desert sun, he could manage to produce a bottle of rum to mitigate the horrid taste of drinking from a brackish water hole. The man who turned up his nose at his Aunt Inès' Tokay, who insisted that his champagne be vintage, and who bought out a wine cellar in Saumur because he liked the Pontet-Canet, now swallowed without a grimace the Algerian *pinard* which had not been improved by being transported for miles on camel-back across the burning desert. And the gourmet who used to eat truffled *pâté de foie gras* with a golden spoon now seemed to relish tinned corned beef which the French army called *singe*—monkey.

The transformation was complete. "The erudite rake" of Saint-Cyr and Saumur, as Henri Laperrine was to write years later, "had become a soldier and a leader, gaily undergoing the toughest ordeals, giving generously of himself, and devoted to his men."

The Fourth Chasseurs d'Afrique never caught up with Bou Amama. The elusive rebel chief vanished somewhere in the vastness of the desert or the trackless ranges of southern Algeria. With his disappearance, however, his influence over the dissident tribesmen also evaporated. The danger that the Senusi uprising might develop into a full-scale revolt passed, and the regiment was withdrawn to base at Mascara.

Foucauld did not welcome the move. He was appalled at the prospect of return to garrison life. Mascara would be Sétif without Mimi. Mascara was a French provincial small town with Arabs in the streets, not an ideal place either to pursue his love affair with Africa or to seek out the secrets of Islamic mysticism. Pursuit of his linguistic studies with Motylinski merely whetted his appetite to learn more about the Arabs at first hand. Poring over military maps of North Africa awakened in him a desire to penetrate deeper into the little-known continent. When his friend Laperrine was assigned to an expedition being organized to move south through Algeria to the Niger, Foucauld applied to join the detail.

Foucauld's Christmas present that year of 1881 was the rejection of his application.

The young lieutenant then went to the division commander with a plan for an expedition of his own. The military maps of Morocco, he pointed out to the general, were largely blank. Less than 15 per cent of the 60,000 square miles had been explored and mapped. Wasn't it time that more was known about this great and rich sultanate adjacent to Algeria? Lieutenant Charles de Foucauld would be glad to undertake such a mission.

The general was not impressed. He reminded Foucauld that the sultan of Morocco was hostile to any travel by Europeans in his domain. The few diplomatic missions were restricted to several large cities. Would-be explorers had been caught and killed.

"There was René Caillié, who traveled disguised as a Mohammedan student, and came back alive," said Foucauld. "There was also the Englishman Burton, who passed as a dervish. There was—."

The general interrupted him with a brusque exclamation. Enough nonsense. The lieutenant was too young and inexperienced to undertake such an expedition, particularly alone as he seemed to be planning. He was still a long way from finishing his training as a cavalry officer. Perhaps in five or ten years. . . .

Foucauld saluted and returned to his quarters, fuming. He was sure that the general's real reasons for vetoing his proposal had been unspoken—that on the basis of his record at Saint-Cyr, Saumur, and Pont-à-Mousson, and because of his defiance of Colonel du Pont at Sétif, he was regarded as unreliable and unstable. Well, he would show them.

On January 28, 1882, he wrote his resignation as second

lieutenant, "voluntarily and absolutely surrendering the prerogatives attached to this rank," and asking permission to withdraw to his home in Paris.

The general endorsed the letter of resignation with a remark that "this officer desires duty only in war time," so that when the viscount's papers were processed through bureaucratic channels, Foucauld's name was not dropped definitively from army rolls, as he thought, but placed on the reserve list.

He was twenty-three years old.

FOUR

RABBI IN MOROCCO

Quand on part en disant qu'on va faire une chose, il ne faut pas revenir sans l'avoir faite.

A man who goes off promising to do a certain thing must not return without having done it.

—Charles de Foucauld

I

Foucauld did not withdraw to his home in Paris, as he had intimated in his letter of resignation. When freed of his military duties in March, he left Mascara for Algiers, armed with letters from his friend Motylinski addressed to men who might help him organize an expedition to Morocco.

The man who took Foucauld to his bosom immediately was a Frenchman with the incredible name of Oscar MacCarthy, curator of the national library in Algiers, who, according to Motylinski, knew more about North Africa than any man alive. MacCarthy was the son of an Irishman who hated the English so much that he joined Napoleon's Grand Army to fight them. After Waterloo he had remained in France and became a naturalized Frenchman. His son Oscar had settled in Algeria in 1849 and when he was Foucauld's age had talked a reluctant governor-general into letting him explore the southern part of the country. He had been thwarted, however, in his effort to map a road across the Sahara to Timbuctoo, and he sympathized with Foucauld's frustration by army brass.

Convinced by MacCarthy that he would need at least a year

of preparation before heading for Morocco, Foucauld had rented quarters on the Rampe Vallée near the Marengo Gardens north of the Kasbah and was arranging lessons in advanced Arabic and Berber when the storm broke in France.

Aunt Inès, who had been overjoyed by Foucauld's reinstatement in the army after the scandal of Sétif, was devastated by her nephew's latest shocking behavior. How could he again wreck his career by a wilful, capricious, gesture? While Cousin Marie de Bondy wrote a tender appeal for common sense, Aunt Inès decided that the time had come for action, not words. She called on her husband to make good their threat of some years standing to have a trustee appointed to handle her nephew's affairs.

Uncle Moitessier brought action in court at Nancy, which was Viscount de Foucauld's legal residence since he had inherited his grandfather's home there. The court was asked to declare the viscount in a "state of prodigality" because since his graduation from Saint-Cyr he had squandered 110,000 francs— $22,000—of his 840,000-franc inheritance. Although a second lieutenant's pay was only a little more than 2,000 francs a year (about $35 a month) Lieutenant Foucauld's monthly expenses often ran to more than $800.

The court agreed that Foucauld was indeed an irresponsible spendthrift and appointed as his trustee a relative of his Grandfather de Morlet's second wife, Georges de Latouche. M. de Latouche summoned the young man to Nancy for an interview which he anticipated would be a tempestuous one.

He was surprised to find the prodigal quite docile, except in the matter of his Moroccan project. Aunt Inès had instructed M. de Latouche to try to dissuade her madcap nephew from his senseless and reckless expedition. In this he was unsuccessful. However, the ex-playboy did agree to live on less than ten per cent of his former budget. If his trustee would underwrite the cost of his expedition, he would manage to get along on a student's allowance of 350 francs a month ($70) out of which he would pay all his living expenses including his Arabic lessons.

Foucauld also asked permission to buy firearms and other gifts for an Arab prince he had been considering as a guide, but M. de Latouche, after toting up the cost, vetoed the proposition.

After a brief and rather strained visit with his family, Foucauld returned to Algiers.

II

Foucauld worked mornings with Oscar MacCarthy in the library, an exquisite example of Eighteenth Century Moorish architecture in the Rue de l'Etat-Major. The building had once been the palace of Mustapha Pasha, one of the last Deys of Algiers. While he could hardly ignore the fine carvings, the cedar panelings, the ceramic fountains in the courtyards, Foucauld was chiefly interested in the dusty, sketchy maps and the musty records of his few predecessors.

Afternoons he spent at the Admiralty, learning to plot latitude and longitude with a sextant, how to use an aneroid barometer, and how to transfer his data to a map. (In this he was already fairly adept; at Saint-Cyr he had scored 11 out of a perfect mark of 12 in topography.)

One of the first steps in his planning was to choose a proper disguise. Obviously he could not go into Morocco as a Christian; that was impossible under current conditions. Most earlier explorers had gone as Moslems, notably René Caillié, but MacCarthy counselled against this. Foucauld's Arabic, while improving, was still imperfect, and his accent would probably betray him. Moreover, he was bound to make some error in customs during the six to eight months he planned to remain in Morocco. Go as a Jew, MacCarthy advised. First of all, the Jews were a rootless people who came from many lands and spoke many languages, all with a foreign accent. Even those from the Mediterranean countries spoke Hebrew with varied accents, so Foucauld's accent would not give him away. Furthermore, the Jews were a small minority in Morocco; with centuries of abuse and persecution behind them, they would instinctively protect Foucauld from the Moslems, even though they saw through his masquerade. Therefore Foucauld would learn Hebrew, in addition to Arabic and Berber, and also a smattering of Ladino which was still spoken as a lingua franca by Jews exiled from Spain. And MacCarthy would find a rabbi to teach Foucauld the rudiments of the religion and customs to go with his assumed identity.

Foucauld's mentor and prospective guide was a man named Mordecai Abi Serour, whose first name the French had Gallicized to Mardochée. Rabbi Mordecai was certainly not chosen for his physical fitness for a hard and perilous journey. He was fifty-four years old, and his long black beard was streaked with white; he was half-blind, he did not hear well, and he was stooped with some sort of rheumatism. However, he did know Morocco (although not as much of it as he pretended), his rabbinical credentials were genuine, and he would make an excellent foil to the inexperience of the pseudo-rabbi.

Rabbi Mordecai had been born in southern Morocco, had studied in Marrakesh, Mogador, and Tangier before going to Jerusalem for the final two years leading to his rabbinate. Back in Morocco, he had decided to exploit a commercial connection he had made with some Syrians in the Holy Land, and abandoned the rabbinate for the market place. He set himself up as a trader in Timbuctoo. In a dozen years he amassed a fortune and was preparing to return to Morocco, marry, and found a Jewish colony in the Sudan when misfortune struck. Several of his caravans were attacked and pillaged. His brother whom he had left in charge of the business in Timbuctoo died, and all properties were confiscated by the local sultan on some flimsy pretext. Mordecai's voyage to Timbuctoo in an effort to recover his assets was in vain. On his return to his home in Aqqa, Morocco, he was captured by Arab bandits, robbed of his remaining fortune (gold dust worth $8,000), and barely escaped with his life.

Having lost caste in his home town for deserting the rabbinate Mordecai moved his wife to Mogador, did some odd jobs for the French Geographical Society, and ended up in Algeria where he taught Hebrew and lectured on the Talmud at Oran and Algiers.

MacCarthy brought Mordecai and Foucauld together in May 1883. Several months of negotiations followed, accompanied by numerous exchanges of correspondence between MacCarthy and Georges de Latouche, who had to approve all expenses before he paid the bills. Latouche also wanted to make sure Mordecai was a man who would see Foucauld safely through the madcap journey and could bring him back alive, for he had little confidence in his ward's practical abilities.

In May an agreement was signed by which Mordecai was to be paid 270 francs a month (about $54) which was a captain's pay and more than MacCarthy himself earned as librarian. Of this pay Mordecai received 600 francs in advance, part was to be paid to his wife in monthly installments during his absence, and the balance on Foucauld's safe return. Unknown to Foucauld, his sister had offered Mordecai, through MacCarthy, another 800 francs to be paid on her brother's safe arrival in Algiers.

Foucauld moved into the cramped quarters which Mordecai shared with his wife and four children to learn something about the customs of the Maghrebin Jews.

His traveling gear was scanty indeed, for MacCarthy had learned by his own experience that there was truth in the old Arab proverb: "A thousand thieves on horseback cannot rob a man who is naked." He carried an instrument case for his sextant, two aneroid barometers, compass, chronometer, and thermometers, and a medicine chest containing basic pharmaceuticals both for himself and to support his role (as first imagined) of Jewish doctor. He carried a bag containing cooking utensils, some provisions, and a change of clothing. For money he carried three thousand francs ($600) in gold and coral.

At dawn on June 10, 1883, Viscount Charles de Foucauld, former second-lieutenant of the Fourth Chasseurs d'Afrique, became Rabbi Josef Aleman, of Moscow, Jerusalem, and Algiers. In Rabbi Mordecai's one-room home he changed into the costume of the Levantine Jew: a long wide-sleeved shirt, linen knickers, a dark Turkish vest, a cowled white robe, white stockings and sandals, a red calotte surrounded by a black silk turban. The wisp of black mustache which had grown into a handle-bar cavalry mustache during the southern Oran campaign had now begun to droop and was augmented with a fringe of soft black beard.

An hour later Rabbi Josef and Rabbi Mordecai went down the steep, narrow, cobbled steps that passed for a street in the *mellah* (the Algiers ghetto) leading to the port and the railway station. While Rabbi Josef, né Foucauld, bought two third-class tickets in his worst French to match his attire, Rabbi

Mordecai was saying a noisy and tearful farewell to his family.

At seven o'clock in the morning the train pulled out for Oran —first stop on the road to Morocco.

III

The Moroccan expedition was marooned for two days in Oran because of the beginning of Shabuoth, the Jewish spring harvest festival which has somehow become associated also with the anniversary of Moses receiving the law from the Lord on Sinai. It was consequently impossible for two rabbis to travel on a holy day. Foucauld records that on arrival in Oran on the evening of the tenth, Rabbi Mordecai had gone to synagogue and brought home to their hotel room a co-religionist who happened to share Mordecai's secret passion for alchemy. Foucauld learned for the first time that his guide was a part-time seeker after the philosopher's stone, and he fell asleep listening to the two men discussing their experiments in the transmutation of mercury into gold.

At sundown on June 12 (Jewish holidays begin and end at sundown), Rabbis Mordecai and Josef boarded a stagecoach for the medieval center of civilization and learning that was Tlemcen. Foucauld had intended to enter Morocco from Tlemcen through the Riff, but Mordecai claimed to have picked up information from his fellow worshippers in Oran to the effect that the Riff was practically impossible for foreigners to traverse. Foucauld accused his guide of stalling and the argument lasted through most of the night journey. Foucauld said he would make a decision at Tlemcen.

They arrived in the ancient city early in the morning, and as they squatted in the dusty, sun-drenched square munching bread and olives, several subalterns of the Fourth Chasseurs d'Afrique came out of the Officers' Club and passed them within spitting distance. Foucauld recognized them all, and was pleased that his disguise was so perfect that one of his ex-comrades-in-arms made derogatory remarks about *les sales Youpins* (the dirty Sheenies). The officers were all sons of aristocratic families and made Foucauld think of his old roommate at Saumur, Antoine de Vallombrosa, the Marquis de Morès, who had just re-signed from the Army and gone off to America to make a fortune

suitable to his title. Morès had been a violent and voluble anti-
Semite and would probably have had a stroke had he seen
Viscount de Foucauld in his miserable role of Rabbi Aleman.

There was no Jewish hotel in Tlemcen, so Foucauld and
Mordecai rented a room for the night in the home of a Jewish
family. Mordecai had located a dozen white-bearded Riffian
Jews and had invited them for a drink so that he might question
them about entering Morocco through the Riff. After several
hours' discussion around a candle and a bottle of opalescent
anise-scented *pastis*, the meeting concluded that the best way to
get into the Riff was through the little fishing port of Nemours.
Mordecai told his co-religionist that he was seeking his wife's
brother who had disappeared two years before and was now
reported to be somewhere in the Riff.

Next day the pair moved on to Lalla Marnia, an all-day ride
by stagecoach, where they slept in the synagogue and inter-
viewed local Riffian Jews. At four o'clock next morning the
stage took them on to Nemours. Here they were advised that it
was impossible for a Jew to get into Riff through Nemours without the protection of a certain Moroccan sheikh who came to
town every month or so and was due in a few weeks. Otherwise
it was better to start from Tetuán.

Foucauld was unwilling to wait for the sheikh and yet was
finally convinced that a direct penetration of the Riff offered
unnecessary risks. Therefore he and Mordecai boarded a small
steamer as deck passengers for Tangier via Gibraltar.

They reached Tangier on the afternoon of June 20, rented
mules, and next afternoon set off with a small caravan for
Tetuán.

His Moroccan journey, therefore, really began on June 21,
1883.

IV

For Mordecai it was a terrifying journey. The aging rabbi
actually knew little of Morocco outside the southern region
around his home town of Aqqa, and a few of the larger cities.
He did know the dangers that beset a traveler who left the
beaten trail, and of course it was Foucauld's purpose to travel
through unknown territory. If there were two roads between

points and one had already been described by earlier geographers, he would take the other.

Foucauld was equipped with letters from the Governor-general of Algeria addressed to all French diplomats and consular officers in Morocco, asking them to give all help to the bearer, but these were apt to be more dangerous than safeguards. If Foucauld was to be attacked, it would be in unmapped territory rather than in the few cities where the French diplomats lived. The letters revealing him to be under French protection, rather than the itinerant rabbi he pretended, would therefore prove to be his death warrant should he fall into the hands of Moslem fanatics.

Taking notes and recording his topographical observations were also risks that might lead to his unmasking. Foucauld described the difficulties in his own words:

"My entire itinerary was logged by compass and barometer. On the road I constantly carried a notebook five centimeters [two inches] square in the hollow of my left hand and a pencil two centimeters long in the other. With these I could record remarkable objects along the way, changes of direction, variations in altitude, the hour and minute of each observation, the rate of speed we were traveling, etc. I wrote thus unobserved all along the way in rolling country, even when we traveled with crowded caravans. I took the precaution of walking ahead or behind my companions so that the fullness of my attire hid the slight movements of my hands. The general contempt accorded a Jew facilitated my being alone."

On arriving in a village, he spent the night (if he could manage to have a room alone) in transferring the descriptions and statistics from the tiny pads to larger notebooks.

"Making astronomical observations was more difficult than logging a route," he wrote. "A sextant is harder to hide than a compass. . . . The altitude and azimuth of sun and stars were taken in villages. By day I would wait for the moment when there was nobody on a roof top; then I would climb with my instruments wrapped in clothing that I said I wanted to air. Rabbi Mordecai stood guard in the stairway to stop anyone who tried to join me, dissuading them with his interminable tales. . . . Sometimes it was impossible to be alone. What stories didn't we invent to explain the sextant? Sometimes it served me to read the future in the skies, sometimes to receive news from absent friends. In Taza it was a preventive against cholera; in the Tâdla it revealed the sins of Jews. Elsewhere it enabled me to tell time, to foretell the weather, to foresee the dangers of the road, and heaven knows what else. . . .

"Observation was difficult in the field, for it was not easy to gain privacy. Sometimes I managed by pretending prayer; . . . I went off at some distance, covered from head to foot by a long prayer shawl, the folds of which hid my instruments. A bush, a rock, or a dip in the terrain hid me for a few minutes. Then I would come back, my prayers finished.

"To sketch the outlines of a mountain or make topographical drawings required even more mysterious procedures. The sextant was an enigma that gave nothing away . . . the slightest sketch would have betrayed me."

Despite his obvious lack of bravery, his geographical ignorance, his complaints about fleas and poor food, and his constant whining about the speed with which Foucauld liked to travel, Mordecai served Foucauld well. Since they lived in Jewish communities, except while traveling when they slept under the stars, Mordecai's glib tongue helped preserve the identity of "Rabbi Josef Aleman." For weeks Mordecai touted his employer as a learned physician specializing in diseases of the eye and with so many cures of blindness to his credit that jealous Christian medical men had hounded him out of Europe. Several times he embarrassed Foucauld by suggesting that he was a faith healer, and overcame the pseudo-rabbi's objections by a reassuring, "You'll see. It always works with somebody."

In one small village Foucauld found that Mordecai's lurid tales of his healing prowess had preceded them. They were preparing to bed down in the tiny synagogue when a woman approached with a little boy in her arms. The boy, she said, had not been able to walk for over a year. The good rabbi must cure him. . . .

Foucauld had always enjoyed masquerading at Saint-Cyr and Saumur, but this was a part he was reluctant to play. He murmured something about being too tired after a long journey, and Mordecai led the woman away, whispering consoling words in her ear.

Next day, while Foucauld was strapping the phylacteries to his forehead and left arm for morning prayer, the woman was back again with her ailing child.

"Pray for her," Mordecai prompted. "Anything. We'll be gone in an hour."

Foucauld had of course mastered the basic prayers of the Hebrew ritual. What was he to recite now? Not, certainly, the *Kaddish*, the prayer for the dead. . . . Why not the *Shemah?*

He stretched out his arms so that the ends of his prayer shawl hung from the tips of his fingers and began the Jewish credo: *Shemah Yisroël, Adonoi Elohaynoo, Adonoi echod!* Hear, O Israel! The Lord thy God, the Lord is one!

The fringed *zizith* of the prayer shawl brushed the face of the child. His eyes lighted up.

"Trust in the Lord," intoned Foucauld, the agnostic.

The boy's face was transfigured. He clutched at the *tallith*. Suddenly he jumped from his mother's arms, clasped the knees of the pseudo-rabbi, and ran down the steps of the synagogue, shouting.

His mother ran after him, sobbing with joy.

"See?" said Mordecai.

Foucauld shook his head. He knew of course that he had performed no miracle, for he had heard of the current work in Paris of Dr. Charcot and his Salpétrière experiments with hysteria and other nervous afflictions. Yet he was everlastingly amazed at the profound and utter faith that these people displayed.

Here was a land of faith for both Jews and Arabs. He had no admiration for the Moroccan Jews, for their bodily uncleanliness or their economic ethics. But he had the utmost respect for their observance of religious rites, their rigid adherence to prayer and ritual, and their trust in God.

As with the Moslems, he envied them their faith.

V

When Foucauld and Mordecai left Tetuán on their rented mules, Mordecai was terrified when he learned the caravan was headed for the holy Mohammedan city of Sheshuan. Why should he not be terrified? No Christian had entered Sheshuan since 1863 when a Spaniard made the voyage—without returning. Moroccan nationalists have explained that Sheshuan had always been considered as a secondary stronghold to protect Islam in Africa if ever the infidels should overrun the north coast. In any event, although some critics of Foucauld's later activities have insisted that his Moroccan expedition was merely an attempt to square himself with the Army by outdoing at its own game the Deuxième Bureau—Intelligence—by mapping this territory solely for its military value, the explorer's own notes were lyrical rather than martial.

Ten days after he left the comparative safety of Tangier and was within a day of the forbidding fortress of Sheshuan, Foucauld was describing the mountainous landscape in the following rhapsodic terms:

"The wheat fields climbed the slopes of Djebel beni Hassan like the tiered rows of an amphitheatre, spreading a tapestry of gold from the valley to the rocky crown. Through the golden wheat many villages gleamed like gems in their garden settings. . . . Everywhere there were gushing springs, cascading through ferns, laurels, fig trees, and vineyards. . . ."

Although Foucauld did not actually enter the Moslem citadel of Sheshuan, he sketched it from across the valley and did sojourn in its Jewish mellah long enough (the night of July 2–3) to be cursed, entering and leaving, by enthusiastic Arab residents who called upon Allah to "Condemn to eternal fires the man who sired you, Jew!"

On July 11 the two-man expedition entered Fez . . . and a blind alley.

For Foucauld, a man in a hurry, who was already fuming over the fact that as a Jew he was immobilized during the Sabbath and holy days when no good Jew, let alone a rabbi, could even take a pencil in hand to transcribe his notes, it was maddening to run into the holy Moslem month of Ramadan. During the month of Ramadan no Moslem may touch food, drink, or woman during daylight hours, and normal life was disrupted.

However, during the unexpected pause, Foucauld came to several decisions. First, he bought two mules at 250 francs each instead of depending upon rented animals. Second, he disposed of his medicine chest. The role of physician, he decided, was too risky; for some reason the Arab mind connected doctors with Christians. Besides, he was tired of acting his way out of the pseudo-medical situations Mordecai was always creating. He also abandoned the dress of the Levantine Jews and assumed the garb of a Maghrebin rabbi, complete with side curls.

Because during Ramadan he could not procure guides to take him to places scheduled on his itinerary, he made two side trips to Taza, three days away, and to Sfru. The journey to Taza made him acquainted with the expensive customs of *anaïa* and *zettet*. The *anaïa,* a lucrative practice since adopted by American racketeers, was the payment for protection—immunity from harm and brigandage. A *zettet* was the important personage of a community (or his agent) who accompanied the traveler from point to point to assure his safety.

In a letter to his trustee Georges de Latouche, preparing him for a request for more money, Foucauld complained that the *zettet* was the most expensive item in his budget, "costing more or less depending upon whether the tribes encountered are more or less dangerous; thus in leaving Taza for another point only six hours journey on the road to Fez, I paid 60 francs. We had to cross the territory of the terrible Riatas. . . ." Yet the expense was necessary, because "without this precaution, the people of the very place you have just left will run after you to rob you before you are a quarter of an hour on your way."

Late in August Foucauld and Mordecai left Fez for Meknès and the province of Tadla. On all previous maps, Tadla had been marked as a city and now that he knew better, Foucauld was determined to visit the provincial capital of Abu-el-Jad and to map the roads and the surroundings.

Foucauld and Mordecai entered Abu-el-Jad on September 6, bearing a letter of recommendation from a high-placed Moslem of Fez to Sidi Ben Daoud, whose influence in the Tadla was greater than that of the sultan himself. In fact, Foucauld commented: "Here there is neither sultan nor *makhzen* (government authority); there is only Allah and Sidi Ben Daoud."

Sidi Ben Daoud sent a grandson to meet the two "rabbis" and received them personally immediately upon their arrival—a circumstance which aroused Foucauld's suspicions at once. Why should this Sheikh of Sheikhs be so considerate to a pair of miserable Jews?

Next Sidi Ben Daoud's son, Sidi Omar, summoned the two "rabbis" to his house, inquired if they had as yet met the leaders of the local Jewish community, and when he received a negative answer, immediately called them together and designated which ones should entertain the visitors. Foucauld noted uneasily that in both Moslem households he and Mordecai had been questioned separately and that there had been many questions about Algeria and French intentions in Morocco.

Foucauld's uneasiness increased when the local rabbis cross-examined him on his rabbinical credentials, his Hebrew accent, and the curious instruments he was now carrying in a goat-skin bag. He was convinced that they were suspicious of his Jewishness, particularly in view of his sponsorship by the great Sidi Ben Daoud.

Next day his uneasiness increased to the point of alarm when a son of Sidi Omar, Sidi Edris, another grandson of the great Sheikh, came to call on him. Sidi Edris had the right to the title of Hadji and wore the green turban of the pilgrim to Mecca. He was, in the words of the Viscount de Foucauld, "a young man of twenty-five, very good-looking despite his being a mulatto, tall, with intelligent features and graceful, supple movements. . . ." He had just come, said the Hadji, to inquire if everything was all right and if the local rabbis were cordial. When Foucauld started to reply, Sidi Edris interrupted to say that it didn't matter, and that he and Mordecai were a thousand times welcome to remain a few days or a few months, as they wished.

The following day the hospitality of the top Moslems became positively frightening: first another call by Sidi Edris, then a summons into the presence of grandfather Sidi Ben Daoud to have tea and imported English biscuits with eight marabouts of the family, then an invitation to Sidi Omar's home.

Ten days after Foucauld's arrival in Abu-el-Jad, Sidi Edris sent for him and gave him letters which he had obviously obtained by pressure on the reluctant local rabbis, introducing "Rabbis Mordecai and Josef Aleman" to Jewish communities further along Foucauld's itinerary. After a sumptuous luncheon, served with great flourish (but without knives, forks, or wines), Sidi Edris told how much he had been impressed by the French cities of North Africa which he had visited on his way back from Mecca. He wondered if it would be possible for him to visit "the Christian continent."

Foucauld was certain that the visit could be arranged and that the Hadji would be more than welcome, particularly if he could reciprocate by bringing back a Christian to Abu-el-Jad where no Christian had been before.

"We have seen Christians before," said Sidi Edris with a sly smile. He added that they had come disguised.

"As Moslems?" Foucauld asked apprehensively.

"As Jews." The smile of Sidi Edris became more enigmatic.

Viscount Charles de Foucauld felt his world collapsing about him. His secret was obviously known to his host. He was at the mercy of a Moslem marabout in a Moslem land where the unauthorized presence of a Christian meant death. What next?

Foucauld stood up. "I must leave," he said.

Sidi Edris begged him to stay. He urged him to move his chair to the window where he could admire the splendid view of the Middle Atlas mountains piled along the horizon to the south. He brought the Frenchman a hand telescope so that he could study the range in better detail. . . . Was this the cat-and-mouse prolongation of sadistic pleasure?

"I must leave," Foucauld repeated. "I must leave Abu-el-Jad."

"I will go with you," said Sidi Edris. "We will leave tomorrow for Kasba-Tadla. I will be your guide to the limits of the Tadla, even beyond. I will take you to Kasba-beni-Mellal."

When Foucauld seemed to hesitate, Sidi Edris went to his desk and wrote a letter to the French ambassador in Tangier, telling him he had acted as host and guide for "two men from your country, and would do the same for all those you may wish to send. The bearers of this letter will give you fuller details. If you wish to see me, send word through the French Consul at Dar-Beïda and I will come at once to Tangier."

The Hadji signed the letter, folded it, affixed his seal, and handed it to Foucauld, urging the utmost caution. "If this should come to the eyes of the Sultan," he said, "he would cut off my hands and tear out my tongue. You must believe that now we are brothers."

Foucauld was deeply touched by this trust, and suddenly realized the reason behind all the consideration—which he had regarded with great suspicion—on the part of the old Sheikh and his sons and grandsons: The elders of the Tadla had seen the handwriting on the wall. The French had already moved into Algeria and Tunisia. Morocco must be next—and welcome. The rule of the Sultan was corrupt and unpopular and a competent impartial government would be a boon to those who believed in the future of a country rich in natural resources. The old Sidi Ben Daoud, his son Omar and his grandson Sidi Edris believed that stability in the guise of a French administration was inevitable, and they were anxious to be in on the ground floor. Hence the red carpet for two "rabbis" who, the Moslems were convinced, particularly after the evidence of the Abu-el-Jad Jews who were willing stool pigeons, were French spies.

From this moment of truth, Foucauld revealed himself completely to Sidi Edris . . . one of the four men during the Moroccan expedition whom he took into his confidence. Two of his confidants were Jews; he revealed himself to the two Moslems without taking Mordecai into his confidence.

Following an exchange of gifts—Foucauld offered a golden Louis and four sugar loaves; and Sidi Edris offered a little slave girl whose service Foucauld had admired—Foucauld, Mordecai and Sidi Edris took the road to the south on the morning of September 17. Sidi Edris was no amateur; he had previously guided many caravans over the roads of the Tadla, but never any group of less than three hundred camels. As guide to the two rabbis, he was a gold mine of information, and in the two books which were to result from his expedition, Foucauld acknowledged that a score of pages were taken practically verbatim from the Hadji's commentary.

On September 23 Sidi Edris bade farewell to his friend at Kasba-beni-Mellal. Foucauld and Mordecai continued their journey to the south and west, skirting the Middle Atlas range to Sidi Rehal, and crossing the snow-covered Great Atlas at the pass called Tizi n' Telouet. They crossed the Little Atlas through the Tizi Agni in late October and saw the Sahara stretching out before them.

On November 14 they reached the oasis of Tisint which was to be the center of several expeditions further south. It was also the scene of his meeting with his second great Moslem friend, Hadji Bou Rhim. From Tisint, Foucauld traveled to Mordecai's birthplace, Aqqa, the southernmost point of his journey, to the great joy of the rabbi. He also made a short trip to Mrimima where he had heard there lived a powerful Sheikh named Sidi Abd Allah Oumbarek who could help him gain passage through the Riff on his return to the North. Hadji Bou Rhim tried to dissuade him from this trip, but the usual Foucauld stubbornness prevailed.

Sidi Abd Allah was impressed by Foucauld's letters of recommendation, but he was even more impressed by the bazaar rumors that the two rabbis were actually Christians, that they were spies preparing for a French invasion, and that they were carrying a fortune in gold. Two gangs of cut-throats actually left Mrimima to take up positions along the road and ambush the travelers when they started back to Tisint.

Sidi Abd Allah immediately made virtual prisoners of Foucauld and Mordecai, setting his four sons to watch over them "for their own protection" from the brigands. Meanwhile the travelers correctly surmised that their hosts were puzzling out some possible manner in which they themselves might successfully plunder the two infidels without violating the sacred obligations of Moslem hospitality. After all, gold is gold, and the inspiration of many a murder. If anyone was to steal the travelers' gold, why should it be the professional brigands? Besides, who would miss these two tattered Jews? Or Christians, whatever they were?

It was in this situation that Viscount Charles de Foucauld found himself on Christmas day of 1883. Although not normally sentimental, he found himself thinking of his mother's last Christmas, when she had made a *crèche* for him in their home in Strasbourg, and he had taken the hand of his three-year-old sister Marie to lead her to the wondrous miniature representation of the three Magi adoring the Infant Jesus in His manger. . . . He also tried to picture his Aunt Inès coming home from midnight mass at Saint-Augustin near her Paris apartment to supervise the Reveillon supper of oysters and white *boudin* with Cousin Marie de Bondy and her family, while Uncle Moitessier led the singing of *Minuit Chrétien* slightly off key. . . . He wondered if this might not be *his* last Christmas. . . .

All week between Christmas and New Year's Day Foucauld and Mordecai slept only in relays. They knew that this sort of thing was no insurance against having their throats cut but at least they would not die without a fight. There were no outright threats, but Sidi Abd Allah and his four ruffian-like sons came to question their "guests" constantly and with knowing leers, spoke of the continuing danger of brigands on the road.

On New Year's Day Foucauld wrote to his sister Marie, whom he addressed as "My good Mimi" (he had not given a thought to his blonde Mimi in many months), wishing her a happy new year and assuring her that he was well and in no danger. "Nor will I be in any danger until my return," he wrote. "The road is long but in no way perilous. If the bad weather which has been delaying me for the past six weeks continues, I may be three months getting home; if the route is easy, I will need only two. . . ."

The wily Mordecai had found a man who could be bribed to carry the letter as far as Tisint, so Foucauld quickly penned a note to Hadji Bou Rhim, telling of his predicament.

"At seven o'clock next morning," Foucauld wrote, "there was a great stir in the village. A troop of twenty-five riflemen and two horsemen marched directly into our courtyard. It was the Hadji, come to rescue me. He had received my note during the night, immediately roused his brothers and relatives, armed them and their servants, set out for Mrimima; and here they were."

Half an hour later Foucauld and Mordecai were on their way to Tisint.

This incident cemented the friendship between Foucauld and Hadji Bou Rhim, to whom he now revealed his true identity. And when Foucauld discovered that his funds were running low and that he would have to seek out the nearest French Consulate to get more money, the Hadji volunteered to accompany him: a mere 500-mile round trip to Mogador on the Atlantic Coast.

Leaving Rabbi Mordecai behind, Foucauld left Tisint on January 9, 1884, with Hadji Bou Rhim and two slaves. It took them nineteen days, crossing the Little Atlas through Iberkaken Pass and skirting the Great Atlas at Agadir-Irir on the sea.

There was some eyebrow-raising at the French Consulate in Mogador when the dirty, ragged, itinerant rabbi announced himself as Viscount de Foucauld, French cavalry officer, who desired to see the consul regarding a draft on the Bank of England. The Jewish clerk-interpreter named Zerbib first forced the unsavory character to sit outside the compound walls, then ordered him to make himself sanitary. He led him to a rather primitive bathroom with a knothole through which consular officers could observe proceedings.

A Monsieur Montel, chancellor of the consulate, was astounded to see (through the knothole) the ragged rabbi taking all manner of instruments from the pockets and folds of his clothing while disrobing for his bath. M. Montel decided there was enough evidence to indicate that the rabbi's claim to be a viscount and a cavalry officer should be investigated further. So the request for money was initiated through Foucauld's sister Marie and the many long tentacles of the Bank of England.

During the waiting period, Foucauld refused hospitality of the consulate staff, preferring to retain his identity of Rabbi Josef Aleman, and living in a boarding house run by a Spanish Jew. However, he surreptitiously dipped into European life now and then, taking a meal or spending an evening in the small European community of Mogador. Once a day he made contact with Hadji Bou Rhim (curiously in his letters he calls him "the chief of my convoy, the Negro, a Sheikh of Tisint") to pay him his per diem and to get a report on the state of the mules, etc.

Foucauld spent weeks working out his geographical and topographical data, his altitudes, his latitudes and longitudes. He also wrote numerous letters to his sister (having discovered that none of the many letters he had addressed to her during the past eight months in care of the Mogador consulate had reached their destination) to reassure her about his health and safety.

Finally, after a six-weeks wait, his money arrived from France and he and Hadji Bou Rhim started back to Tisint from Mogador on March 14. This time the explorer followed the course of the Sous river south of the Great Atlas in order to map new territory. He reached Tisint on March 31, and found Rabbi Mordecai in good shape following his long rest.

Despite Mordecai's impatience to take the shortest route home, Foucauld went north over a completely different itinerary, crossing the Little Atlas through the Tizi n' Haroun, following the Dades and Todra valleys to Ksar-es-Souk, and re-crossing the Great Atlas through mile-high Tizi n' Telremt. This time he followed the Muluya valley along the southern slope of the Middle Atlas, heading for Debdu, the first (or last) Moroccan trading post before reaching the Algerian border.

On May 12, within a few miles of the end of their journey, Foucauld was walking ahead of his small caravan, taking notes, when he was set upon by two of his Moslem escorts. Valiant counter-attacks by Mordecai (who showed himself no poltroon) and the third Moslem member of the escort who insisted on honoring his *anaïa,* saved Foucauld's life, but not his fortune. The two ruffians made off with all his money, and he was forced to sell his two mules and rent two more in order to make the final few days' march to the frontier.

On May 23, 1884, he crossed into Algeria at 10 o'clock in the morning and a few hours later he was in Lalla-Marnia. Mordecai immediately entrained for Algiers. Foucauld made for the divisional headquarters of the French Army to re-establish himself as an ex-cavalry officer and shed his masquerade as Rabbi Josef Aleman. He had some trouble getting through the noncoms guarding the officer of the day, but finally succeeded in facing a lieutenant about his own age who looked down his nose at him with obvious distaste.

"Well, well, Maumené," said Foucauld. "Still a lieutenant, I see. You should have paid more attention to your studies at Saint-Cyr and Saumur. Maybe you'd have another stripe by now."

The officer of the day stared at his former classmate in amazement for a moment, then sprang up and clapped the wretched "rabbi" on the back.

"Foucauld!" he exclaimed. "Piggy! Still up to your old masquerading, I see. We'll get you a bath and some civilized clothes and you'll tell us all about it."

The celebration at the junior officers' mess in Lalla-Marnia that night equalled anything that Saumur or Pont-à-Mousson had ever known.

VI

The reunion of Charles de Foucauld with Oscar MacCarthy in Algiers was somewhat less raucous, but it was nevertheless a joyous one. The scholarly librarian was not only delighted to welcome his protégé home safely from a hazardous journey, but he was amazed and enchanted by the great mass of information the young man had brought back.

During his eleven months as Rabbi Josef Aleman, Foucauld had:

Traveled nearly 2,000 miles on foot and on mule-back, some 1,400 miles farther than previous explorers, whose data he corrected. He found, for instance, that the River Dra, in the extreme south of Morocco, deviated by at least 50 miles from the course shown on the earlier maps of the German explorer Rohlfs.

He had logged the latitude and longitude of 40 localities and corrected the longitude of five others.

He had fixed the altitude above sea-level of 3,000 points, where only a few dozen had been previously recorded.

He had described in lucid and sometimes poetic terms the geography of the virtually-unknown sultanate.

He had outlined the social and racial structure of the various tribes and their political relationship with—or independence of —the Sultan.

He had made a sociological and statistical study of the Jews in Morocco.

He had mapped all the roads he had traveled (and some of those he had learned by questioning other travelers), indicating the travel-time by foot and mule of each stage. He had done the same for the principal rivers and their tributaries.

He had made more than one hundred sketches.

He had made a census of the number of horses and firearms possessed by the various tribes.

He was not yet twenty-six years old.

VII

Rabbi Mordecai Abi Serour permanently retired from the teaching of Hebrew and the Talmud when he collected his handsome fee for returning the viscount to Algiers safely. He invested his money in retorts and alembics, chemicals and mercury in order to continue indulging his experiments in alchemy. He never succeeded in transforming base metals into gold before he died, poisoned by mercury fumes.

Foucauld talked M. de Latouche into allowing him to pay a pension to the rabbi's widow until she too died several years later.

FIVE

BETROTHAL AND THE SALT MARSHES

He that loveth not, knoweth not God, for God is love.

—I St. John, 4, viii

I

The Viscount Charles de Foucauld who returned to France early in June 1884 was received with something akin to awe by all of his family except Aunt Inès Moitessier who stood in awe of nothing and no one. Aunt Inès was glad to see her nephew return safe and sound, naturally, but she was very busy closing up her Parisian town house preparatory to leaving for her summer home in the south, to say nothing of arranging a suitable match for Charles' sister Marie who was now nearly twenty-three and must be married soon if she was not to face spinsterhood.

His sister Marie and his cousins, Viscountess Marie de Bondy and Countess Catherine de Flavigny, found him a new and glamorous character—lean, brown, his hair now parted on the left, an enigmatic smile half hidden by a bushy, drooping mustache. Fond as he was of his family, he felt himself somewhat of a stranger among them, and the strangeness must have been apparent in his appearance and demeanor, despite his fashionably high-buttoned jacket and vest and the pearl stickpin in the tight knot of his cravat. The virus of Africa was in his blood for good.

In white tie and tails he dutifully attended Aunt Inès' last salons of the season, but he could hardly wait to go to suburban

Sèvres to present Oscar MacCarthy's letter of introduction to Henri Duveyrier, vice president of the French National Geographical Society.

Duveyrier was a man who had had much the same experience as Foucauld. He was an older man—he was just over forty—but had also been a protégé of MacCarthy's. At eighteen he had explored the Sahara. At twenty-one he had written a book on the Tuareg and was awarded the Legion of Honor. Ill health had forced him to become an arm-chair geographer, however, and the recent death of a woman he had loved all his life but whom parental objections had prevented his marrying, had made him increasingly bitter. Foucauld's visit was like a breath of his own youth, and the two became great friends.

Foucauld planned to spend July with his family at the Château du Tuquet near Bordeaux, then return to Algiers to write his book which he felt should be done on African soil. He also wanted to be near MacCarthy and his library. Toward the end of the month, however, he fell ill with a mysterious malady which was diagnosed as "mucous fever" and was immobilized for the month of August and well into September.

Autumn found him in Algiers however, working hard on the book—and seriously contemplating marriage.

It was apparently love at first sight. The girl stepped into his life quite by accident. He had called on a retired army officer, an old Sahara hand named Major Titre, a geographer of note, to discuss some maps. As the two men were talking, the major's daughter came into the room, a winsome, dark-eyed girl of twenty-three in a pastel dress and a big wide-brimmed straw hat such as the shepherds wear in the Jurjura mountains.

The given name of Mlle. Titre has not been recorded in the eighty-odd years that have intervened, but there is no doubt that Charles de Foucauld saw in her the answer to his hopes and the materialization of his dreams. He was, she wrote many years later, the great love, the only love of her life. And to him, she was not only the incarnation of the love he had been vainly seeking all his life, but she represented stability. Major Titre and his motherless daughter lived in a charming little villa near the Porte du Sahel among the palms and eucalyptus of the hills behind Algiers. From the small but gay garden there was an exquisite view of the city and the blue Mediterranean. What more could a man ask? Here was peace and security for life. Here was a happy end to his restlessness.

Foucauld asked the geographer for his daughter's hand and set about assiduously to woo her. She would make an excellent wife. She came of a good bourgeois family of Lyons. She had been born a Protestant but had become a pious Catholic. The agnostic Foucauld told her he would not interfere in her practice of whatever religion she wished, and she told him she was sure that in time he would return to the church. He would then laugh and talk about his fiancée's hobby—water-colors.

Charles gave his family in France no inkling of his romance and impending marriage. He knew he would be going home in December, for his Aunt Inès had at last found a proper mate for his sister Marie and had set the wedding date for December 30. He planned to go to Paris for a family Christmas, his first in years, and stay for the wedding. He looked forward to general approbation. They would all be delighted that he was to settle down at last.

He was surprised to find that they were not at all pleased. Oh, his sister Marie was not *dis*pleased, since she was about to be married herself to a man of Aunt Inès' choosing, Viscount Raymond de Blic, an innocuous chap of good family and sound fortune. But Aunt Inès was personally and volubly shocked. First of all, a Foucauld must not be a traitor to his class. True, she herself had married a rich plebeian, but had she not secured aristocratic husbands for both her daughters and for Marie Inès de Foucauld, Charles' sister? And was Charles now going to dilute his blood line by marrying a plebeian?

Furthermore, Aunt Inès continued, had Charles forgotten that he was by court order still a ward of M. de Latouche who could at will contract or cut off his allowance? How could a Viscount de Foucauld marry under these circumstances? A Viscountess de Foucauld could not be found washing her own dishes or scrubbing her floors. A Viscountess de Foucauld must be dressed by the best couturiers of Paris, not by some by-the-day seamstress of Algiers. She must have servants, her own carriage, and a good address. . . .

Foucauld was flushed and tight-lipped as he stalked from

his aunt's presence. The old Foucauld contrariness had been aroused. Nothing, but nothing could now stop him from marrying dark-eyed Mlle. Titre!

He was overlooking his cousin Marie de Bondy.

Cousin Marie intercepted him on the stairway of the town house in the Rue d'Anjou. She took him gently by the hand and led him into the dining room where there was a Christmas tree, an Alsatian Christmas tree which was as rare in Paris as it was common in Strasbourg. There was also a crèche, like the crèche his dear mother used to prepare in the years before she died. The lights from the Christmas tree made liquid reflections in Marie's eyes.

"My poor Charles!" she said, taking both his hands. "You love this girl very much, don't you?"

"Very much."

"Then you must give her up."

Foucauld blinked. "You are talking nonsense, Cousin," he said.

"I am talking sense. If you love her you have no right to make her unhappy."

"But we are very happy together. We—."

He stopped, struck by the look of infinite sadness in his cousin's tear-filled eyes. He had always sensed that her own marriage, which her mother found so eminently suitable, had not been happy. She had never complained, and she had dutifully borne the Viscount de Bondy four fine children, but—.

"What will you do after you finish your book, Charles?"

"I don't know yet."

"Are you going back to Morocco?"

"I'd like to, but I'm afraid it's impossible right now. Henri Duveyrier has got me quite excited about the oases of the Sahara and the salt marshes of Tunisia. . . ."

"You see? How can you marry when at any moment you will be rushing off to the Congo or Madagascar? This poor girl will have a phantom for a husband. You should never marry, Charles. Never!"

For a long silent moment Charles de Foucauld stared wistfully at the cousin to whom he had declared, as he danced with her on her nineteenth birthday, "You are the most beautiful girl in the world and I love you. As soon as I come into my inheritance I intend to marry you." Had that been only fifteen years ago?

Suddenly he smiled broadly.

"You talk as if you'd like me to become a monk," he said.

Marie de Bondy did not smile. "Well, why not?" she said.

Cousin Charles laughed heartily.

On the next to last day of 1884 Marie Inès de Foucauld became the Viscountess de Blic with appropriate pomp and solemnity.

On January 9, 1885, the secretary-general of the French National Geographical Society announced that the society's gold medal would be awarded to the Viscount Charles de Foucauld for his exploration of Morocco, and that the explorer, who was in Paris, would perhaps like to say a few words to the meeting. Foucauld, however, did not address the distinguished gathering. He was already on his way back to Algiers.

He did not see Mlle. Titre on his return. Instead he explained to her father that since he was planning another journey of African exploration, he would like, with infinite regrets, to withdraw his offer of marriage. He hoped Major Titre, as a geographer and explorer himself, would understand that this would be best for all concerned.

II

When Spring came to the Mediterranean and the amphitheatre of hills surrounding Algiers was bright with roses and mimosa, Foucauld was deep in his book. He did not even return to Paris for the ceremony of accepting his gold medal from the Geographical Society. He knew it was to be an elaborate ritual, attended by many notables, and that his Aunt Inès would never understand his reluctance to accept kudos for a work that he had not yet completed. He asked his new friend Henri Duveyrier to receive the medal for him, but that veteran explorer, reinvigorated by his contact with the younger man, was off again in Africa for the first time in years.

It was finally Olivier de Bondy who on April 24, 1885, accepted the medal from the hands of Count Ferdinand de

Lesseps, builder of the Suez Canal, then president of the Geographical Society. At least the family could bask in reflected glory.

By midsummer Foucauld had practically completed his book with its sheaf of maps and sketches, but he hesitated to turn it over to his publisher quite yet. He came home to spend a month or so with Aunt Inès, to rest, to think, to talk with Cousin Marie de Bondy, to try to find out whey he felt a stranger in his own country among his own family. He came to the conclusion that he would never settle down (the name of Mlle. Titre was never mentioned) until he had seen the desert peoples of whom Henri Duveyrier had written—the fanatical M'zabites of Ghardaïa, the Berbers of the oases, and the Tuareg of the Saharan plateaux. Perhaps, too, he would complete the mission which Duveyrier had never undertaken and Lieutenant Laperrine of the Fourth Chasseurs had never completed—crossing of the Sahara from north to south, pioneering a route linking French North Africa with the colonies of the Niger and the Congo. By the end of August he had made his preparations for a new expedition. On September 14 he sailed for Algiers from Port Vendre.

This time he headed due south from Algiers. There was no need for secrecy or disguise. Although he was traveling through country that was not exactly friendly, it was technically under French control and Foucauld had the co-operation and protection both of the army and the colonial ministry. He had in fact planned to travel in style, or at least comparative style, considering the lack of comfort in transport and accommodations at that time. He had written a friend in Africa, asking him to procure two camels, two horses, and an Arab attendant, but had to make do with two mules and one Arab. He made the first 300 miles by stagecoach, and arrived at the charming little oasis of Laghouat in the natty attire of a Parisian sportsman. Further south at Ghardaïa there was a reunion with Captain Calassanti-Motylinski, the language officer of the Fourth Chasseurs d'Afrique who had first interested Foucauld in the Arabs and Berbers.

Motylinski was delighted that the seeds he had planted had borne such splendid fruit. He showed Foucauld the ancient and curious civilization of the M'zabites, a dissident sect of Moslems, who over the years had created a small civilization of their own with its own superstitions and even its own architecture; even their mosques were different. The town of Ghardaïa was built on a hill like a pyramid, topped by its great mosque with its curious pyramidal minaret. Foucauld was fascinated by the thousands and thousands of date palms that surrounded the oasis, watered by hundreds of ancient wells, some of them 200 feet deep. The creak of pulleys which were the heart of the ingenious old irrigation system, was as characteristic a sound in the M'zab as the muezzin's call to prayer.

Motylinski accompanied Foucauld 200 miles further south to El Goléa, where Henri Duveyrier had barely escaped assassination a score of years earlier, and where few Christians had been since. They found a French army officer trying to set up a system of communications between desert outposts and coastal bases by using carrier pigeons—unsuccessfully; the birds refused to fly over the Sahara.

The two men traveled over the dreary dunes of the Great Eastern Erg, through the date-rich oases of Wargla and Tuggurt, where they parted company on December 5. Foucauld crossed over into Tunisia. He was determined to see the great salt marshes—the shotts of El Gharsa and El Jerid.

Whether by design or accident, Foucauld was to spend the Christmas holidays in the Jerid, that country between Saharan steppes and dunes, the date-palm oases and the shotts. Often he left his party to sleep under the blazing stars of the desert night, to woo the solitude he was coming to love, to commune with himself, to seek in the silent vastness of Africa the secret of his own restlessness. For the second Christmas in three years, he went to sleep in the heart of Islam, with prayers to Allah and the chant of the muezzin echoing in his ears.

SIX

IN QUEST OF TRUTH

*Tu cherches Dieu? Tu ne le chercherais pas
si tu ne l'avais pas déjà trouvé.*

*Are you seeking God? You would not be
seeking Him if you had not already found
Him.*

—Blaise Pascal (1670)

I

Foucauld sailed for France from Gabès, on the east coast
of Tunisia, in mid-January, 1886. After a brief visit in Marseilles with his old friend of cavalry days, the Duke of FitzJames,
he went on to Nice to spend a month with his sister, Marie de
Blic, who was wintering on the Riviera with her husband and
first child. On February 19 he returned to Paris.

He rented a ground floor apartment at 50 Rue de Miromesnil
not far from Aunt Inès' town house. The furnishings of the
rooms were symbolic of Foucauld's schizophrenic existence during the next two years. The walls were hung with fire-arms and
textiles brought from Algeria, sketches and water-colors of
Morocco, and family portraits. There was no bed; Foucauld
slept on a Moslem prayer rug on the floor, wrapped in his
burnous. But in the great mirrored mahogany clothespress there
hung evening clothes of the most stylish cut, silk scarves, elegant
topcoats and top hats.

By day Foucauld worked at the last draft of his book on
Morocco. Curiously enough, his revised pages did not include
any of the data he had accumulated on his journey through the

oases of southern Algeria and Tunisia, although one of the reasons he had originally advanced for the trip was to be able to compare the terrain with similar parts of Morocco; El Goléa is approximately the same latitude as Tisint. As a matter of fact, the log-books of Foucauld's second African expedition were given to Duveyrier who left them to the French Geographical Society, and they saw publication only twenty years after Foucauld's death when Father Georges Gorrée wrote a book called "In the Footsteps of Charles de Foucauld."

At night Foucauld led an active social life which centered around the town house of Aunt Inès at the corner of Boulevard Malesherbes and Rue d'Anjou, just a stone's-throw from the Madeleine. Aunt Inès was no longer the dazzling young beauty whose portrait had been painted by Ingres not once but twice— in 1851 and again in 1856—but she was still an extremely handsome woman whose Sunday "at homes" were attended by the cream of Parisian society and the world of politics, arts and letters.

Aunt Inès' guests were all eminently respectable, respectably pious, and in unanimous awe and admiration of Aunt Inès' wit, influence and determination. Aunt Inès was not at all shy about using her friends to help her friends and relatives. The Prime Minister was a frequent dinner guest at the Moitessier town house, and it was hardly a coincidence that M. Moitessier's nephew Louis Buffet had become a cabinet minister at the age of thirty, one of the youngest on record, or that his brother Aimé should hold an important government post.

One regular at Aunt Inès' Sundays and dinners intrigued Charles de Foucauld: the Reverend Father Huvelin, Abbé of St. Augustin, the parish church of Aunt Inès and her family. The Abbé seemed to be the answer to the two things that had contributed most to Foucauld's youthful agnosticism: in provincial France religion was woman's business; men went to church rarely, perhaps for midnight mass on Christmas Eve because it was fashionable, for Easter, or for a wedding or funeral of a friend; otherwise churches were largely peopled by elderly ladies with black shawls over their heads. Furthermore, religion had always seemed to Foucauld a thing of emotion rather than reason, and he had grown up when France was groping through an "age of reason"; he could never adjust to the logic of the Trinity—that Three should equal One God.

His African experience had destroyed his feeling that men were outside religion. Both the Moslems and the Jews excluded women from active participation in religious practices. Only a man could pray effectively.

Abbé Huvelin was certainly a man. Moreover, he was a man of reason, a graduate of the famous École Normale, and a man whose sermons were not addressed to sentimental and timorous old ladies but attracted intellectuals to the St. Augustin church when he was preaching. He was a relatively young man when Foucauld first met him—he was still in his forties—although he looked older than his age. He had a round face, topped with bushy, wavy hair, yet he could never be called baby-faced, for his features were pinched with pain. His thin lips seemed to be constantly on the point of crying out, and his piercing eyes might have seen all the world's sadness and tragedy. He had been disabled in youth by what had been then diagnosed as "rheumatic paralysis" and he seemed in himself to be a symbol of universal suffering.

Far from being a self-pitying cripple, however, the Abbé was a compassionate educator, an apostle to the godless *cognoscenti* of the Second Empire and the Third Republic. His message to his parishioners was: Never ask God to comfort you; ask Him to give you strength to bear your allotted burden. Perhaps his strongest appeal to young Foucauld was the fact that he had converted Émil Littré.

Littré had been a man after Foucauld's own heart. Littré had been not only an intellectual and an agnostic, but an active apostle of Positivism, a follower of August Comte who rejected from his philosophy everything that could not be accepted by the senses or by ordered reason. Littré was a philologist, a translator, and a man of letters whose election to the French Academy in 1871 provoked the resignation of Monseigneur Dupanloup. Littré had been a senator and the author of the monumental *Dictionary of Medicine and Surgery* and *Dictionary of the French Language*. And yet before he died in 1881, while Lieutenant Foucauld was chasing the elusive Bou Amama through Southern Oran, the illustrious Littré had begged Abbé

Huvelin to lead him back to God. Perhaps this was the man to lead Foucauld out of the unhappy morass, the godless, restless uncertainty in which he had been floundering these recent years.

Foucauld did not approach Abbé Huvelin directly for some time. First of all, he was busy correcting the galleys of his Moroccan book. Second, he was still dependent upon Cousin Marie de Bondy in matters of the spirit. He read and reread the dog-eared copy of Bossuet's *Elévations sur les Mystères*, which Marie had given him at the time of his First Communion. He bought more Bossuet—*Discours sur l'Histoire Universelle* and *Méditations sur l'Evangile*. He discussed them with his cousin. In their long and frequent tête-à-têtes his long yearning seemed to become sublimated. "You are lucky to believe," he said. "As much as I seek the light, I cannot find it."

"Pray," said Marie de Bondy.

Sometimes on his way home from Aunt Inès' brilliant soirees, before discarding the white tie and tails for the comfort of his Moroccan burnous in the privacy of his bachelor quarters, he would drop in at a church. In the candle-starred quiet of the ecclesiastical night, he would follow the counsel of his beloved cousin. It was always the same prayer: "If Thou art my God, make Thyself known to me, O Lord!"

There was no answer.

Still he persisted in his search. He discussed Islam with his friend Henri Duveyrier, to whom he admitted that he had even considered becoming a Moslem. Much as he admired the faith of the Moslems, however, he was deterred by the fact that such religiosity seemed to lead only to a sordid way of life. Nor was he attracted by the idea of a Moslem paradise with its houris and its fountains gushing wine; it was too close to his own pre-Moroccan youth.

Perhaps, he thought, he did not know enough about the religion into which he had been born. True, he had learned his catechism as a boy and gone through a Jesuit school. Yet ever since he had reached the age of reason, he had studiously avoided delving into Christian doctrine until quite recently. Perhaps if he knew more. . . .

One morning in late October, 1886, unable to sleep, he arose very early and sauntered aimlessly up the dawn-quiet Rue de

Miromesnil. As he turned into the Boulevard Haussmann, his pace quickened, and by the time he reached the Place Saint-Augustin, he knew that he was not wandering aimlessly at all. His steps seemed to be directed. Ahead of him, surmounting the three byzantine arches of the entry, was the great rose window of Saint-Augustin church.

He strode into the church and went directly to the confessional he knew to be occupied by the Abbé Huvelin. He bent over slightly to speak through the grille.

"Monsieur l'Abbé," he said, "I have no faith. I have come to ask you to teach me."

"Kneel!" ordered the priest. "Confess your sins to God and you will believe."

"But that is not what I came for, Monsieur l'Abbé. . . ."

"On your knees!" said Abbé Huvelin. "Confess!"

Viscount Charles de Foucauld, the cadet who made a shambles of discipline at Saint-Cyr and Saumur, the subaltern who defied the French army because of a blue-eyed blonde, the man who braved death in hostile Morocco, knelt obediently and humbly recited the guilty details of his lurid past.

"Have you breakfasted?" asked Abbé Huvelin at last. "No? Good. Then go to Communion."

Foucauld seemed a little dazed as he rose to his feet, but he walked toward the altar rail with a light, buoyant step.

II

There is no doubt that what Foucauld later called his "second first Communion" marked a turning point of his life.

His conversion, like so many other recorded experiences, was instantaneous, like a great light suddenly bursting upon him after so many years of wandering in the dark. His festering doubt vanished as though it had never existed. The great weight of brooding incompleteness, the heavy sense of imperfection—he had never experienced any feeling of guilt or sin—was abruptly lifted. He truly felt himself a new man.

For a while there was no external sign of the change except that he now attended Mass regularly and his friends noted that he seemed to smile more frequently. He went about his daily affairs as usual. He finished reading the proofs of his book on Morocco; he argued with his publisher over the number of maps and illustrations to be included in the volume, and ended by paying for the cost of the additional plates out of his own pocket.

He went to Dijon to stand as godfather for his sister Marie de Blic's second son, named for him, and spent the summer with his cousin Marie de Bondy, her atheist husband and their four children at their country home, the eighteenth-century Château de la Barre, some miles south of the Loire. And he often visited his friend Henri Duveyrier at Sèvres.

With Duveyrier he discussed future projects of exploration, and in fact seemed to be toying with the idea of becoming a professional geographer and explorer. For this he would have to regain control of his own fortune in order to finance the costs. In the Autumn of 1887 he wrote to a friend, complaining that the extra expense of subsidizing the publisher of his book, added to the cost of his trip across southern Algeria and Tunisia, had made a big dent in his budget. "My income is sufficient to cover these extraordinary expenses, but barely," he wrote. "Although I have not borrowed a sou since my return from Morocco, neither have I saved anything. I would like to get out from under the trusteeship with which I have been saddled for the past five years. As long as my trustee has control, I cannot consider another journey, and since my book is about to appear, it is high time that I began thinking of new expeditions."

He wrote in a similar vein to Emil Maupas, Oscar MacCarthy's assistant in the Algiers Library: "I am still vaguely concerned with the Moslem countries and intend to visit them again. I am reading Arabic and studying the countries of the Levant in general, but I have as yet no set plans. . . . Just as I miss greatly the good friends I left in Algiers, I also miss the blue skies, the warm sun, and the dazzling sunlight. . . ."

During the winter of 1887–8 Foucauld's Moroccan work was published in two volumes—*Reconnaissance au Maroc*, a book of some 500 pages and more than 100 sketches; followed by *Itinéraires au Maroc*, a supplement of maps, tables, etc. Immediately glory descended upon the little apartment in the Rue de Miromesnil. Letters of congratulation arrived from friends, army associates, and strangers. There were citations from learned societies and universities, queries from French and foreign geographers, cautious applause from politicians (who were not quite sure what French colonial policy should be), enthusiastic orders for books from the French general staff, invitations to dinner from distant relatives who knew that their suddenly-famous cousin had a weakness for pâté de foie gras and rack of Alsatian kid, and requests for papers to be read before erudite groups. Foucauld answered them all with polite notes of thanks and regrets.

He did accept an invitation to lunch from his explorer friend Duveyrier to meet fellow explorers and officers of the Geographical Society, but he specified the menu that he, as a pious Catholic, could properly eat—during Lent!

He conferred frequently with his spiritual guide, Abbé Huvelin.

And he went again that summer of 1888 to the Château de la Barre to absorb strength from the great love of his life, a pure and spiritual love, as he himself described it, a love which was hopeless in a worldly sense, but which in its sublimation was largely responsible for Foucauld's new life, his new freedom, his new happiness.

"You must love God, my cousin," Marie de Bondy had once said. "No other love is worthy of you or of me."

"But I do not believe in God, Marie."

"You will, Charles. You must."

And now at last Charles de Foucauld did—passionately—much to the amusement of Cousin Marie's husband, Viscount Olivier de Bondy, and even their sons who were growing into cynical adolescence.

On August 10, 1888, Foucauld accompanied the Bondys on their annual picnic (via four-in-hand) to Fontgombault, some 30 kilometers away, where the air was invigorating, the fruit and local preserves excellent, and the eleventh-century monastery, then occupied by Trappists, a favorite charity of Cousin Marie. While Viscount de Bondy and his children were scouting the countryside for the sweetest yellow plums, Viscountess de Bondy and Viscount Charles de Foucauld were kneeling in prayer in the eleventh-century chapel.

Foucauld was particularly taken by the abbot of the old monastery, a young man of great charm and piety whose religious name was Dom Albéric. He was even more impressed by the patched and threadbare poverty and humility of the Trappist monks. Their abject submission recalled the words of Abbé Huvelin who in one sermon had said: "Jesus has achieved the ultimate in abnegation and self-effacement. No one can go lower."

All the way home Foucauld was silent and Cousin Marie de Bondy was beaming. She was sure she had achieved her goal. Cousin Charles had not only returned to the fold but he was obviously on the point of giving himself entirely to God. Although he had not said a word since they left the monastery, she knew exactly what he felt and what he was thinking.

She was greatly shocked next day when Charles received notice from the Ministry of War, reminding him that he was still a reserve officer in the French Army and that he should report for duty with the 19th Chasseurs for summer maneuvers.

Charles too was startled and not a little disturbed. He had forgotten that his resignation from the Chasseurs d'Afrique at Mascara was a qualified one—that he had agreed to serve again in time of war, which meant that he was still on call and therefore obligated to take periodic training. For days he brooded silently while Marie de Bondy watched anxiously for his decision.

On August 22, less than a fortnight after Foucauld's impressive visit to the Trappist monastery at Fontgombault, an orderly rode up to the Château de la Barre, leading another horse on which there were voluminous saddlebags. The orderly dismounted, tethered both horses, and carried the bags into the château.

An hour later he came out again accompanied by Lieutenant Charles de Foucauld, resplendent in the scarlet breeches, sky-blue tunic, shiny high boots and plumed kepi of a cavalry officer.

Foucauld swung briskly into his saddle, and turned to wave

briefly to Marie de Bondy who stood at the window with her husband. The sun flashed on the lieutenant's sabre as he rode off for three weeks in the field.

"A splendid, martial-looking figure, your pious cousin." Olivier de Bondy chuckled.

Marie de Bondy bit her lip and said nothing.

III

In October, 1888, the tribunal of Nancy, with the approval of the family, annulled the appointment of Georges de Latouche as trustee and returned control of the Foucauld fortune to the Viscount himself.

So one month after his thirtieth birthday Foucauld had all the money he wanted. He could organize a dozen expeditions to explore the unmapped lands in the far corners of the world. Or, since his superiors rated him as an outstanding officer as a result of the summer maneuvers, he could return to the gay army life with its intensive carousels and expensive women. Actually he did neither. His sextant, compasses, and other tools of exploration he presented to Marie de Bondy's sons as souvenirs. His gaudy uniform he put way forever. And he had not touched a woman since the day of his "second First Communion."

Shortly after the Nancy tribunal restored him to full financial competence and two years to the day from the morning he had first knelt in Abbé Huvelin's confessional, Foucauld again sought out his spiritual guide at the church of Saint-Augustin.

"Father," he said, "I should like to dedicate my life to God."

Abbé Huvelin shook his head sadly. "You are not yet prepared, my son. You cannot yet be sure."

"From the moment I believed there was a God, I knew that I could not help living for Him alone."

"You must not make such an important decision impulsively. You must think carefully."

"I have been thinking for two years, Father."

"You have been many things in your short life, my son. But when you leave the world to give yourself to God, there is no return."

"I have made up my mind, Monsieur l'Abbé."

Again the priest shook his head. "Prepare," he said. "Travel. Walk the sacred ground where Our Lord has walked. Pray where He has prayed. When you return, we will discuss your future."

Once again Foucauld bowed to the will of Abbé Huvelin. He would make a piligrimage to the Holy Land.

SEVEN

A LONG FAREWELL

There is strength in my weakness.
—St. Agatho, Pope 678–682 A.D.

I

Foucauld reached Jaffa early in December, 1888. After clearing Turkish customs, he hired two horses and a guide and set off for Jerusalem. He found the Holy City covered with a light snowfall when he arrived on December 15. He checked in at a Franciscan pilgrims' hostel, but he did not sleep there. Instead he spent the night praying in the Church of the Holy Sepulcher, prostrate on the stone floor.

For a week he roamed the narrow, twisting, cobbled streets of old Jerusalem. He prayed in the Garden of Gethsemane and climbed the Mount of Olives. He followed the Via Dolorosa to Golgotha.

On Christmas Eve he was in Bethlehem, kneeling at the Shrine of the Nativity.

In January he rode horseback into Galilee. He fell in love with Nazareth and its evocation of the youth of Jesus, returning for a second visit after he had completed his tour of the Holy Land.

Everywhere he collected souvenirs for his family—pressed flowers from Gethsemane, a bit of earth from the Mount of the Beatitudes, crucifixes made from olive wood in Bethlehem.

By March, 1889, he was back in France, more certain than ever that he would devote the rest of his life to the service of God. He was fairly certain also that his was to be a life of monastic abnegation rather than of preaching. In order to compare the rule of the various religious orders, Foucauld made four retreats in four different monasteries.

For Easter he prayed at the eleventh-century Benedictine monastery in Solesme, on the Sarthe river. Trinity Sunday found him at La Grande Trappe, mother house of the Cistercians. In October he spent a week in another Trappist monastery, Our Lady of the Snows, high among the firs and beeches of the Cévennes chain of the massif of Central France. Still undecided, he spent part of November with the Jesuits at Clamart, on the southern fringes of Paris. On his return home he wrote to his sister in Dijon:

"Yesterday I came back from Clamart and following the formal, unreserved and positive advice of the father who was guiding me, I have finally, calmly and confidently reached the decision I have been pondering for so long: I shall become a Trappist.

"I have made four retreats in four monasteries and in all of them I was told that God was calling me and that He was calling me toward the Trappist order. My heart leans in the same direction, and my spiritual guide agrees. The matter is now settled, and I am so informing you. I will enter the monastery at Our Lady of the Snows where I spent some time recently. When? The date is not yet fixed as I have various things to put in order. Especially must I go to tell you goodbye. . . ."

Foucauld went to Dijon to say farewell to the Blic family on Dec. 11. He lingered for a fortnight, basking in the warmth of a family Christmas which he would never experience for himself. "Let us grieve," he said at last to his sister, "but let us thank God for our grief."

After New Year's Day he arranged with the family attorneys to deed his entire fortune, over which he had just regained control, to his sister Mimi.

He distributed all his personal belongings among his various relatives.

On January 14 he wrote to his sister: "Goodbye, my good Mimi, I am leaving Paris tomorrow. . . . Pray for me, and I will pray for you and yours. We must not forget one another as we draw closer to God."

Early next morning Foucauld took Communion at Saint-Augustin. Kneeling beside him at the altar rail was his beloved cousin Marie de Bondy. Together they listened while Abbé Huvelin celebrated mass.

There were tears in Marie de Bondy's eyes as they stepped into the wan winter sunshine of Place Saint-Augustin. This would be their last day together. There would be no tomorrow to share.

Together they roamed the gray streets of Paris like the lovers they had never been nor would ever be. They wandered aimlessly down the cold, wind-swept Champs-Elysées, under the leafless trees of the Tuileries gardens. They said little, for there was no need for words. Their hearts were full of the great and pure love which Marie had transmuted into a burning passion for God. The man she had rescued from himself she was giving to the Lord. The joy of the sacrifice must outweigh the sorrow of parting.

As the early January dusk settled quickly over Paris, they were back again at Saint-Augustin to bid farewell to Abbé Huvelin. They knelt as the crippled priest blessed them.

Hand in hand and in silence they walked the few blocks up the Boulevard Haussmann, past the intersection of the Rue de Miromesnil where Foucauld had lived, to the corner of the Avenue Percier where stood the town house of Viscount Olivier de Bondy, Marie's husband. Here they said goodbye.

That night Foucauld wept as he sat alone atop the tall, double-decked horse-drawn bus that rolled down the Grands Boulevards toward the Gare de Lyon.

"This sacrifice has cost me all my tears," he was to write later. "Since that time, since that day, I no longer weep. I seem to have no more tears to shed, except sometimes when I remember. The wound of the fifteenth of January is always the same. The sacrifice of that day remains the sacrifice of every hour."

When Viscount Charles de Foucauld got off the bus at the Place de la Nation, he was a poor man. The gay, spendthrift of the Fourth Hussars owned only the clothes on his back, the few personal effects in his pockets, and enough money to buy a third-class ticket to La Bastide-St. Laurent, the railway station for the Trappist monastery of Our Lady of the Snows.

II

Foucauld did not find it easy to give up the world. On his arrival at Our Lady of the Snows, before he had been received into the Trappist community, he sat down to say goodbye again to the world. For him the world had become Marie de Bondy.

"Where was I at this time yesterday?" he wrote to his cousin. "I was still close beside you, saying farewell to you. Hard as it was, it was still delightful, for I could still see you before me. . . . I cannot get used to the idea that I have said goodbye to you forever. . . . Nevertheless, it is the truth, I know it to be the truth, I want it to be the truth, and yet I cannot believe it. At nine in the morning, at four o'clock, at this moment, always, I feel so close to you—and my eyes will never again look into yours. . . .

"I must gain strength from my weakness, use this weakness itself in the service of God, thank Him for this pain and offer it to Him for His solace. May He accept this sacrifice from an humble and contrite heart that it may benefit all His children, particularly you. I ask him with all my heart to increase my pain if I can bear a heavier burden so that He may draw comfort therefrom and that His children, you above all, may get a little more good from it. . . .

"I am incapable of thanking you for all your kindness. I am unworthy of it. In fact, how can I thank you for the sweetness of these last days, of these last hours, of yesterday? . . . May we be reunited some day at the feet of our Lord, communing with Him as we did yesterday morning, receiving His blessing as I received yours last evening. Sweet benediction!"

This was the last letter Foucauld wrote before entering the Trappist community, the last which he would be able to send sealed and unread by the Superior. In the morning he would be shrouded in the anonymity and silence of the Cistercians, buried behind the pale granite walls of Our Lady of the Snows—at the age of thirty-two.

EIGHT

THE RESTLESS TRAPPIST

Je veux crier l'Evangile toute ma vie.

I would shout the Gospel all my life.
—Charles de Foucauld

I

Foucauld had chosen to be a Trappist because he found the rule of the order to be the strictest and the most trying, and he had chosen Our Lady of the Snows because he considered it the poorest monastery he had visited. He was resolved to lead a life of poverty, humility, abnegation, and self-effacement—as close to the suffering of Jesus Christ as he could manage.

On St. Albéric's day, ten days after his arrival at the monastery, he took the white cloak of the Trappist novice and the religious name of Brother Marie-Albéric. He asked Dom Martin, the Abbot, to give him the most menial tasks. He swept out the chapel (not very skilfully at first), waited table in the refectory, carried boughs, made wreaths for the Perpetual Adoration, burnished candlesticks. He arose at two in the morning to pray, spent most of the day at worship, went to bed at seven in the evening. His spare time he spent reading (systematic rereading of the Bible and other religious literature), writing to his cousin Marie (the letters were of course read by Dom Martin before they were mailed) and letting a few of his friends know what had become of him.

The meals were indeed meager, particularly for a man who had been practically weaned on fine wines and choice food. The Trappists lived on thin gruel, dry bread, and vegetables cooked in salted water. There were no eggs or meat, no milk, no wine, no butter or oil. During Lent the regime was reduced to one meal a day, and Brother Albéric cut his own ration still more by limiting himself to bread and water.

On Easter Monday of 1890 he wrote to his sister: "I should not say that I have borne up well under cold and hunger, for I have not even felt either. Of the Lenten routine (one meal a day at four-thirty) I have only this to say: I found it agreeable and pleasant, and I was not hungry for one day. However, I did not really overeat.

"As for my soul, it is in the same state as when I wrote last, except that the good Lord is giving me even more support, my body as well as my soul. I have no burden to bear; He bears all. I should be indeed ungrateful to our most gracious Father, to our most gentle Lord Jesus, if I did not tell you to what extent He has taken me into His hands, enfolded me in His own peace, keeping me from all confusion and protecting me from encroaching sorrows. . . . The Office, the Holy Mass, prayer (in which my own sterility has been so painful to me) have been very sweet for me, despite the innumerable distractions of which I have been guilty. . . . Manual labor is a great comfort because of its resemblance to the work of Our Lord. . . ."

Brother Marie-Albéric had not been long at Our Lady of the Snows before he began making plans for an even more desolate life. He asked to be transferred to a Trappist monastery in Syria which he had been told was even more impoverished, where life was even more primitive, and which would entail the self-punishment of exile from the France he loved.

"I cannot bear living a life of ease and honors," he wrote to his friend Henri Duveyrier, "when Our Lord's was the ultimate of suffering and scorn. I cannot travel through life in first class when He whom I love traveled in the lowest. . . ."

Six months after he became a Trappist his request was granted. On June 26 the Abbot accompanied him to Marseilles. Next day he sailed for Alexandretta in steerage.

Twelve days later, on the eve of his arrival, he wrote to his family: "Tomorrow . . . I will say farewell to this sea, my last link with the land in which you all live and breathe."

A Trappist from Our Lady of the Sacred Heart met the boat

and accompanied Brother Marie-Albéric on muleback for the two-day journey over the Amanus mountains to the monastery. The Aleppo road was not only a dangerous winding trail barely scratched into the mountainside, but was also frequented by brigands who lay in ambush for caravans. Three armed Turks accompanied the Trappists as far as the Beilan Pass through which had passed the armies of Darius and Alexander, and later the Romans and the Crusaders.

Late in the afternoon of the second day the two monks reached the Lazarist mission at Akbès, and four miles farther on the Trappist monastery of Our Lady of the Sacred Heart at a place the French spelled Cheïkhlé and the Turks pronounced Shurley.

The monastery was a far cry from the solid granite quad that was Our Lady of the Snows. Brother Marie-Albéric described it in his letters home as "a collection of little thatched houses of planks and adobe. . . . a hodgepodge of barns, animals, and shacks huddled closely together as protection against forays by brigands, shaded by large trees and watered by a spring pouring from a rock. . . ."

Our Lady of the Sacred Heart was staffed by twenty bearded monks who also looked after some fifteen orphans, largely Kurds and Armenians, between the ages of six and twelve. The monastery had been founded eight years previously as a possible refuge for Trappists in case the Church-State conflict in France should result in exile for the order. It was surrounded by pine-and-oak-clad mountains, but the monks had reclaimed enough flat land to plant some wheat and barley, a little cotton, and an excellent vegetable garden to take care of the Trappist diet. They had also cultivated a small vineyard which produced a delightful white wine, but since there was no market locally and the cost of distribution was prohibitive, the vintage was stored for medical emergencies. The monks of course did not touch a drop, except the privileged few who were picked to taste and grade the vintage each autumn.

In summer the monks slept in the hayloft, its loose flooring making them one with the animal sounds and smells drifting up from below. In winter they moved to the garret above the refectory, which was perhaps more satisfactory aromatically, but, since the refectory was roofed with galvanized iron, often covered with snow, was no more comfortable. Neither the straw pallets nor the moss-stuffed comforters were much help against the sharp chill of the mountain nights.

Brother Marie-Albéric worked at first in the fields. He picked cotton, weeded the kitchen garden, gathered stones that hindered the cultivators of the wheat and barley. He cut wood, dug potatoes, harvested the grapes. He washed dishes and clothes, and, when the Abbot judged that he might need a respite from his manual labors, he sewed for the orphans.

The spectacle of Viscount Charles de Foucauld darning socks and sewing buttons on the underwear of little Armenian orphans would have delighted his former comrades-in-arms. He could picture their startled expressions: Maumené, the champagne-bibbing, fun-loving accomplice of his masquerades; Morès, now the Duke of Vallombrosa, his old roommate; Fitz-James, Lyautey, Laperrine, Pétain. . . . Well, they could laugh their heads off. Brother Marie-Albéric relished every minute of it.

Foucauld had in fact carried on a sporadic correspondence with Vallombrosa-Morès since he had become a Trappist novice. The Vallombrosa fortune had been badly mangled in the collapse of the Union Générale, a failure which Rightest politicians attributed to dishonest Jewish bankers and thus strengthened Morès' congenital anti-Semitism. Morès had gone to America to mend his financial fences, married Medora Marie Hoffmann, daughter of a New York banker, and gone West to raise cattle. He settled in the Dakotas, named a town Medora after his wife, shipped his herds to Chicago, but could not make a go of it. He soon abandoned the stockyards for the Boulevards, but his restlessness sent him to India to hunt big game and to Indo-China to survey a railroad. At last report he was back in Paris again, trying his hand at politics, writing anti-Semitic pamphlets, working for General Boulanger, and stumping the slaughter-house district with a gardenia in the button hole of his frock coat. . . .

It all belonged to another world. . . .

Brother Marie-Albéric had also been in correspondence with Henri Duveyrier. He was worried about the old African explorer. Duveyrier had been brooding. The announcement of a new African project revived some of the bitter attacks of his old critics, men who blamed him for the tragic annihilation of the Flatters expedition and other massacres of Frenchmen by the Tuareg. Duveyrier's writings on the Berber peoples had conveyed the idea, said the critics, that the Tuareg were gentle, trustworthy, loyal tribesmen, thus misleading the French who found out too late that they were actually cruel and treacherous warriors.

Bitterly Duveyrier withdrew further within himself. He cancelled his new African expedition and never ventured beyond the walls of his garden in suburban Sèvres. More than ever he mourned his lost love.

Brother Marie-Albéric tried to comfort him by letter. He spoke of the great peace he himself had found in God. He suggested that his friend go to see Abbé Huvelin, a man of great learning whose academic attainments would surely appeal to a man of science like Duveyrier. There was no reply.

Then one day near the end of Brother Marie-Albéric's second year in the Syrian monastery word came from the Secretary-general of the French Geographical Society that Duveyrier had killed himself.

Brother Albéric was profoundly shocked, for Duveyrier was one of his four or five true friends.

"You console me," he wrote to Secretary Maunoir, "in telling me how little he was conscious of his actions during the last days of his life. I hope that God in His infinite goodness will have mercy upon him. He was, as you say, a man of great character, of exalted soul, of tenderest heart."

On Candlemas Day, February 2, 1892, Brother Marie-Albéric took his simple vows. His head was shorn to tonsure. Dom Martin, Abbot of Our Lady of the Snows, on an inspection tour from France, presided over the ceremony. "Our Brother Marie-Albéric," wrote Dom Martin later, "would seem to be an angel in our midst. He wants only wings."

Dom Louis de Gonzague, prior of the Syrian monastery and Dom Martin's brother, was also impressed by the new novice's godliness. Two days after the rites, he wrote to Marie de Blic in praise of her brother: "His confessor, our revered Father

Dom Polycarpe, who will soon have behind him fifty years of religious profession and thirty years as a Superior, has assured me that in all his long life he has never encountered a soul belonging so completely to God."

This hierarchal praise, sincere as it must have been, was not without ulterior motive. The Trappist authorities had decided that the novice who had once called himself Charles de Foucauld was definitely the executive type and would have a great future in the organization. As soon as he could decently be promoted—say in four months—he would be made Master of Novices. Ultimately he would become Prior of the Cheïkhlé monastery. . . .

Before he could achieve the higher ranks, the novice would of course have to be ordained so that he could administer the sacraments. Arrangements were made consequently for Brother Marie-Albéric to study theology with the learned Father Destino, Superior at the Lazarist monastery at Akbès. Brother Marie-Albéric was impressed by the erudition of Father Destino, a Neapolitan who had been professor of theology at Montpellier. He did not, however, take to the program his superiors had laid out for him. "What did Saint Joseph know about theology?" he grumbled.

He persisted, however, and made the daily eight-mile round trip between Cheïkhlé and Akbès without giving up his prayers, meditation, or manual labor. After some months of this routine, he wrote:

"The studies interest me, particularly the Holy Scripture, which is the word of our Celestial Father. Dogmatic theology as well, which concerns the Holy Trinity, Our Lord, the Church, and which draws close to God. . . . But these studies are not nearly as good as the practice of poverty, abjection, or the imitation of Our Lord which may be gained from manual labor. However, since I am doing this as a duty, after having resisted as much as possible, it is evidently what the Good Lord expects of me at this moment."

Brother Marie-Albéric was indulging in understatement. Whether or not the Good Lord expected more of him, he was giving his full measure of abnegation and self-sacrifice. During his first years in Syria, there were three successive epidemics of cholera morbus which not only swept the villages but which invaded the monasteries as well. Nursing cholera patients is not only a wearing job but a nasty one, yet the former fop of the Fourth Hussars did it with a will and loving care. He soothed fevered limbs, washed pain-racked bodies, prayed for tormented souls, and comforted the dying. In the midst of death, he thought for the first time of consecrating not only his life to God, but his death as well.

It was during one of the cholera epidemics that we find him for the first time eager for martyrdom. Surprised and somewhat chagrined that he had escaped the scourge, he wrote to Marie de Bondy that the Good Lord had evidently found him not yet ready for death.

II

After three years in Syria, Brother Marie-Albéric was practically certain that he would never take his final vows as a Trappist. The order which he had chosen for its harsh rule, its stark poverty, and rigorous piety was becoming too soft for him.

In May, 1893, a Papal order which authorized the Trappists to add a little oil and butter as seasoning for their vegetables, saddened Brother Marie-Albéric. Writing to Marie de Bondy, he complained that "for several weeks now our cherished cooking with simple salt and water is a thing of the past. I don't know what kind of grease now goes into our food. . . . A little less mortification means so much less offered to the Good Lord; a little more spent on feeding us means so much less to give the poor. . . . Where will it all stop? And where are we headed? God have mercy on us."

The oil-and-butter concession was only part of a voluminous new *Usages and Constitution of the Order* promulgated by Pope Leo XIII, and when a copy of the entire document reached Syria, Brother Marie-Albéric was not at all pleased with the Trappist reforms. "May it be said between you and me," he wrote to his beloved cousin, "this is not at all the poverty that I would want nor the abjection of which I have dreamed. . . . My needs in this respect have not been satisfied."

His dissatisfaction was increased when he was sent to comfort the family of a Christian Syrian peasant who was dying of cholera a few miles from the monastery. When he saw the misery, the filth, and the bare subsistence which marked the lives of these simple people, he burst into tears. It was with a deep sense of shame that he left the wretched hut of the cholera victim to re-enter what seemed to him the comparative luxury of his austere Trappist cloisters.

Immediately he began to formulate plans for what was to become a life-long obsession: a congregation more austere than the Trappists, closer to the life of Christ. The subject dominated his correspondence—with Abbé Huvelin, his Cousin Marie de Bondy, his sister, and several of his ecclesiastical superiors—for the next few years.

On October 4, 1893, he wrote: "In view of the fact that it is impossible here to live a life of poverty, of abjection, of humility, of real disinterest, I might even say even of contemplative assimilation of Our Lord at Nazareth, I wonder if Our Lord gave me these desires merely that I should sacrifice them to Him, or whether, since no current order of the Church provides the possibility of leading the life which He Himself led in this world, I might not be able to recruit a few souls to form the nucleus of a small congregation of this kind. . . ."

The rules would be simple but hard. Absolute poverty. Manual labor, sufficient to maintain the brothers on a subsistence level, but enough to give generously to the poor. Prayers without end, but no service with choir, "which merely confuses foreigners and offers little aid to the sanctification of the ignorant." Communal life, yes, but in small groups; "populous monasteries inevitably assume a material importance hostile to abjection and humility." And there was to be no hierarchy—everyone was to be a Little Brother or Little Sister of Jesus.

Brother Marie-Albéric's idea met with little enthusiasm. His spiritual guide, Abbé Huvelin, was particularly dismayed by his protégé's rule: Two meals a day (porridge at eleven in the morning, cooked with salt and water only; half a pound of bread at six; nothing more, except that on Sundays and non-fast holidays a little milk and butter might be added to the porridge, and a touch of honey or fruit added to the evening bread. Nothing more. Beverage: only water.

Abbé Huvelin was at first cautious; then vehemently opposed

to his convert's ideas. On January 29, 1894, he wrote: "Continue your theological studies, at least until your diaconate. [The good Abbé was determined that his charge should achieve priesthood.] Apply yourself to the interior virtues up to the point of complete humility. As to the exterior virtues, practice them as regards your obedience to the rule and to your superiors. We will talk about your other questions later. Moreover, you are not fitted—but not in the least fitted—to be a leader of men."

Brother Marie-Albéric, for the nonce resuming his Foucauld crest and its *Jamais Arrière* motto, did indeed refuse to retreat. He continued to bombard Abbé Huvelin with his arguments. And as the fifth anniversary of his simple vows approached, the date on which he was scheduled to take his final vows as a Trappist—Feb. 2, 1897—it was evident that something had to give way.

Abbé Huvelin wrote to his colleagues, expressing his uneasiness. "Evidently," he wrote to a friend in July, 1895, "he will not go on. He will become more and more convinced that the voice of God is calling him. The beauty of the goal to which he believes himself committed will obscure all obstacles, especially those which are insurmountable. . . . I am frightened by the life he wishes to make his, by the Nazareth which he wants to make his home, by the group which he wishes to gather around him. But I have no hope of saving him for the Trappists."

Brother Marie-Albéric continued to write letters.

III

The years 1895 and 1896 were years of death for Brother Marie-Albéric—very personal and poignant death.

In March there came news of a demise which, ten years earlier, might have changed his whole life. The news was communicated with all apparent dispassion and received with equal objectivity.

His beloved cousin Marie informed him that her lawful wedded husband, the Viscount Olivier de Bondy, father of her four children, had departed this life surrounded by his family and—despite his sometime agnosticism—the rites and comforts of the Holy Mother Church.

Cousin Charles de Foucauld replied in kind as Brother Marie-Albéric—formally, with great sympathy, and with the knowledge that he had no need to refer his cousin to the source of all comfort—to God and to Jesus Christ.

It was a curiously impersonal letter of condolence, but what else could he do? He had already said farewell many times to the great love of his life. He could add nothing to the letter he had written to Marie on the first anniversary of his leave-taking in Paris.

On that anniversary he had written several times during the day, recalling what they had been doing together at that exact moment of his last hours as Viscount Charles de Foucauld.

"So our last day had arrived, and was already nearly gone. . . . At this very moment, at five o'clock, I was beside you for the last time in this world. Praised be Our Lord Jesus for giving me the strength to make this sacrifice! . . . How well I remember your clock that marked my last minutes. . . ."

He had thanked her again for her parting gift of a rosary, and had declared: "I thank God for making you so kind to such an unworthy creature as I. . . . May Our Lord Jesus Christ eternally bless you . . . your four children, Olivier, and those you love."

When Olivier de Bondy died in that March of 1895, the old Charles de Foucauld had in a worldly sense already been dead five years.

A little more than a year later Brother Marie-Albéric received another shock. He was never really surprised by anything that his old roommate and fellow cavalry officer, Antoine de Vallombrosa, Marquis de Morès, ever did. Vallombrosa was amazing, impetuous, and unpredictable. During recent years, however, the news of Vallombrosa had been disquieting. When his hero, General Boulanger, killed himself in exile in 1891, Vallombrosa's anti-Semitism rose to hysterical heights. He became editor of the anti-Semitic paper *L'Assaut* and wrote pamphlets which got him three months in jail for libel. On his release he wrote violent pieces for the *Libre Parole* which rode the wave of anti-Semitism leading to the Dreyfus affair. He fought a series of duels with Jewish army officers including Dragoons Captain

Crémieux-Foa and Camille Dreyfus. He killed Captain Armand Meyer.

When Captain Alfred Dreyfus was arrested and convicted of treason on what proved to be forged evidence, Morès-Vallombrosa lost interest in the whole business and decided to go in for international intrigue. It was a return to his first love—to Brother Albéric's great love—Africa. In Southern Algeria Morès organized a large and complex expedition to cross the Sahara into Sudan and the Egyptian Sudan. He hoped to negotiate with the Tuareg for a caravan route to Lake Chad. His ultimate goal, however, was Khartoum where The Mahdi was still firmly entrenched ten years after having thrown out the British under "Chinese" Gordon. Morès hoped to make a deal with The Mahdi whereby they might jointly replace British influence in Egypt with French influence.

Morès' caravan was organized at Ghardaïa on a grand scale—camels, camel drivers, interpreters, Ajjer and Hoggar Tuareg with their slaves, Chambaa with their women, riflemen, swordsmen, horsemen, water carriers, a provision train. . . .

They had not gone far before the Tuareg decided to kill the leaders and take over the rich caravan for themselves. Morès, wounded, backed against a palm tree, and faced his attackers single-handed, loading and reloading his pistol, pouring fire into the treacherous tribesmen until a Tuareg shot finally severed his spinal cord.

As the Trappist novice prayed for the soul of his old schoolmate in June of 1896, he wondered again if his dear and revered friend Henri Duveyrier might indeed have been mistaken in his estimate of the character of the Tuareg.

His doubt lasted only an instant. Duveyrier had not been mistaken. The Tuareg were fundamentally good people. They were Moslems. They had not had the advantage of knowing Jesus Christ. They needed to understand love in its deepest and Christian sense. They needed help.

Antoine de Vallombrosa, Marquis de Morès, had in reality died an unselfish death. His mission to Africa had been a selfless one, ultimately to bring French civilization to an underdeveloped people. He had been partly motivated by love of adventure, true, but above all by his love of France. If only he had died for love of Jesus Christ. . . .

More than ever Brother Marie-Albéric was sure that God did not intend him to live and work among the theologians of Akbès or in the truck gardens of Cheïkhlé. His destiny, he was convinced, lay among the Moslems.

IV

In the autumn of 1895 the Sultan of Turkey ordered a general blood-letting among the Armenians and other native Christians of Syria and elsewhere in the Ottoman Empire. In November Brother Marie-Albéric wrote of the events in stunned, horror-stricken phrases:

"We are in the midst of atrocities, wholesale massacres, arson and pillage. Many Christians have been real martyrs, for they died voluntarily, without defending themselves, rather than deny their faith," he wrote his family.

"The wretched land has been left in frightful distress. The winters here are very severe and I don't know how these unfortunates who have lost their homes to fire and their worldly goods to plunder will be able to keep from dying of cold or hunger. . . .

"I am writing to you for alms—not for us, God forbid, for I shall never be poor enough—but for the victims of persecution. By order of the Sultan, nearly 140,000 Christians have been massacred in the last few months. In Marash, the town nearest to us, the garrison slaughtered 4,500 Christians in two days. We, our brothers at Akbès, and all Christians within two days' travel should have perished. I was not worthy of dying. Pray that my conversion may be complete, that another time, despite my wretchedness, I may not be rejected at the gates of heaven which already stand ajar.

"Europeans here are protected by the Turkish Government, so we live in safety. They have even posted a detachment of soldiers at our door to see that we come to no harm. How painful it is to be on such good terms with those who butcher our brothers . . . !"

As the months crawled by, Brother Marie-Albéric knew that he would never in all conscience be able to take his final vows as a Trappist, a ceremony scheduled for February 2, 1897, the fifth anniversary of his simple vows. He pleaded by letter with his spiritual guide in Paris, asking advice and especially permission to seek release from the Trappist order.

At last in June, 1896, came a letter written on Abbé Huvelin's twenty-ninth anniversary of becoming a priest. Father Huvelin regretted that his protégé was not to follow in his footsteps to the priesthood, but grudgingly gave his permission to seek dispensation:

"I had hoped, my dear child, that you would find what you sought among the Trappists, that you would find sufficient poverty, humility, and obedience to be able to follow the life of Our Lord in Nazareth. . . . I am still sorry this is not to be. There is too strong an urge which is pushing you toward another ideal. . . . I do not believe that you can stop this. Say so to your superiors. Simply state your thoughts. . . . Show them my letter. Speak up. . . . I pray for you."

Brother Marie-Albéric immediately wrote to the Trappist Monastery at Staouëli near Algiers, upon which the Cheïkhlé monastery was now dependent. He also wrote to Abbé Huvelin, thanking him for his advice and enclosing a revised draft of his regulations for the proposed congregation of the Little Brothers of Jesus, which he was still determined to found.

Back came the stern disapproval from Paris: "Your rule is absolutely impractical. . . . The Pope even hesitated to approve the Franciscan rule, which he found too severe, and as for yours! To tell the truth, it frightened me! Live in the shadow of some community in whatever abjection you desire, but do not, I beg of you, write any rules!"

Although disappointed by Father Huvelin's continued rejection of his idea of founding the Little Brothers of Jesus, Brother Marie-Albéric was delighted with his permission to seek release from his preliminary Trappist vows. He requested dispensation from Dom Sebastien Wyart, Trappist Superior-general at Rome, and was told to proceed to the monastery at Staouëli to await orders.

He took the first boat out of Alexandretta, and spent his thirty-eighth birthday at sea. He reached Marseilles at five o'clock on the afternoon of September 23, 1896, and although it was the first time in seven years that he had set foot on French soil, sailed for Algiers an hour later.

The monastery at Staouëli, a dozen miles along the coast westward from Algiers, was headed by Dom Louis de Gonzague, former prior of the Trappists in Syria, friend and admirer of the unhappy novice. After two weeks Dom Louis informed Brother Marie-Albéric that the orders had arrived from Rome. Pending a final decision by the Superior-general, Brother Albéric was to study theology for two years at the Gregorian College in Rome.

"My wishes have not changed one iota," he wrote. "In fact, they are firmer than ever. Yet I obey unquestioningly, with deep gratitude, and with confidence that following this long ordeal the will of God will become clearly manifest. . . ."

V

Brother Marie-Albéric was happy to be in Rome, fountainhead of Catholic thought, city of the martyrdom of Saint Peter and Saint Paul. He was not happy, however, with his theological studies. He lived at the mother house of the Cistercian Order in Via San Giovanni in Laterano. He went to school with young clerics little more than half his age.

"Old, ignorant, and rusty in Latin," he wrote three weeks after his arrival in Rome, "I have great difficulty in following the courses. . . . I shall be an ass in theology as in all else. . . ."

He foresaw a long pull ahead.

"God willing, I shall very probably spend three years here," he wrote shortly before the end of 1896. "This year I am taking only philosophy, which I consider as a task to be accomplished the best I can, obediently and gratefully, while still desiring with growing passion another life. . . ."

The Superior-general, however, had apparently conceived of the theological studies merely to test the discipline and obedience of the restive Brother Marie-Albéric. When the novice had been three months in Rome, Dom Sebastien Wyart summoned him for a personal interview. Apparently impressed by the younger man's sincerity and godliness, the Superior-general released Foucauld from his Trappist vows and confided him to the counsel of his spiritual guide.

By the end of January, 1897, Abbé Huvelin had repeated his earlier advice: Return to the Holy Land and live alone.

"I prefer Capernaum or Nazareth or some Franciscan monastery," he wrote to Foucauld. "Live in the shadow of the monastery but not in it, using only its spiritual resources, and living in poverty at its door. Do not dream of grouping a company of souls around you, and especially not of giving them a rule. Live your own life, and if other souls come to you, live the same life together, without regulating anything. On this point I am very decided. . . ."

Early in February, Charles de Foucauld, no longer Brother Marie-Albéric and no longer bound by Trappist vows, took his own personal vows of perpetual chastity and poverty.

Superior-general Dom Sebastien Wyart gave him his own cross, and the Cistercian Order gave him a steamship ticket for the Holy Land.

Turning his back on the temptation to visit his loved ones in France, he announced his plans only in a letter to his sister and brother-in-law, the Blics: "The new life which I am about to begin will be much more hidden, much more solitary, than that which I am leaving. I want only you to know where I am, so tell no one that I am in the Holy Land; say only that I am in the East, living a life that is very withdrawn, writing to no one. . . ."

He left Rome for the heel of the Italian boot, embarking at Brindisi on February 17, 1897.

NINE

HANDY MAN IN NAZARETH

*C'est dans la solitude que Dieu se donne
tout entier.*

*It is in our solitude that God gives himself
to us completely.*

—Charles de Foucauld

I

Small boys ran after him as he trudged the narrow, cobbled streets of Nazareth on his way from the post office to the convent of the Clarist Sisters. When they shouted gibes and insults at him, Brother Charles of Jesus glowed with satisfaction, and when they pelted him with stones, he was delighted. The more he was humiliated, the more he was mocked and mortified and stoned, the closer he felt to the humble abnegation of Our Lord Jesus Christ Whose feet trod these very cobbles almost nineteen centuries before. He thanked God for the privilege.

The Arab urchins' unholy glee was not without some basis, for Brother Charles might well have passed for an animated scarecrow. He had dressed himself in what he believed approximated the attire of a simple artisan of the time of Christ: a white woolen cap with a twist of ragged turban, a long hooded blouse of blue-and-white striped cotton, blue denim trousers, open sandals, a huge rosary dangling from a wide leather belt, and Dom Sebastien's cross hanging around his neck.

Brother Charles of Jesus, as Foucauld now called himself, had landed at Jaffa on February 24, 1897. He had made his way to Nazareth on foot, begging his food as he passed through

Ramleh, Bethlehem, and Jerusalem, sleeping in the fields. It took him ten days to reach the shores of the Sea of Galilee, but it was like coming home.

He stopped at the Franciscan hostel, hoping to be allowed to stay as a servant, but he was turned away. The Franciscans were their own servants. However, they directed him to the convent of the Clarist Sisters, whose gardener had recently died.

Mother Marie de Saint-Michel of the Poor Clares at once engaged the queer-looking pilgrim whom she found prostrate on the floor of her chapel, praying. She knew, in fact, the identity of her new handyman. The sexton of the Franciscan hostelry had recognized the traveler from his visit nine years before and warned Mother Marie that the man who would apply for a job as gardener was actually Viscount Charles de Foucauld. She kept his secret.

Foucauld described his duties in a letter to Marie de Bondy:

"I serve the Mass and the benediction of the Holy Sacrament, I sweep up, I run errands, in a word I do what I am told to do. On Sundays and holidays I have no duties so I can pray all day long. I live in a wooden shack outside the cloister. This is exactly the life I have been seeking."

The wooden shack was actually a small tool shed. He had refused to sleep in the gardener's room which was within the compound and, he found, much too elegant. He even discarded the straw pallet and blanket which he had at first taken into the shed and thereafter slept on a bench with a stone for a pillow.

As for food, he was unable to resist entirely the pleadings of the Mother Superior, who was the descendant of an old aristocratic family. Née Edith de Miomandre, she had first served as a Clarist Sister in Périgord, ancestral province of the Foucaulds. On Sundays and holidays he consented to take his meals with the Poor Clares—black coffee in the morning, dinner at noon and supper in the evening. "On other days," he wrote to Abbé Huvelin, "I live on bread. Up to now I have been eating two meals of bread, but there is so little mortification in my life, I suffer so little, that I have decided that during the winter I shall eat only one, as I did among the Trappists. . . ."

Brother Charles arose in the middle of the night after five

hours of sleep. Until Angelus he prayed in his shed, then went to pray at the Franciscan chapel, situated in what had once been the house of the Holy Family. He returned to the Clarist convent in time for seven o'clock Mass. His duties during the day were not heavy. He went for the mail only twice a week. His function as gardener, for which he had been hired originally, gradually grew less and less as he demonstrated that he definitely did not possess a green thumb. On the contrary, his inept watering and fertilizing ruined a whole flower bed. His horticultural activity was subsequently limited to spading, raking, and the occasional pruning of the cypress.

He spent more and more time in his tool shed, reading, writing, praying, meditating. The man who was bored and confused by theological studies now plunged deeply into the reading of theology. He read and reread the works of Saint Augustine. He read the *Imitation of Christ.* He wrote commentaries on the Scriptures. He wrote hundreds of pages of meditations and self-examination. He composed a 600-page manuscript called "Considerations on the Festivals of the Year." He wrote letters —hundreds of them. He reveled in his solitude and obscurity.

"The more I have abandoned everything which was once my comfort," he wrote, "the more happiness I have found. . . . I live in infinite peace, an overflowing peace which submerges me. . . . If you only knew the joys of a religious life, in what state of jubilation is my soul!"

Charles de Foucauld had found anonymous happiness at last.

He did not find it incongruous that his jubilation should be closely linked with thoughts of death, for his was the joy of love, the selfless love of Our Lord, a love for which death would be merely the ultimate expression. A few months after moving into his tool shed in Nazareth, he wrote: "Imagine that you should die a martyr, divested of everything, lying naked on the ground, unrecognizable, bloodied and riddled with wounds, tortured and violently slain—and wish that it might be today."

This thought Brother Charles later condensed into a maxim which he carried with him through the rest of his life, hand-printed on the fly-leaf of his breviary: "Live as if today you were to die a martyr."

II

The anonymity of Brother Charles of Jesus was not quite perfect. So strange a figure, a caricature of a tatterdemalion who spoke such impeccable French with a cultured accent, was bound to arouse widespread curiosity, and all sorts of rumors were current in the Nazareth bazaar.

One day in the post office he was accosted by a lay brother from a Salesian monastery who said: "I hear you had a very good job back home in France."

"Ah?"

"Yes, a job as Count. Is it true?"

Brother Charles smiled. "I'm just an old soldier," he said.

Reports of the piety of the extraordinary handyman who served the Poor Clares in Nazareth finally reached the ears of Mother Elisabeth of Calvary, Abbess of the Clarist convent in Jerusalem and superior of the Clarist order in the Holy Land. Mother Elisabeth wrote to Nazareth for details and received such a glowing reply that she was suspicious. She had great confidence in Mother Marie de Saint-Michel, of course, but pious frauds were not uncommon and she wanted to make certain that this was not just another adventurer posing as a holy man. She asked that the handyman be sent to Jerusalem so that she could see for herself. Mother Marie de Saint-Michel thereupon invented a mission—an important letter to be delivered to the Mother Superior by hand—that would take Brother Charles to Jerusalem. He insisted on making the journey on foot. He refused to take provisions with him; he would beg for his daily bread.

Early in July 1898 Brother Charles reached Jerusalem by way of Samaria. He was not a very prepossessing character. Badly-fitting sandals had left his feet lacerated and swollen. Sleeping in the fields had not improved the state of his one and only garment, already showing wear after more than a year in the Holy Land. His scraggly beard, already showing a few silver strands, was now gray with the dust of the road. His receding forehead was red and peeling from the impact of the July sun in Palestine.

Despite the unappetizing externals, however, the Clarist Abbess of Jerusalem immediately found the key to the character of this unusual handy man: his eyes. Deep sunken in his thin, narrow face, the dark eyes burned with a great passion, an unworldy love, an immeasurable tenderness incongruously blended with an indomitable resolution.

Mother Superior Elisabeth immediately understood this self-made waif who stood before her. After all, she was only a dozen years his senior, and she came from the same background. She too had her roots in Périgord, the land which produced the ancestral Foucauld stubbornness. A woman of great charm and great drive, of great piety and ambition, she prided herself on her knowledge of human nature and her ability to win humans to God. Within minutes of their first meeting, she had the silent hermit, the man who wanted only solitude and obscurity, talking his head off like a tipsy second lieutenant of the Fourth Chasseurs d'Afrique.

Whether it was their common Périgourdine ancestry or merely the overwhelming personality of a great and good soul, Mother Elisabeth soon learned his life story; his mother's death when he was a child, his over-indulgent grandfather, his brief army career, Morocco, Abbé Huvelin, his conversion, the Trappists. . . .

"You must stay with us for a few days to rest your poor bleeding feet," said the Abbess. "The chaplain's room is yours for as long as you like."

But Brother Charles refused. There was a vacant shack outside the compound, was there not? A shed next to that occupied by the Negro watchman and his wife? He would be glad to stay there for a short rest before starting back to Nazareth.

That night Mother Elisabeth confided to one of her Clarist Sisters:

"Nazareth was not mistaken. He is truly a man of God. We have a saint in our midst."

III

The impression which Brother Charles had made upon Mother Elisabeth did not fade with his return to Nazareth. Here was a man whose great talent, intellect, and saintliness was being wasted. He must be shown how to give greater service to God. Two months later she summoned him again to Jerusalem.

"I don't know why she sent for me," he wrote to his family in France, "for I can be of little use to her. I think she is merely being charitable toward me, so that she in her turn may overwhelm me with kindness. She is a saint. . . . What beautiful souls are created by the Good Lord, and how good He is to let me meet them! What gems of moral beauty there are hidden away in these cloisters, and what lovely flowers bloom there for God alone! . . ."

It cannot be entirely a coincidence that the women who had the most influence on the life of Charles de Foucauld were older women. Psychologists, of course, would say that this is because he constantly sought to fill the need created by the loss of his mother when he was six years old. Yet in both the case of Marie de Bondy, whom he wanted to marry and who succeeded in transmuting his love for her into love for God, and of Mother Elisabeth of Calvary, who induced him to take a vital step which even his beloved spiritual adviser had been unable to do, there was something else involved. In both cases there was an obvious mutual attraction, on a high moral plane, but so strong that it might well be termed a pure and spiritual love.

On his fortieth birthday—September 15, 1898—he was summoned to what was apparently a decisive interview with Mother Elisabeth. She told him that he was not giving full measure of himself to God; that he should think seriously of taking the orders; that he could never achieve fulfillment until he became a priest.

Brother Charles protested: "To be a priest, I would have to show myself. I am made for the hidden life."

Mother Elisabeth answered by quoting from the Sermon on the Mount:

"A city set upon a mountain cannot be hid. Neither do men light a lamp and put it under a bushel, but upon the lampstand; and it giveth light to all in the house. Even so, let your light shine before men, in order that they may see your good works and glorify your Father who is in the heavens."

Brother Charles made no comment. He could not very well

argue with the words of Jesus, yet he did love his obscure solitude.

"Think about it," said the Abbess.

During their first interview, Charles de Foucauld had confided in Mother Elisabeth his hopes and plans for the Little
Brothers of Jesus. The Abbess did not share Father Huvelin's
objections. In fact, she approved. She even suggested a first
recruit: a novice he had known at the Trappist monastery at
Cheïkhlé, who was now reported to be in Jaffa. Brother Charles
could bring the novice to Jerusalem and they could form the
nucleus of their little colony just outside the Clarist convent
walls.

Brother Charles immediately left for Jaffa, to find that his ex-
Trappist friend had just left. He followed the trail to Alexandretta, where he also arrived too late. When he finally made
contact, the former novice declined the honor of being the first
adherent of the Little Brothers. Abbé Huvelin was right;
Foucauld's proposed rule was too severe for human endurance.

Returning to Jerusalem, Brother Charles settled down for a
while in the shack next to the watchman's cottage outside the
convent walls.

"My life here is the same as at Nazareth," he wrote to his
family, "except that I am even more alone, which is still better.
The convent is two kilometers from Jerusalem on the road to
Bethany, on an admirable site beside the Vale of Kedron across
from the Mount of Olives. All Jerusalem is spread beneath its
windows—Gethsemane, the whole Mount of Olives, Bethany,
the mountains of Moab and Idumea which rise like a dark wall
beyond the Jordan. . . ."

He was kept busy with odd jobs and particularly with paint-
ing and drawing—talents which he had almost forgotten since
he made the last sketches for his work on Morocco. He painted
religious subjects, he did a symbolic series of nine medallions
representing the life of Mother Elisabeth, he made sketches for
a new monastery. With the chaplain's permission he received
his own key to the chapel so that he might on occasion spend all
night in prayer.

Mother Elisabeth did not lose sight of her original objective:
to win Brother Charles to the priesthood. She was a woman of

great determination as well as great spirituality. She was accustomed to leadership. She was a builder and organizer. She had founded three convents for the Poor Clares since she had left Périgord: at Paray-le-Monial in the upper reaches of the Loire Valley in France; at Nazareth, which she had turned over to her protégée, Mother Marie de Saint-Michel; and at Jerusalem. Mother Elisabeth was not giving up easily on the ordination of her pious handyman.

At regular intervals she pointed out to him that if he became a priest, the world would be richer by at least one more Mass every day. She accused him of selfishness in keeping to himself alone the gifts which he had nurtured and brought to fruition by long spiritual labors. Why did he persist in refusing to become a missionary to carry the Word to the dark places of the earth?

For answer Brother Charles walked silently to the solitude of his green shanty outside the walls.

Mother Elisabeth then ordered her Poor Clares to pray daily that God allow Brother Charles to see the light and take the orders.

Next time he saw her, Charles said: "If you are that determined, why not write to my spiritual guide? I can't very well write to Abbé Huvelin myself, because for years I have been saying 'no' to the same plea. It is only God's will that I can follow."

Mother Elisabeth wrote to Paris. So did Brother Charles. It took some time before the answer came back across the Mediterranean.

Abbé Huvelin was perplexed. Of course, he wanted Foucauld to become an ordained priest; he had wanted it for many years. But he was uneasy about Jerusalem, even uneasy about Mother Elisabeth. The Abbess was of course a woman of God, a saintly woman, and yet. . . .

"I wish you would go back to your hutch in Nazareth," wrote Abbé Huvelin.

Mother Elisabeth was in complete agreement—as long as Brother Charles would take the orders. As a matter of fact, she had been thinking that perhaps he had better go north again. She even had a suggestion that would not only take him back to

the region that he preferred, but might well lay the cornerstone
for his dream project, a home for his Little Brothers. How
would he like to take title to the Mount of Beatitudes on the
shore of the Sea of Galilee? What a perfect spot for a holy
hermitage, an isolated place where the nucleus of the Little
Brothers of Jesus might grow, and yet a shrine which might indeed become a goal of the really hardy and saintly pilgrims.

Brother Charles was intoxicated by the idea. Was it really
possible that he might set up a shrine on the Mount of Beatitudes?

It was indeed possible, said Mother Elisabeth, and immediately put him in touch with the Franciscan authorities charged
with custody of the Holy Places of the Holy Land. The Franciscans in turn put him in touch with their Jerusalem business
agent, a man named Lendli, who said he could secure title to
the Mount of Beatitudes site for 13,000 francs—the equivalent
then of $2,600.

Charles de Foucauld's enthusiasm knew no bounds. He wrote
to his brother-in-law, Viscount de Blic, asking him to send him
the 13,000 francs at once. He worked feverishly on a plan
whereby he would transfer title of the Mount of Beatitudes to
the Franciscan order, thereby insuring that it would remain in
the hands of the Church. He would erect a shrine there, staffed
by a priest and a servitor, so that Mass would be said daily in
perpetuity. He saw himself as the poor and obscure servitor, and
had in mind as priest a Maronite who had attached himself to
Brother Charles, but whom Sister Elisabeth vetoed after con-
firming her suspicions that he was half mad. And around this
beginning would grow the Little Brothers. In fact, Brother
Charles had resumed work revising his rule so that it might
secure even Abbé Huvelin's approval. As he finished his draft on
the Feast of the Sacred Heart, he rechristened his dream order
the Little Brothers of the Sacred Heart of Jesus.

In his own words, Charles de Foucauld recorded his thinking
about the project:

"I believe it my duty to try to buy the probable site of the
Mount of Beatitudes. I can see clearly that either because of
obstacles raised by the Turkish Government or because of their
current expenses, the Franciscans cannot promise to establish

there now or in the foreseeable future an altar with a tabernacle and a chaplain. . . . I see nothing better than to propose that I undertake to maintain on the summit of the mount an altar, a tabernacle which would house in perpetuity the Blessed Sacrament, and a chaplain charged with celebrating Mass daily. My proposal would entail the condition that whenever the Franciscans are willing to assume the maintenance of the altar, tabernacle and the chaplain, the premises would be immediately transferred to them by me or my heirs.

"I had first thought of installing there a hermit chaplain in a poor lodging, and to move in beside him as servitor and sacristan. But I realize that I can under no conditions impose these expenses upon my family. I must therefore find some other solution. I see only one: that is to become myself the poor chaplain of this poor sanctuary."

Viscount de Blic's 13,000 francs arrived and was immediately paid over to Mr. Lendli.

Abbé Huvelin's reaction also arrived, full of reservations, cautions, worry, and the word that Cousin Marie de Bondy was also very much worried about the whole deal. "Please, please," pleaded Abbé Huvelin, "return to Nazareth."

But Brother Charles had already left for Nazareth of his own free will. Mother Marie de Saint-Michel of the Clarist Sisters had written that there was trouble over the title to the land upon which his tool-shed sanctuary stood. Would Brother Charles come and help straighten things out?

Brother Charles came at once.

IV

The land dispute was ultimately settled in favor of the Poor Clares, largely because Brother Charles re-established residence in the tool shed.

Brother Charles' own status as a prospective landowner was making less progress. Inexplicable delays, curious complications, and requests for new documents were forever coming up. Foucauld suspected that the Turkish government was behind the delay, and he was right.

The Sublime Porte had long had the eccentric hermit under surveillance. Turkish censors had been reading all his incoming and outgoing mail, and they were puzzled as only Orientals can be puzzled. Here was a penniless pilgrim, a ragamuffin who lived in a shanty outside the Clarist convent, yet who wrote and received letters to and from Viscounts, Marqueses, Generals and Archbishops. Furthermore, Turkish intelligence reported that Brother Charles of Jesus was actually none other than Viscount Charles de Foucauld, a former officer of the Fourth Hussars and Fourth Chasseurs d'Afrique, who had undertaken a hazardous mission into Morocco, obviously for the purpose of mapping the interior for the French Army. Here was a supposed penniless religious ascetic who, overnight practically, was able to plunk down 13,000 francs on an otherwise worthless piece of real estate—worthless except that it was a mountain top. It would be an ideal observation post, a visual signal station (overland telegrams still had to go through Turkish censorship, and the wireless telegraph had not yet been perfected). Obviously, the whole transaction must be subject to the most careful scrutiny. . . .

Meanwhile Brother Charles was busy convincing himself that his decision was correct, despite the continuous bombardment of objections from Abbé Huvelin. Brother Charles wrote them all down in his spiritual diary under alternate headings of *Here* and *There*. Samples:

"*Here* my status is in itself of the lowest; *there*, in my eyes, it would be of infinitely high stature for nothing for me is higher than a priest. But where could I best imitate Our Lord: The priest can more perfectly imitate Our Lord, Who as sovereign priest offered Himself daily. I must place humility where Our Lord placed it . . . practice it where He practiced it—in the priesthood.

"*Here* I have more distractions due to my surroundings. . . . *There* I could spend part of each night at the feet of the Blessed Sacrament. . . . Although *here* my abjection may at first glance seem greater, *there* I should submit to a thousand more humiliations. *Here* in my own right I am superior to my current status. *There*, as an ignorant, inept priest, I should be, in my own right, far below my capabilities. . . ."

In June 1900 Brother Charles had made up his mind to the point of no return. He walked to Jerusalem to put his problem before the Patriarch, Monseigneur Piavi. First of all, he needed the Patriarch's permission to be ordained in his diocese. Second, he needed the Patriarch's authority to establish his hermitage atop the Mount of Beatitudes. And finally, he wanted the Patriarch's approval of his rule for the congregation of the Little Brothers of the Sacred Heart which he expected to grow on the sacred mountain top.

Even Abbé Huvelin had hedged on this latest project. His perennial *no* was to some extent tempered in his latest message: "My child, I do not have the wisdom to advise you on this. I can see only objections, and I am frightened by the basic principle underlying your devotion and your piety."

When Brother Charles arrived at the door of the Patriarchate, his only garment was beginning to show the signs of more than three years of wear. His ill-fitting sandals had finally disintegrated beyond repair; he had thrown them away and for the last fifty miles had been shod only with two blocks of wood fastened to his feet with straps. His trousers were out at the knees and patched with paper. He was badly sunburned, and the unbearded portions of his thin face, including the expanding forehead which was rising into his receding hairline, were red and peeling. His Excellency Monseigneur Piavi was not only unimpressed, but he was secretly angry with his underlings for having let this scarecrow into his inner sanctum.

His Excellency listened impatiently while Brother Charles expounded his case, then said: "We will consider the matter. Please withdraw now."

Brother Charles withdrew. As he wrote later: "I saw the Patriarch and told him what I had to say. So, although he dismissed me in a rather cavalier manner, I am quite content. I could not be at greater peace or more happy."

The Patriarch did indeed keep his promise to consider the matter. He was in fact rather surprised by the report brought back by his investigators. The strange tatterdemalion with the blazing, hypnotic eyes was not just one of the religious crackpots who seemed to thrive in the Holy Land. He was a man of parts, of education, of fine background, of moneyed family, and of long and undisputed piety. Monseigneur Piavi immediately

sent after Brother Charles, summoning him to another interview for further discussion of his plans—too late.

Whether or not the device on the old Foucauld coat of arms—
Jamais Arrière—seeped into Brother Charles' subconscious at
this time, will never be known. It is a matter of record, however, that Brother Charles did refuse to turn back. He had
accepted the Patriarch's initial dismissal as a token of the Divine
Will. God apparently did not approve of his plan to become a
priest and remain in the Holy Land as chaplain of a shrine on
the Mount of the Beatitudes. There was no use, therefore, in
returning to discuss the matter further with His Excellency. He
had made up his mind to become a priest; there was no Divine
indication of disapproval of this decision. Therefore, if he was
not to become a priest in Jerusalem, he would return to France.

First of all he sought out Attorney Lendli to recover the
13,000 francs he had paid for the Mount of the Beatitudes, so
that he could return the money to his brother-in-law. In this,
too, he met with rejection. Either through the machinations of
the Turkish government or the skulduggery of some sharp real-
estate operators, Brother Charles owned nothing but a receipt
for 13,000 francs. The man whose signature was on his receipt
had fled Jerusalem. Title to the Mount of the Beatitudes had
been sold to somebody else. God's will was indeed evident.

"Stay in Nazareth," cabled Abbé Huvelin.

But Charles de Foucauld was no longer to be deterred from
his new purpose. *Jamais Arrière!* Bidding farewell to the saintly
women of the Poor Clares, he made his way to Jaffa. On a hot
August day of 1900, his breviary in his hand and a basket containing a loaf of bread and a handful of dried fruits on his arm,
he embarked as a deck passenger on a ship bound for Marseilles.

V

Paris—for the first time in ten years! The Church of Saint-
Augustin—for the first time in ten years!

Abbé Huvelin was not at the church when Foucauld arrived.
Neither was he at the parsonage around the corner in Rue de
Laborde. He was at Fontainebleau nursing a bad case of gout,
but at word of his convert's arrival, he hurried to meet him.

The priest had expected to give Foucauld a tongue-lashing

for disobeying his cabled orders to remain in Nazareth. Instead, he was more startled than displeased. He scarcely recognized the gaunt, sun-burned man in the tattered oriental masquerade. There were touches of gray in his beard now, and he was beginning to lose his hair. But the disarming smile and the fervent glow in his deep-set eyes were the same as they had been when Foucauld was a dapper man-about-town, seeking the Truth. Besides, he was going to take the orders. Abbé Huvelin forgot his projected reprimand and enfolded the penitent in his forgiving embrace.

The two men had much to discuss after ten years. They spent the next twenty-four hours together. As Abbé Huvelin described it: "He dined and slept at the house, lunched with me, and took off for Our Lady of the Snows and Rome. . . . He is a very godly soul. He wants to be a priest and I showed him how. He had very little, too little money; I gave him some. He was well acquainted with my opinion of his actions, as I had made it clear by cable. However, he is being impelled by something much stronger, and I can only admire and love him."

At the Trappist monastery of Our Lady of the Snows, the ex-novice was welcomed with open arms by Dom Martin, the Abbot. Dom Martin secured the necessary number of clerics to vouch for Foucauld as a man of great virtue and obtained permission of the Bishop of Viviers for Foucauld to prepare for ordination in his diocese, which included the monastery. Dom Martin also persuaded Foucauld to abandon his oriental beggar's rags for the more conventional black cassock of the lay Trappist brother.

Foucauld then entrained for Rome for a brief visit with theologians who had been his professors before his departure for Nazareth. He wanted advice on his course of study for the priesthood, on his plans after ordination, and also on his revised rule for a congregation of the Little Brothers of the Sacred Heart. At Rome he lived in a boarding house at 105 Via Pozetto, across the street from Saint-Claude-des-Bourguignons where the Fathers of the Blessed Sacrament practised perpetual adoration. Thus he could spend most of his time at prayer or at study in the presence of the Eucharist.

He spent his forty-second birthday on his knees before the

Blessed Sacrament, his big theological tomes open on the floor in front of him.

He returned to France by way of his sister's home in Burgundy, and also had a brief visit with Marie de Bondy—their first meeting since she had become a widow. He reached Our Lady of the Snows on September 29 and went immediately into retreat. On October 7, the Feast of the Holy Rosary, he received minor orders from Dom Martin and once more assumed the white robe of the Trappist novice and the name of Brother Albéric. On December 22 he became subdeacon.

Father Léon Laurens, assigned to teach Brother Albéric the ritual of the Mass, complained that an infinite number of rehearsals was necessary because at the first words pronounced at the foot of the altar—*Introïbo ad altare Dei*—Foucauld would instinctively go into a trance-like mystical union, his spirit soaring in prayer. He would then kneel and beg forgiveness for being so stupid.

Shortly before Easter of 1901 he became a deacon and in May began his thirty-day retreat which marked the end of his preparation for the priesthood. On June 9 he was ordained at Viviers, the episcopal see, in the presence of the Bishop, Monseigneur Bonnet, and Dom Martin who had accompanied him from the monastery.

Next day he celebrated his first Mass at Our Lady of the Snows. His sister Marie de Blic came down from Burgundy for the occasion and received Communion at the hands of her brother.

It was a great day for Mimi de Foucauld de Blic who, after Mass, sat with her brother in "a good session," her eyes bright with tears of joy.

It was a proud day for Dom Martin, Abbot of Our Lady of the Snows, to see the culmination of ten years of religious life of "our dear and saintly hermit," begun in these very cloisters.

It was a solemn day for the Reverend Father Charles de Foucauld, for his real career was about to begin.

TEN

HOME TO AFRICA

Flattery is easy in Africa, but praise must be hard-earned.

—L. Durand-Reville, Académie
de la France d'Outremer

I

The new recipient of the Holy Orders had no intention of settling down in some village parish on the banks of the Rhône; there were plenty of priests in the diocese of Viviers to which he was attached; there were plenty of priests in France, in fact. There were also plenty of priests in the Holy Land, so that to return to Nazareth, which he loved, would be an act of self-indulgence. Where then should he go except where the need was the greatest? Africa.

In all Morocco, a country as large as France with a dozen million inhabitants, there was not a single priest. In the Sahara, an area seven or eight times that of France, there were perhaps a dozen missionaries. The call was loud and clear.

The Bishop of Viviers, who was now his superior, was quite ready to approve a roving mission for Father de Foucauld, but there were a number of obstacles. First, Morocco was out of the question. Foucauld would have to be content with some post in Southern Algeria near the Moroccan border. Second, Foucauld would have to obtain permission from ecclesiastical, civil, and military authorities before setting up his altar in French North Africa.

The White Fathers, founded by Cardinal Lavigerie in 1874, claimed religious jurisdiction over the Sahara and French West

Africa, and the hierarchy of this missionary order looked with some suspicion upon this eccentric free-lance who wanted to set up in their territory a new, austere, and as yet unapproved order.

The civil authorities, represented by the Governor General of Algeria and the Bureau of Native Affairs, had great reservations about missionaries. First of all the policies of the Third Republic were generally following an anti-clerical line leading to the imminent separation of Church and State. Furthermore, it was the policy of French civil authority in Africa not to meddle with the religion of the Moslems. The White Fathers were already there on tolerance.

The French Army, too, was committed to non-interference with the Mohammedan religion. Moreover, Army brass was somewhat less than enthusiastic about the military record of the ex-cavalry officer turned priest.

Father de Foucauld decided that the best way to get into the desert was to offer himself as chaplain for some army unit stationed at a distant outpost. To this end he wrote in August 1901 to Monseigneur Bazin, apostolic vicar of the Sahara and Sudan, explaining his project:

". . . The memory of my comrades who died without the sacraments and without a priest during the expeditions against Bou Amama (in which I took part) twenty years ago, urges me imperatively to leave for the Sahara as soon as you will have granted me the necessary authority. . . . I humbly ask two things of Your Grace.

"1. Authority to establish a small public oratory in one of the little French garrisons without a priest between Ain Sefra and Twat. I should reside there to administer the sacraments and serve the sick.

"2. Authorization to gather about whatever companions, priests or laymen, Jesus might send me, and to practice with them the adoration of the Very Blessed Sacrament there exposed.

"If you deign to grant me this double request, I should reside in this humble oratory without the title of curate, vicar, or chaplain, and without any subsidy, living as a monk, following the rule of Saint Augustine either alone or with some brothers, living in prayer, poverty, labor and charity, without preaching, without going out except to administer the sacraments, in silence and in cloister.

"My aim is to give spiritual succor to our soldiers, to prevent their souls being lost through lack of the last sacraments, and *especially* to sanctify the infidel peoples by carrying among them Jesus present in the Blessed Sacrament just as Mary sanctified the house of John the Baptist by carrying Jesus there. . . ."

Monseigneur Bazin referred the matter to Monseigneur Livinhac, Superior-general of the White Fathers, whereupon letters of high recommendation went out to Monseigneur Livinhac from Dom Martin, Abbé Huvelin, and the Bishop of Viviers. Curiously enough, all three clerics noted not only Father de Foucauld's great piety but also his military service and his aristocratic family. For good measure, letters also went to Monseigneur Guérin, Prefect Apostolic of Ghardaïa.

When there was no immediate response from North Africa, Father de Foucauld decided to go to Algiers and plead his case in person. He sailed from Marseilles early in September 1901, carrying with him the fittings for a portable altar, a few books, some canvas for tenting, fifty yards of rope and a small bucket for use in desert water holes.

He was met in Algiers by his old friend Dom Henri, prior of the Trappist monastery at Staouëli, and Monseigneur Guérin, the young apostolic prefect.

Guérin was greatly taken by Foucauld from the moment of their first meeting. "I regard the entrance of this saintly priest into the territory of the prefecture in my trust to be a blessing of God," he said. "A veritable saint like Charles of Jesus cannot help doing good."

He took the new arrival to Saint Joseph's monastery at Maison Carrée, a few miles east of Algiers. Saint Joseph's, the mother house of the White Fathers, was surrounded by vineyards which produced a first-rate wine. Here Father de Foucauld was presented to Monseigneur Livinhac, Superior-general of the missionary order.

Despite the enthusiastic introduction by the Prefect Apostolic of Ghardaïa, Monseigneur Livinhac was rather cool to Foucauld and his plans. First of all, the missionary concept of the White

Fathers was radically different from the austere example of the ex-Trappist. The White Fathers were interested in the material as well as the moral welfare of their converts. In their schools they taught the Arabs trades as well as the catechism, weaving as well as The Word. Furthermore, the White Fathers believed in the good life between tours of duty. The hostel at Maison Carrée was in effect a rest house for missionaries on leave after two or three years in the glaring wastes of the desert. It was a charming retreat set in a mosaic of palm-shaded nooks and corners, sun-bright buildings, and blazingly-colorful flower beds. The White Fathers on leave ate well and drank deeply of the excellent wine grown in their own Algerian vineyards. This was hardly the sort of community into which an ex-Trappist who lived on dry bread, dried dates, and water would seem to fit.

Of course the fact that Foucauld was not actually a member of the White Fathers also bothered Monseigneur Livinhac. Here was an unattached priest, responsible to the Bishop of Viviers who had ordained him scarcely three months earlier, barging into the well-established community of Cardinal de la Vigerie, wearing the garb of his own upstart congregation of which he was the only member: a white gandurah, the front of which was emblazoned with a red heart surmounted by a cross —the insignia of the unauthorized Little Brothers of the Sacred Heart; a white tarboosh draped with sun-protecting flaps for ears and nape; loose sandals, and an out-size rosary dangling from a broad leather belt.

And the rule that this lone eccentric had written for his non-existent order—what would it do to the missionary work of the White Fathers? Eagerness to shed a martyr's blood. . . . Willingness to starve to death if necessary. . . . Absolute obedience to Father de Foucauld, "despite his unworthiness. . . ."

No, no. This man was an egomaniac or a simple lunatic. He should not be allowed to function in White Fathers' territory, no matter how earnestly Monseigneur Guérin pleaded his cause. There was one way to put him off without taking responsibility for rejecting a pious Christian. . . .

"We will consider the matter," said Monseigneur Livinhac. "If the Governor-general of Algeria authorizes your mission to

Southern Oran, we would be most happy to add our ecclesiastical approval."

The risk seemed slight. The anti-clerical civil authorities of the Rue Berthezène were not likely to give free rein to this wild-eyed zealot.

Father de Foucauld retired to the other side of Algiers to await the decision. He accepted the invitation of Prior Dom Henri to be his guest at Staouëli. He would feel more at home among the Trappists where he could pray all night and dine on a handful of barley, if that be his desire, without having to refuse ungraciously a glass of wine tendered by a missionary wishing to share his month of relaxation.

Dom Henri, however, was not going to allow his old friend Brother Charles, erstwhile Brother Marie-Albéric, to sit tranquilly by while awaiting a decision. Dom Henri was a man of action.

"You are an old soldier, Brother Charles," he said. "Is it not true that old soldiers always respond to the call of a comrade?"

"I have never traded on my brief service to France as an officer," said the ex-lieutenant of the Fourth Chasseurs d'Afrique.

"I understand the present chief of the Bureau of Native Affairs in Algiers is an army officer named Lacroix," said Dom Henri. "Perhaps you know him."

"Lacroix," said Father de Foucauld. "Not Henri Lacroix by any chance?"

"Major Henri Lacroix, yes."

"Do I know him? Henri Lacroix was a classmate of mine at Saint-Cyr! But that was nearly twenty-five years ago. He may not remember me."

As if anyone could forget the plump, well-heeled cadet who swilled champagne, read Aristophanes, and ate *pâté de foie gras* with a golden spoon!

"Jog his memory," said Dom Henri. "You may need him."

The Prior himself carried Foucauld's note into Algiers, and Major Lacroix, overjoyed to hear from his old classmate, immediately came out to Staouëli to see him. There was a subsequent reunion at Major Lacroix's villa at which Foucauld broke down and drank some Algerian wine with Mme. Lacroix's excellent French cooking. . .

The Chief of the Bureau of Native Affairs had no trouble in securing permission for Father de Foucauld's mission from the Governor-general of Algeria and the Commander of the Nineteenth Army Corps, into whose territory the priest wanted to go. With the civil and military authorizations granted, the Superior-general of the White Fathers added his ecclesiastical approval as he had promised.

On October 15, 1901, Father de Foucauld left Algiers for Beni-Abbès, a small garrison on the edge of the desert some 400 miles south of the Mediterranean coast. He would take the train westward to Oran, then change to the new railway that snaked south along the Moroccan frontier to Ain Sefra in the Ksour range of the Atlas mountains. From Ain Sefra he still had nearly 140 miles to go before reaching his destination. Foucauld wanted to travel the last lap on foot, but Major Lacroix objected. Humility or not, no Frenchman, even a priest, must enter the desert walking like an indigent nomad. He was representing not only God and the Church but France as well. Major Lacroix telegraphed ahead to make sure horses would be provided for Foucauld when he reached the rail head.

Inasmuch as he was indebted to his old classmate for expediting his mission, Foucauld could not gracefully object.

At Ain Sefra, Foucauld was met by General Cauchemez, French commander of the region, who insisted that he stay over a few days and rest up for the long journey overland. The general installed his guest in the quarters of the Bureau of Native Affairs—a sunny commodious room with a soft white bed. It was only several days later that he learned the bed had not been slept in. Foucauld had for so long been a stranger to the comforts of a mattress and linen sheets that he preferred to sleep on the floor.

He rode out from Ain Sefra mounted on a mare of the Makhazan cavalry. He was accompanied by a convoy led by Lieutenant Huot of the Bureau of Native Affairs. On the second day of his journey he crossed a village the name of which brought a tightness to his throat, a tear to his eye, and a prayer to his lips: Duveyrier—named for his old friend, scholar and geographer, fearless explorer of unmapped wastes who did not have the courage to face life.

Half way to Beni-Abbès, the commander of the garrison at the oasis of Taghit galloped out at the head of a troop of Arab cavalry to meet the old hussar turned priest. Captain de Susbielle had told his horsemen: "You are going to greet a French marabout who comes here out of friendship for you. Salute him with honor." As the Arabs presented arms, Foucauld returned the compliment in the best cavalry manner. He galloped to meet the Arabs, his white gandurah flapping in the wind, reining in his mount in front of the captain, forcing the animal to rear in salute in the finest Saumur tradition.

Next morning, his gluteal muscles still sore from the unaccustomed horsemanship, he celebrated Mass—the first Mass ever said at Taghit—before an awed and powerful assembly of both Christians and Moslems.

At twilight of the fourth day he came upon Beni-Abbès. He halted on a little rise, looking down on the oasis, where the Saura, one of the mysterious underground rivers that underlie the Sahara desert, come to the surface for a few hundred yards to make things grow, then disappear again. Father de Foucauld looked out over the oasis, a lovely green grove of ten thousand date palms which had put their taproots down fifty yards—the length of Father de Foucauld's emergency water supply rope. He gazed at the little white-walled communities of a few hundred houses of the Arabs adjoining the oasis. He could smell the water, a sweet fragrance which every man who has ever known the desert has come to love. He turned to the west, where the vanishing sun was draping a purple glow over the rocky hammada, the stony plateau which stretched out toward Morocco, the country of his youth. To the east the astounding pink waves of sand, the turbulent sea of giant dunes that were the beginning of the Great Western Erg, faded into the sudden desert night. The stars were already pricking through the incredibly deep blue of the African sky.

Father de Foucauld dismounted, sank to his knees, and thanked God for allowing him to return to Africa, the excitingly

beautiful land which should be God's country if only the Word
of God were known.

He had come home.

II

It did not take Father de Foucauld long to choose the spot for
his chapel and hermitage. He refused to live within range of the
guns of the French garrison—three companies of sharpshooting
riflemen and a service company. He could not of course live
within the oasis, since life there would be too comfortable. His
understanding with Major Lacroix and the Bureau of Native
affairs precluded his settling within the Moslem community. He
picked out a barren area—fifteen acres which he ultimately
bought for a thousand francs, provided by Marie de Bondy, who
did not even question the somewhat exorbitant price in view
of current Saharan real estate values. He celebrated Mass for
the troops the morning after his arrival—an exhilarating experience, for he was after all the only priest within 300 miles!

Foucauld found several springs and a few abandoned wells on
the property he had picked out. He immediately put his water
supply in order, then set about building his hermitage and lay-
ing out a vegetable garden.

He began building his chapel with his own hands. He described it in a letter to his cousin who had financed the construction: "Flat roof built of palm-tree trunks covered with
palm-leaf thatch—very rustic, very poor, but well-proportioned
and charming. Four palm-trunk uprights support the roof and
provide a handsome frame for the altar. A kerosene lamp hangs
from the one at the left of the altar, brightening the darkness. A
tent of heavy dark-green canvas is suspended from the ceiling to
protect the altar against the rain, which is fortunately very rare.
The roof is largely protection against the sun. . . ."

When the post commander, Captain Emil Louis Regnault,
returned from patrol, he was so happy to have a chaplain in his
area that he assigned details of his men to help Foucauld in his
building project. They made sun-dried bricks. They gathered
flat stones from the hammada. They dug and chopped and
sawed and sweated, but no more than did the architect and master builder.

Father de Foucauld himself did the altar piece—a canvas work in the spare but eloquent design and the true, economic line of his Moroccan sketches—a Christ with arms outstretched to embrace and give Himself to all the world. On the breast of the Saviour, Foucauld had painted the scarlet sacred heart and the cross growing out of it, which he had made his trademark. At the left of the altar he depicted Saint Joseph. At the right there was a niche containing an alarm clock—the clock of the hermitage which the Arabs soon came to call *Khawa*—fraternity. Father de Foucauld painted a heart and cross on the front door, added the Latin phrase "Jesus Caritas," and called his hermitage the Fraternity of the Sacred Heart.

On the walls of his chapel Foucauld hung the fourteen Stations of the Cross, done in red, black, and blue ink on cloth or heavy paper tacked to stretchers made of wood from packing cases.

On December 1, 1901, Father de Foucauld celebrated his first Mass in his new chapel. It was packed with officers and men from the garrison of Beni-Abbès, some curious, many devout, many hungry for the spiritual life they had been missing for so long. Wrote one soldier: "He recited the *Domine non sum dignus* with such feeling that we all wanted to cry with him."

The mud chapel of Beni-Abbès measured about 45 feet in length, 13 feet in width and 13 feet in height. While his establishment was expanding, Foucauld slept at the foot of the altar "curled up like a dog at the feet of his Master." Little by little he added outbuildings, including narrow cells in which he would sleep for the few hours he allowed himself to rest. When an officer of the garrison asked how he could possibly sleep since there was no room to stretch out at full length and relax, he replied: "Did Jesus have room to relax on the Cross?"

The cells for the Little Brothers—who never came—were just as narrow. The room for the passing travelers was bigger. There was also a building for non-Christian birds of passage, for Foucauld said: "I want everyone—Christians, Moslems, Jews, and pagans—to look upon me as their brother—the universal brother."

Brother Charles of Jesus, as he was again calling himself, lived on bread and water, with an occasional can of condensed milk or a handful of dates. His visitors were always given barley, dates, flour, and a few vegetables he managed to grow in the back lot. His own expenses ran to seven francs a month— less than $1.50. The money he received from his sister and his cousin Marie de Bondy from time to time he used to feed and clothe the poor of the village or, when he could put enough aside, to buy freedom for some slave.

Foucauld was shocked and saddened by the fact that the institution of slavery was flourishing in Southern Oran. What's more, he found that the Arabs and Berbers in Algeria treated their slaves far more cruelly than did the Moroccans. He wrote long letters to his most influential friends in France, particularly to Henri de Castries, asking them to lobby for legislation in the Chamber of Deputies which would outlaw slavery. This hardly endeared him to French authorities in Africa, who were committed to non-interference in local customs, nor to the Arabs who resented the French marabout's attempt to change their social structure and to deprive them of their property.

On January 8, 1902, Foucauld purchased his first slave, a lad of about twenty, and gave him his freedom. As the bargain was concluded on Saint Joseph's Day (for 400 francs), Foucauld renamed him Joseph du Sacré Coeur. Joseph seemed deeply grateful to his liberator, who cooked and cleaned for him, washed his clothes, and waited on him, as he did for all visitors to his Fraternity, black or white, well or ailing. In fact, he gloried particularly in caring for the ailing, the more repulsive the better.

Joseph showed his gratitude by learning to sing Christian hymns and asking to be instructed in the Catholic religion so that he might be baptized into the faith. Foucauld must have had some doubt about Joseph's sincerity for he shipped him off to Saint Joseph's at Maison Carrée for instruction by the White Fathers; it seemed the appropriate thing to do, inasmuch as the beginning of what might be his first conversion occurred on Saint Joseph's Day. The White Fathers, however, promptly returned him as shiftless, unreliable, untruthful, and interested in Christianity merely as a means of living without work.

Foucauld was not in the least discouraged. He records that some twenty slaves a day came to his Fraternity. He fed them

all, clothed those he could, and bound up the wounds made by
chains, whips, or branding irons. Some of the slaves had run
away and were quickly reclaimed by their masters. Most of them
begged Foucauld to buy their freedom as he had bought Joseph's.

He gave away most of his own clothes. Knowing this, Dom
Henri, the Trappist prior of Staouëli, sent him a cassock, two
shirts, twelve towels and a cloak merely as a loan, so that he
could not give them away. He tried to get some of the officers
of the garrison to contribute a few francs of their monthly pay
so that he could buy barley to feed his slaves and the few travelers who began to drop in. The officers of the garrison, when
they saw the miserable fare on which the priest lived, used to
send him vegetables and other nourishing food, but he gave
them all to the slaves.

He continued to buy slaves and set them free. During the
years 1902 and 1903 he mentions the liberation of four other
slaves besides Joseph. One was a gawky Negro lad of fifteen,
Paul Embarek, who did his best to learn how to become a Christian but never quite seemed to make it. Another, a boy of thirteen called Pierre, six years a slave, also seemed on the road to
conversion, but decided to go home to his family. The only
proselytes who continued to live at the Fraternity were a little
Negro girl whom he baptized at the age of three and one-half
and renamed Abd-Jesus (servant of Jesus) and a blind, simple-
minded old septuagenarian he called Marie.

III

The daily routine of the hermit of Beni-Abbès, as he detailed
it to his Prefect Apostolic, Monseigneur Guérin, in September,
1902, was as follows:

"Get up at 4 o'clock (when I hear the alarm clock ring, which
is not always!). *Angelus, Veni Creator*, prime and tierce. . . .
[Until ordered otherwise by Monseigneur Guérin, Foucauld at
first arose at 3 A.M.]

"At 6 o'clock, a few dates or figs and discipline; immediately
followed by an hour of adoration of the Very Blessed Sacrament.
Then manual labor (or its equivalent—correspondence, various
copies, extracts from authors worth keeping, reading aloud, or

the expounding of the catechism to one or another), until 11 o'clock. Then sext and nones, some prayers, and self-examination until 11:30.

"11:30, dinner.

"Noon, *Angelus* and *Veni Creator* (the last is chanted; you will laugh when you hear me; without wanting to, I have composed a new tune).

"The afternoon belongs in its entirety to the Good Lord and the Blessed Sacrament, except for an hour given to necessary conversation, replies to this or that question, cooking, the sacristy, etc.—the essentials of housekeeping and charity; this hour is divided throughout the day.

"Noon to half-past twelve, adoration; from 12:30 to 1:30, Stations of the Cross, a few vocal prayers, reading of one chapter each of the Old and New Testaments, a chapter from *The Imitation*, and a few pages from some spiritual author (Saint Theresa, Saint John Chrysostom, San Juan de la Cruz, all in rotation).

"From 1:30 to 2, written meditation on the Gospel.

"From 2 to 2:30, moral or dogmatic theology.

"From 2:30 to 3:30, hour reserved for the catechumens.

"From 3:30 to 5:30, adoration. This is the best moment of the day, after Mass and the night. My work is done, and I tell myself that I have only to contemplate Jesus . . . This is an hour full of sweetness.

"At 5:30, vespers.

"At 6 o'clock, supper.

"At 7 o'clock, I expound the Gospel to a few soldiers, prayers and benediction of the Blessed Sacrament with the holy ciborium, followed by the *Angelus* and the *Veni Creator*. The soldiers then leave, after a brief conversation in the open air. Then the Rosary, and if I have not had time to say it before my explanation of the Holy Scriptures, the Night Song. I go to sleep about 8:30.

"At midnight I get up again (if I hear the alarm clock) to chant the *Veni Creator*, recite the Matins and the Lauds—another very sweet moment, alone with the Bridegroom. In the profound silence of the Sahara, under these vast heavens, this

hour of intimacy is one of infinite peace. I go back to sleep at
1 o'clock."

Foucauld was both surprised and pleased to find so many soldiers coming to his primitive chapel for Mass, for confession,
and for his informal evenings to listen to his exposition of the
Gospel. In every case, he sent the soldier a letter, asking him to
come back whenever he felt like it and could get away from the
garrison. These letters he signed "Brother Charles of Jesus," because he felt that if the men considered him as a real chaplain,
probably with officer rank, they would feel shy. For this he was
rewarded by a continuing stream of pious French soldiers, and a
reprimand from Abbé Huvelin who reminded him that he was
now an ordained priest and must sign "Father de Foucauld,"
rather than "Brother Charles," which implied a lay rank only.

Father de Foucauld did not neglect the officers. He occasionally took a meal at the officers' mess, particularly when he
needed a little extra money for his charities—he was now feeding
seventy-five indigents a day, aside from his freed slaves. He
needed help, manpower rather than money. Woman power if
he could get it, although he hesitated to ask for nuns to be sent
to this primitive oasis.

"If I do not ask you to send me a few White Sisters," he wrote
to Monseigneur Guérin, "it is only because I know that wherever you can provide them, you do so, and that you will never
have enough to place them everywhere they are needed.

"I am still alone. I need companions, but apparently I am not
sufficiently faithful so that Jesus could give me even one. I do
my best to follow the little rule that you know so well. . . ."

The little rule which everyone knew so well was still the
willingness to starve to death, to shed blood gladly on African
soil, to obey Father de Foucauld blindly, despite his unworthiness. There were no takers.

In May of 1903, Father de Foucauld wrote in his journal:
"Thirty years ago today I celebrated my first Communion, receiving the Good Lord for the first time. . . . What favors have
been showered on me in those thirty years! How good the Good
Lord has been! How many times have I received Jesus between
these unworthy lips! And now I may hold Him in my miserable
hands! And now I serve an oratory where night and day I may

rejoice in the Blessed Tabernacle, where every morning I may consecrate the Blessed Eucharist, where every evening I may give the benediction! And now finally—and especially—I have permission to found my order! What grace!"

The permission which Father de Foucauld found so exciting was word from Monseigneur Guérin that he was free to establish his long-cherished Little Brothers of the Sacred Heart of Jesus. The young Prefect Apostolic of Ghardaïa may have undertaken this action on his own responsibility, believing that Father de Foucauld's austere rule would make implementation of the permission unlikely. In any event, he could send no recruits in response to the plea from Beni-Abbès for dedicated men.

The White Fathers at Maison Carrée could do no better. Neither could the Trappists. Dom Martin sent regrets from Our Lady of the Snows. Dom Henri at Staouëli warned Father de Foucauld that his proposed rule was too much for human endurance. The Bishop of Viviers was of no help either.

When Monseigneur Guérin made a second appeal on Foucauld's behalf to Our Lady of the Snows, the Trappist Abbot replied:

"You exhort me to give him an aide, a companion. For the moment I cannot, but even if I could, I should hesitate. As you know, Monseigneur, my esteem for the heroic virtues of Father Albéric is deeply rooted in a close association of twelve years. The only thing that astonishes me about him is that he has performed no miracles. I have never seen, outside of books, such saintliness on earth. But I must confess that I question somewhat his prudence and his discretion. The austerity which he practices and which he expects from his companions is such that I am inclined to believe that any neophyte would succumb from it in a very short time. Moreover, the concentration which he himself practices and which he wants to impose on his disciples strikes me as superhuman to the extent that it would drive the disciple mad before he died from the rigors of asceticism. . . ."

One of the Trappists of Staouëli wrote: "His life is so austere that those among our superiors who have the sincerest affection for him judge him to be more admirable than imitable. . . ."

Despite alternate joys and discouragement, Foucauld continued to work and pray and hope.

For Christmas of 1902 he received a bell for his chapel, paid for by Marie de Bondy ("Not to exceed 25 francs in cost," Foucauld had written) and sent by the White Fathers at Maison Carrée. The bell came packed in a small barrel and was supposed by the commander of the military supply train which brought it camel-back from the railhead at Ain Sefra to Beni-Abbès to be wine for the Mass. Consequently the barrel was protected from the desert sun by a canopy of leaves and sprinkled with water at regular intervals. When he checked to see if it had soured and found the bell instead of wine, Foucauld was delighted. The bell was installed with care and tolled with jubilation.

In February 1903 bands of Moroccan marauders attacked several Arab settlements in the vicinity of Beni-Abbès, and Paul Embarek, the freed slave, ignominiously ran away from Father de Foucauld.

Two Trappists from Staouëli made plans to join Father de Foucauld's Little Brothers of the Sacred Heart of Jesus, but they never came.

At Easter of 1903, Brother Charles was still the only priest within 300 miles. On that date he wrote in his diary:

"I am still without postulant, without novice, without nuns. . . . Unless the grain of wheat fall into the ground and die, it remaineth alone; but if it die, it bringeth forth much fruit. . . . Reign in me, Heart of Jesus, that I may die . . . in bringing forth fruit for Thy glory!"

ELEVEN

THE GYPSY YEAR

*Everybody should be the censor of his own
conscience.*

—Francis Cardinal Spellman

I

The hot desert air was vibrant with the roll of drums, the
brassy call of bugles, the squeal of camels and the curious bird-
like cries of Arab women. Thick dust clouds rose above the
thunder of hoofs as the Makhzan cavalry galloped past, followed
by a crack troop of swift Mehari. Gunfire crackled in salute to
the Commander-in-chief of the Saharan Oases, come to Beni-
Abbès on an inspection tour.

Major Henry Laperrine was an imposing figure as he sat ram-
rod straight on his white horse, gravely returning the salutes.
Despite the hot sun glinting on the four gold stripes of his kepi,
his well-tailored uniform of scarlet and blue was buttoned
tightly to his high collar. The officer with the keen, intelligent
eyes and the Vandyke beard was quite obviously a man of stature and authority.

After receiving the salaams of the local caïds, Major Laperrine rode to outpost headquarters for brief military formalities.
Then:

"I would like to see your hermit, Father de Foucauld," he
told Captain Regnault.

"He never leaves the confines of his mud hermitage, *mon
Commandant,*" said the captain.

"Then *I* shall call on *him,*" said the Commander-in-chief of
the Saharan Oases.

A pack of mongrel dogs yapped at the heels of Major Laperrine's white steed as he approached the low wall of sun-dried brick (erected by Father de Foucauld with his own hands) which surrounded the bleak desert acreage consecrated to God and Jesus Christ. The Major strode into the compound and found the Reverend Father bathing the open sores of a diseased Harratin—the half-breed offspring of a Berber and a Negro slave.

For an instant Laperrine was shocked. Could this gaunt, brown, balding fellow with missing teeth have anything in common with the plump, spoiled, indolent cadet of Saint-Cyr whom he had known twenty-five years ago? Could he possibly be the once dashing fellow second-lieutenant of the Fourth Chasseurs d'Afrique who had shared with him the hardships and perils of the pursuit of Bou Amama?

"Henry!" said the Reverend Father Charles de Foucauld.

"Piggy!" exclaimed the majestic Commander-in-chief of the Saharan Oases. "How you have changed!"

"And you!" said the former lieutenant of the Fourth Chasseurs d'Afrique, staring at the imposing figure of a born commander.

The two men fell into each other's arms—the dirty, ragged servant of God, and the resplendent symbol of the nascent French commonwealth in Africa.

They pushed open the rickety wooden door upon which was inscribed "Jesus Caritas" above the Sacred Heart surmounted by the Cross. And far into the night—interrupted, at times, by Father de Foucauld's religious duties—they talked of what had happened to both of them in the twenty-odd years since they had parted company, not terribly far from the God-forsaken corner of the desert in which they were now reunited.

Laperrine's record was spread upon the official books for all to see. But Ex-second Lieutenant Charles de Foucauld wanted to hear all the details from the professional soldier himself.

After Foucauld had left the army in a pet when he was refused permission to accompany Laperrine on an expedition across the Sahara to Timbuctoo—a mission which, incidentally, had not yet been accomplished in the intervening twenty-odd years—Laperrine had been promoted to first lieutenant of the First Spahis, assigned to Senegal, made captain of the second

Dragoons in 1891, transferred to the Second Sudanese Spahis two years later, and assigned to the Saharan Spahis in 1897. It was here that he first made his reputation as a soldier of the desert by organizing the Meharists, the crack camel corps of the French colonial army. He had always looked upon the camel as a weapon of war since Napoleon's early use of the animals in the army of Egypt, a Napoleonic policy which had not long endured. He understood the camel. He had learned the tricks of the Chaamba, Berber camel drivers who had long been a scourge of the French and had been part of the treacherous conspiracy that led to the assassination of Foucauld's old roommate, Vallombrosa-Morès. And he had transformed the Chaamba from professional cut-throats into a pro-French corps of desert police by the simple fact of giving them his trust, a uniform, and his orders. In 1899 he had been given command of the Seventh Chasseurs, and in 1901 he had become top man of the Saharan Oases. The whole southern area of the Algerian Sahara—Twat, Gurara, and Tidikelt—were under his command.

Laperrine still dreamed of crossing the Sahara from North to South to link French North Africa with Equatorial Africa. He had recently received authorization for such an expedition via Timbuctoo, but at the last minute the orders were countermanded. He had reapplied for authorization and laughingly told Foucauld that this time he would avoid opening any messages from Paris until after his return.

The two men had much in common besides a great love for Africa and a few years of Saint-Cyr, Saumur, and a short African campaign. They were idealists. Laperrine was wholeheartedly and single-mindedly devoted to the image of France as the great civilizing influence. Foucauld was whole-heartedly and single-mindedly devoted to the ideal of living in imitation of Christ so that his example might instill a love of Jesus among a people who had never known Him. Laperrine believed their two ideals complemented each other. After all, despite the strong anti-clerical trend in Paris, France was still a Catholic country, and Laperrine would like to appear religious in the eyes of the Moslems who, seeing no priests among the occupation forces, concluded that the French were a godless people.

Laperrine offered to take Father de Foucauld along with him

to Timbuctoo. He also painted a glowing picture of opportunities among the Tuareg who had never seen a priest. Three of the six Tuareg tribes—the Iforas, of Eastern Adrar; the Hoggar Tuareg of the Djebel Ahaggar, and the Taïtok of Ahenet—had already pledged loyalty to France during the past year, and were therefore open to Christians. The headman of the Hoggar—called the Amenokal—the most warlike of all the Tuareg, was due soon at In Salah with all his nobles to engage in a peaceful ceremony of allegiance. Things had changed considerably since the Flatters massacre, generally attributed to the Hoggar Tuareg.

After Major Laperrine left Beni-Abbès to continue his inspection tour, Father de Foucauld thought long and hard about the Tuareg. The idea of being the first man to carry the Cross among them excited him. These were the people whom his friend Duveyrier had found cordial and sympathetic but who had cut the Flatters expedition to pieces. These were the people who had murdered his old friend and roommate Vallombrosa-Morès. He would take them the concept of Christian love.

Brother Charles began looking through his meagre belongings for the book which Major Lacroix had slipped into his baggage when he left Algiers for the desert. The book was a grammar of the Tamashek language. Tamashek was the Berber dialect spoken by the Tuareg. Could it be that the major's gift was an omen?

II

Following Major Laperrine's departure, Father de Foucauld looked forward eagerly to another distinguished visitor on a tour of inspection: his ecclesiastical superior, the Prefect Apostolic of Ghardaïa, Monseigneur Charles Guérin. Monseigneur Guérin was expected in the first weeks of 1903, but he was detained by travel difficulties and the hospitality of lonely White Fathers just as eager as Father de Foucauld for companionship, spiritual talk, and a rare chance for confession.

Major Laperrine came and went. The weeks dragged on. Foucauld wrote letter after letter, inquiring, pleading, explaining. "Don't let the others monopolize you," he wrote in May. "There are currently three officers' messes in Beni-Abbès. The first few days they will fight over you. But it goes without saying that you and your suite—including your camels—will stay at the Fraternity. You will be at home here. Captain Regnault at first insisted on putting you up at the *bordj* of the Arab Bureau where you would be more comfortable, but I told him that your place was under the roof that sheltered the Blessed Sacrament, and he understood. But your cook will not be idle. Unless your chef gets his hand in, you would have to eat my cooking and I should not like to poison you.

"I will receive you as a poor man would receive his tenderly beloved father, which is to say very poorly. . . . But you will be master here, and if you like, I will be your guest. You will be completely free to do as you wish."

Foucauld went on to explain that he had baptized his blind old catachumen Marie because he thought she was dying. She was very ill and the doctor was away. "Fearing she would die, I baptized her, upon her clearly expressed desire, after having her recite in Arabic the Pater, the Credo, the Acts of Faith, Hope, Charity and Contrition, and having her again ask formally to be baptized."

Marie did not die. In fact she outlived Father de Foucauld.

Father Guérin finally arrived at Beni-Abbès on May 27, accompanied by Father Voillard and their retinue. He also brought with him Paul Embarek, the ex-slave who was liberated by Father de Foucauld and who had deserted him under fire. The Prefect Apostolic had found the gawky lad repentant at one of the southern oases and had brought him back to Beni-Abbès, sheepish and contrite.

Father de Foucauld was reluctant to receive him at first, for, as he explained to Monseigneur Guérin, "I will never baptize him. He will remain a catachumen as long as he lives, for he is incapable of understanding the mystery of the Eucharist."

However, "seeking direction . . . from the conduct of Our Lord with Judas Iscariot," the priest forgave him and welcomed him into the Fraternity once more.

Monseigneur Guérin, some years Foucauld's junior, was a wiry, intense priest with a dark, heavy, somewhat scraggly beard hiding most of his deeply-lined face. His piercing gray eyes were topped by heavy eyebrows. He wore a white sun hat with a wide floppy brim and the usual white gandurah of the White Fathers. He and Father Voillard remained in Beni-Abbès for five days. On May 31, Pentecost, the Prefect Apostolic celebrated Mass in Father de Foucauld's makeshift chapel, and Foucauld noted in his diary: "For the first time in centuries, perhaps for the first time in history, there are three priests at Beni-Abbès."

When he left on June 1, Monseigneur Guérin took with him little Abd-Jesus, the Negro slave child purchased and baptized by Father de Foucauld. Abd-Jesus would be raised by the White Fathers at Maison Carrée.

After his superior's departure, Foucauld listed the principal points made by Father Guérin in discussing the work at Beni-Abbès:

"1. Speak much to the natives . . . always in a manner to better their souls, to lift them up, to bring them nearer to God, to prepare the soil for the Gospel.

"2. Take advantage of temporal alms-giving by giving spiritual alms for the good of the soul along with material alms.

"3. Install benches and shelters in the courtyard so that visitors are not forced to stand. Conversation while seated is apt to be more intimate and serious.

"4. The work of proselyting in Moslem countries should not be restricted to children but extended to grown men. The seeds of the Gospel sown in the souls of children will not germinate except in soil that has been worked or at least is friendly disposed. . . .

"5. While working to convert the poor, do not neglect the rich. Our Lord did not neglect them. Neither did St. Paul, his imitator. . . . If they become Christians, it is not just for a daily bowl of soup. . . .

"6. I build too much. Stop. Don't add to my buildings.

"7. The Moslems of the Sahara accept their false religion solely by *confidence* in their ancestors, their marabouts and those who surround them, only because of the *authority* exercised by those they trust. We must try harder to win their trust and to acquire more authority. . . . For this three things are needed: to be very saintly; to be seen often with Moslems; to talk much. . . ."

Point No. 8 was in the form of a question obviously much dis-

cussed by Fathers Guérin and de Foucauld: "To bring the Moslems to God, must we seek their approval in certain things they
esteem? For example, is being audacious, a good horseman, a
good shot, and rather ostentatiously generous? Or rather in
practicing the Gospel in abjection and poverty, traveling about
on foot without baggage, working with the hands as did Jesus
in Nazareth, living in penury like a humble laborer? . . ."

Father de Foucauld reached the conclusion that it is not from
a Chaamba camel driver that one should learn to live, but from
Jesus.

III

Three weeks after the departure of Monseigneur Guérin,
Foucauld received a letter from Major Laperrine which made
him wildly excited over the possibilities of a mission to the
Tuareg. At one of the oases on his itinerary Laperrine had come
across a Tuareg woman "of noble family" who had saved the
lives of a number of wounded survivors of the ill-fated Flatters
expedition. After the death of Colonel Flatters and most of his
men, the survivors under Lieutenant Dianoux gave battle at
Amguid to a group of Tuareg under Attici-ag-Amellal, the
Amenokal of the Hoggar Tuareg. The Tuareg woman took the
French wounded into her home and barred the door to Attici
who, himself wounded at Amguid, wanted to put the Frenchmen
to the sword. The woman, whose name was Tarishat Oult Ibda-
kane, nursed the Christians back to health, then saw that they
were repatriated through Tripolitania.

"She is now in her early forties," Laperrine wrote to Foucauld, "is reputed to be very influential, and is well known for
her charity."

This demonstration of Christian mercy by a Moslem woman
convinced Foucauld that he must by all means take God to the
Tuareg.

"Is not this woman ready for the Gospel?" he wrote to Monseigneur Guérin. "Should we not write to her, saying that her
charity which she so often practices and which moved her to
shelter, nurse, defend, and repatriate the wounded of the French
mission twenty-two years ago, is known to us and fills us with
joy and thankfulness to God?"

Foucauld then drafted a letter which he proposed that his superior send to Tarishat. It began:

"Giving thanks to God in admiration of your practice of charity toward men, we write you this letter to tell you that hundreds of thousands of Christian priests and nuns, when they hear of you, will bless you and sing your praises to God. These men and women who have renounced marriage and all worldly goods to devote their lives to prayer, meditation of the Word of God, and to the practice of charity, will pray that God may cover you with favors in this world and with glory in heaven. . . ."

He also suggested that the Pope might wish to write to Tarishat also.

A few days later his mind was made up and his plans took definite form. On June 24 he wrote to Monseigneur Guérin for permission to enter the heart of the Tuareg country and settle there, at least until the White Fathers could send priests into the region. "I would pray there," he wrote. "I would study the language and translate the Holy Gospel. I would fraternize with the Tuareg and live without enclosure. Every year I would go north for confession. On the way I would administer the Sacraments at all army posts and speak of God to the natives. . . ."

Within the week he also wrote to Abbé Huvelin in Paris, asking his blessing on the mission to the Tuareg, and to Major Laperrine, seeking military authorization.

On July 13 he received a reply from Abbé Huvelin, unusually liberal for the tight rein-holder that Foucauld's spiritual guide had become: "Go where you believe the will of God calls you."

On July 22 Major Laperrine sent his authorization, although he qualified his action somewhat in a communication to Captain Regnault at Beni-Abbès nearly a month later: "I authorize de Foucauld to come to the Tidikelt [a jurisdiction which at that time included the Hoggar] although technically I have no right to do so. However, I shall probably get away with it with no more than a few threats and insulting letters from every echelon to the highest. I have become accustomed to kicks in the behind. I have a special file for them."

On August 1 an answer finally came from Monseigneur Guérin. Surprisingly, he wanted more time to think the matter over. Father Foucauld suspected that the reflection was being done in Maison Carrée, where Monseigneur Livinhac was taking the long view, surveying the whole picture of the newly-opened territory of the Hoggar and adjoining areas. This, after all, was the province of the White Fathers. . . .

Before final word came from the Prefect Apostolic, a new element had intervened in the life of Father de Foucauld.

IV

Since the beginning of July 1903 Moroccan razzias had been raiding the Algerian side of the border with increasing frequency. Father de Foucauld, in fact, had been complaining to both ecclesiastical and military authorities that the Algerian-Moroccan frontier was a one-way street. Moroccan bands were continually coming across, while he (Foucauld) had continually been refused permission to cross the line and visit his old friends only a hundred miles or so away—the Moslems who had befriended him during his expedition to Morocco a score of years before.

In mid-July a razzia of some two hundred camel-mounted raiders struck at an Algerian detachment of fifty riflemen from Adrar at three in the morning, killing half the company. Captain Regnault struck southwest from Beni-Abbès in retaliation with a hundred Camel Corpsmen and horsemen, found the raiders in the dunes of Tabelbala, and killed a score of them.

Father de Foucauld, who had never entirely shed his scarlet trousers and blue tunic of the Chasseurs d'Afrique, studied the maps like an old strategist and decided that the Moroccan marauders would strike next at Taghit. It was an exposed post, hard to defend because of its location in a hollow surrounded by hills, and it was, like all French outposts in North Africa, undermanned. Father de Foucauld asked Captain Regnault to send him to Taghit, where, he said, he might soon be needed.

Captain Regnault refused. The roads were unsafe, he said, and he could not spare the men to escort the priest. Father de Foucauld's reaction was two-fold. First, he removed the Blessed Sacrament from the tabernacle in his little chapel, to be able to keep it constantly under surveillance in case of an attack. Second, he sent an unofficial (and clandestine) note to Captain de Susbielle, the handle-bar-mustachioed commander of the outpost at Taghit, where Strategist de Foucauld expected the next razzia would strike. The message was concise: "Send for me."

This was on August 12, 1903. For the next week no courier came through to Beni-Abbès. They were quite busy up the line. Captain de Susbielle, with 470 men and two three-pounders for all artillery, was fighting off a force of 6,000 Moroccan raiders commanded by the Sherif of Matrara and accompanied by 3,000 service troops, if women, children and camp followers could be called troops. The attackers included 500 ruffians on camel-back, most of them armed with breech-loading rifles, and 600 pack camels. Captain de Susbielle, outnumbered twelve to one, had a tactical problem on his hands.

"Captain," said Father de Foucauld, when word finally came through to Beni Abbès, "you must let me go to Taghit. Men must be dying there who need spiritual comfort."

"Sorry," said Captain Regnault. "I can't spare either a horse or an escort."

"Then I will go on foot," said Father de Foucauld. "Alone."

This time Captain Regnault had his way. The ex-lieutenant of the Fourth Hussars did not bite his nails while awaiting news of the battle. He prayed—for nearly a week.

When the news finally came through, it was good news. Reinforcements from Beni-Abbès and from the Foreign Legion Mounted from El Morra had saved the day for Captain de Susbielle. The Moroccan marauders had withdrawn with 1,200 casualties.

"The finest feat of arms in Algeria for forty years," was Father de Foucauld's comment. "And yet—."

The reservation referred to the fact that nine French had died without benefit of last rites, and twenty-one wounded were without spiritual comfort. And the only chaplain of the Western Sahara just eighty miles away. . . !

On September 2, twenty miles north of Taghit, another Moroccan raid jumped a Foreign Legion convoy, knocking out forty-nine men. This time Captain Regnault gave Foucauld a horse, for Captain de Susbielle had requested his presence. Foucauld rode the eighty miles in twenty-three hours non-stop, from ten one morning until nine the next. On arriving at

Taghit he unpacked his portable altar, said Mass, then strode into the shed serving as base hospital to comfort the wounded.

An ex-officer of the Chasseurs d'Afrique did not have to be told that a priest could not expect a very warm welcome from a bunch of wounded Foreign Legionnaires. They were not only unbelievers, as he had once been, but they were men without roots, and they were men in pain. He was not surprised at the chorus of catcalls and obscene epithets which greeted his entry into the hot, humid gloom of the makeshift ward. He did not wince at the rank effluvia of sweat, suppurating wounds, excreta, and the urine-stained pallets on which some of the wounded lay naked except for their bloodied bandages.

One of the Legionnaires raised his voice in a ribald marching song and his companions joined in. Father de Foucauld, who knew the words of all the bawdy barrackroom ditties, smiled tolerantly, listened for a moment, then raised his hands for silence.

"You're mistaken, boys," he said. "That verse should begin with 'Le Duc de l'Aquitaine et toute sa compagnie. . . .' "

There were more catcalls and rude noises, but there was also genuine and sympathetic laughter. Some of the men liked the priest who knew the marching songs better than they did.

During the ensuing days Father de Foucauld patiently won the respect and even friendship of the Legionnaires. He washed and rebandaged their wounds, listened to their troubles, ran errands for them, wrote letters for them, prayed for them and, for those who asked him, with them. Some of the ambulatory cases came to Mass. During the more than three weeks that he remained at Taghit, most of the wounded received Communion at his hands.

One day he rode to the battlefield to bless the graves of the officers and men buried there.

Another day he inspected the mural decorations and pornographic pin-ups in the ward. Some of these had obviously been created for his particular benefit, for they included priests and angels with anatomical emphasis designed to shock the saintly. His only comment was an occasional word of praise for the anonymous artist's talent, but with a stick of charcoal he improved an occasional error of perspective or bad draftsmanship and incidentally eliminated the obscene details.

In his spare time (he slept only five or six hours a night) he wrote a monograph entitled: "The Gospel Presented to the Poor Negroes of the Sahara." There was nothing patronizing in the work, as the title might seem to indicate. It was written in simple prose such as the following extract:

"The three great mysteries of the Holy Trinity, the Incarnation, and the Redemption, are completely incomprehensible to the mind of men. This is not surprising. As the small child understands less than the adolescent, and the adolescent less than the adult, so does a man understand less than an angel, and an angel less than God. A small child has his view cut off by a wall two cubits high, an adolescent by a wall three cubits high, and a man by a wall of four cubits. God sees over all walls, and His view is infinite. . . ."

An hour after Father de Foucauld had left to return to Beni-Abbès on September 30, 1903, Captain de Susbielle received word that some army brass was due at Taghit at sundown. He immediately dispatched an orderly to post guest quarters to make sure Father de Foucauld's room had been put in order for the new arrivals.

The orderly was back in five minutes. "There's nothing to put in order, *mon capitaine*," he said. "The bed has never been slept in."

V

Father de Foucauld returned to the Taghit area several times during the next few months for humanitarian and ecclesiastical duties. He reported to Monseigneur Guérin that all Catholics among the wounded had behaved in exemplary manner as far as their religious obligations were concerned. One of the Foreign Legion wounded—a German Protestant—had died of his wounds. Foucauld pleaded with the dead lad's commander to write a personal letter to his mother in German before she could receive the cold impersonal notice reading: "The Ministry of War regrets to inform you. . . ."

Father de Foucauld's main concern during the last weeks of 1903, however, was the solution of his problem of the Tuareg.

Should he go to Tidikelt and to the Hoggar? Should he remain in Beni-Abbès, where he knew he was needed and where he felt at home and at peace? Major Laperrine was urging him more and more strongly to accompany him on one of the "journeys of domestication," as he called his expeditions into the regions recently giving titular allegiance to France but not yet entirely pacified. Laperrine was in fact suggesting a date early in January.

Father de Foucauld went into retreat during December to take stock of himself, to meditate, and to come to a decision. He also wrote to Abbé Huvelin in Paris, seeking advice again. His great resolution of the summer seems to have been dissolved by the Taghit interludes into agonizing indecision. However, putting the facts and the arguments on paper for his spiritual guide did much to clarify his own feelings:

"You will recall," he wrote, "that I was going to leave in September when I was summoned to serve the wounded at Taghit. Now that calm seems to have been re-established, should I proceed with my original plan? . . . If Monseigneur Guérin could and would send another priest, I should certainly not go. My duty clearly calls for my remaining at Beni-Abbès . . . but I believe that he has no one to send.

"Under these circumstances, should I not go to the Far South to set up transient quarters where I could spend two or three or four months a year and en route administer or at least offer the Sacraments to the garrisons, and to display the Cross and the Sacred Heart to the Moslems while talking to them about our holy religion?

"At this moment, nothing would be simpler for me. I have been invited, I am expected. But nature down there is at its most repulsive. I shudder—and I am ashamed of it—at the thought of leaving Beni-Abbès and the calm at the foot of the altar in order to plunge into these journeys for which I have now developed the greatest horror. If I did not believe with all my heart that such words as *pleasant, painful, joy* and *sacrifice* should be eliminated from our dictionary, I should say that I am a little sad at the thought of leaving Beni-Abbès.

"There are many logical arguments against it: I would leave the tabernacle at Beni-Abbès empty. There might be fighting here in my absence, although this is not likely. Should I divert myself with travel which is not good for the soul? Do I not glorify God more in worshipping Him in solitude?

"Despite the contrary arguments of logic and of nature, I feel a great and growing interior urge to make this voyage.

"A convoy is leaving for the South on January 10. Should I take it? Should I wait for another? There may be none for several months, and I have reason to believe that I would find it harder to join the next one.

"I beg of you, write me a line in this regard. I will obey you. . . ."

January 10 came and went—without word from Abbé Huvelin.

On the morning of January 13, 1904, a convoy of fifty soldiers commanded by Lieutenant Yvart of the Second Chasseurs d'Afrique prepared to leave for Adrar, capital of the Twat oases, 250 miles to the south. At the last moment Father de Foucauld decided to go along. He loaded a donkey with his portable altar, the essentials for Mass, a square of canvas, and saddlebags containing barley, flour, salt, dates, his books, a new pair of leather sandals and two pairs of espadrilles. He refused the horse Captain Regnault had offered him, but accepted a spare donkey. He would go on foot beside his animals. So would young Paul Embarek, his vagrant catachumen, whom he was taking along to serve the Mass.

As the desert sun rose above the palms of Beni-Abbès, Father Charles de Foucauld, now in his forty-fifth year, started walking into the unknown.

VI

Eighteen days of marching under the sweltering African sun. Eighteen nights of shivering in the chill of a desert winter. Eighteen days and nights to remind Charles de Foucauld that he was no longer a dashing cavalier or intrepid explorer but a middle-aged priest. The physical limitations of his mortal frame, however, were in no way a match for his soaring spirit. He was a pioneer for Christ. When he reached the oasis of Adrar on February 1 and was greeted by his old friend Major Laper-

rine in person, he was as chipper as a subaltern on his first tour
of overseas duty.

Laperrine persuaded Brother Charles to take up residence at
headquarters, bribing him, if that is the word, by turning over
a whole room for his use as chapel. He also shook his head in
admiration of his old friend's log of the long journey, a repeti-
tion of his Moroccan expedition, with sketches, statistics, and
figures on distances, latitude and longitude, location of wells
and water holes, number of palm trees, even notes on the native
populations and how they might be aided by the distribution
of seeds.

Major Laperrine reported to Captain Regnault that Father
de Foucauld was "in very good health. He is working hard at
his Tuareg language [Tamashek]. Since his arrival he has
picked my archives here clean. What's more, he has been a very
good boy. He has let himself be persuaded to eat with us at the
mess and has been quite gay in the process. He has even
agreed to sleep in a bed. . . . I have promised to take him
along on my next tour, and if I see that he gets along with the
Tuareg, I shall turn him loose. I am only sorry he did not arrive
a fortnight earlier, for then he would have met Moussa-ag-
Amastane [the Amenokal of the Hoggar Tuareg] and might
have gone back to the Hoggar with him. . . . My dream is to
make him the first priest of a Hoggar parish. . . ."

In the meantime Laperrine insisted that his old friend do his
homework under the best possible conditions. The best possible
place to study Tamashek, said the Commander of the Oases, was
Akabli, a crossroads of the caravans some 160 miles to the east of
Adrar. Tamashek was the language of commerce at Akabli,
because most of the traffic through the oasis was Tuareg in
origin, and there was a particularly erudite scholar who was just
the man to teach Foucauld not only Tamashek, the spoken
language, but also Tifinagh, the Tuareg script deriving from
old Numidian characters.

So after only a week's rest, Father de Foucauld was again on
the desert trails with his portable altar, his provisions, his
donkeys, and his catachumen servitor, Paul Embarek. Lieutenant Besset commanded this convoy, which made a roundabout

The Early Years

'If Thou art

my God

make Thyself

known to me.'

Charles as a boy of six

Cadet de Foucauld
at Saumur

On his return
from Morocco

Charles at the time
of his conversion

Hermit of the Desert

Brother Charles in front of
his first Saharan hermitage

Brother Charles with Paul
Bonifa and little Abd-Jesus

'I want everybody—
Christians, Moslems,
Jews and Pagans—
to look upon me as
their brother.'

The hermit of the Sahara

Charles with a slave he freed

Scenes

(Service Photographique du Service d'Information et Documentation du Gouvernement General de l'Algérie.)

A band of Tuareg meharists

A Tuareg man

Lhote

of the Hoggar

O.C.R.S.

This is the Hoggar, stark but beautiful

Charles' Hermitage at Asekrem

The forbidding landscape of Asekrem

Tamanrasset

O.C.R.S.

The bordj of Père de Foucauld at Tamanrasset

'Have confidence that the destiny

God has reserved for you

will be the best for His Glory,

for your soul, and for the

souls of others.'

itinerary through In-Salah and Tit, taking twelve days to cover what should have been a 150-mile journey.

Father de Foucauld had almost a month in Akabli before Major Laperrine stopped by to pick him up on his next "domestication tour." With his basic grounding in Berber, dating back to Sétif and the idle weeks in Evian with Mimi after his repatriation, Foucauld was already confidently fluent in spoken Tamashek, which was after all a Berber language. And he was already sufficiently advanced in Tifinagh (in which script, he had been told, no book had ever been written) to begin a draft translation of the Gospel.

On March 14 Foucauld started south again in the caravan of the Commander of the Saharan Oases. Laperrine had a long list of Tuareg chiefs to visit and convince of the friendship of France—it would be the first time any of them had seen the brilliant uniform of a French hussar flanked by the cassock of a priest, and the Koran did revere Jesus as a prophet—but the goal of this particular trip was his lifetime dream of pushing through to Timbuctoo.

On Laperrine's insistence, Foucauld consented to ride a swift Army camel. The old explorer's log was a long list of oases, dates, and distances: March 15, bivouac in the dry bed of the Wadi Keraan after a day's march of 30 miles. . . . March 16, Tin Tenai wells. . . . 17 to 20, bivouac in the desert. . . . April 1, Good Friday eve, camp at the In-Ziza Oasis, where the pure water and the presence of many caravans caused Father de Foucauld to speculate on the advantages of founding his Little Brothers of the Sacred Heart there where during a good rainy season the vegetation is lush. "Four years ago after the rains," he recorded in his diary, "there were 500 tents here for several weeks—Hoggar, Ahenet, and Iforas Tuareg. . . ." Six days later he decided that the Timissao wells were even more favorable.

As they advanced deeper into Tuareg country, tribal chiefs came to call on the imposing Commander-in-chief and the humble priest. Some were friendly, some reserved, others suspicious and even surly. One former enemy who had never quite made peace with the French—Marabout Abidin—did not even deign to call but sent his representative. Nowhere, however, did they encounter open hostility—until they reached the frontier between Algeria and the Niger Territory of French West Africa.

On the evening of April 16 the Laperrine party was making camp near the desert wells of Timiawin when a company of Sudanese riflemen rode up under the command of two French officers. Their spokesman, Captain Théveniaut, informed Major Laperrine that he had orders to prevent, by force if necessary, the advance of the Algerian expedition to Timbuctoo.

Laperrine could appreciate the irony of the situation—that after having crossed nearly five hundred miles of desert populated by potentially hostile tribesmen, the first open enmity and threat of bloodshed should come from one of his own kind.

This family fight, based on bureaucratic jealousies, would have been comic were it not for its tragic implications. After all, there had already been fratricidal bloodship in the Niger Territory; in 1901 a French colonel and captain had been killed by French bullets at Zinder—because of a question of prerogatives.

Father de Foucauld listened with admiration as Laperrine patiently discussed the matter with Théveniaut, carefully delving into the heart of the matter. The basic problem was simple enough. The Governor of the Niger was responsible to the Ministry of Colonies. The Governor-general of Algeria answered to the Ministry of the Interior. The line of demarcation between the two territories had never been clearly drawn further East than the longitude of Lisbon, which was a thousand miles west of the Timiawin wells. The Governor of the Niger believed that boundaries should be settled on ethnic rather than geographic lines. Therefore he even resented the fact that the Iforas Tuareg, who lived on both banks of the Niger, had pledged allegiance to France through Algerian authorities rather than through him.

It was a difficult decision for Laperrine to make. He ranked Captain Théveniaut and was therefore not obligated to obey him. However, he believed the question was one to be settled in Paris and not by force of arms in the desert. Reluctantly, therefore, he gave up his dream of being the first man to cross the Sahara from north to south, from the Mediterranean to Timbuctoo. In the morning he and his expedition would turn north again.

That night Father de Foucauld wrote in his diary, referring to Captain Théveniaut and his companions: "After having fraternally shaken their hands on our arrival, I shall leave tomorrow without bidding them goodbye. . . . I shall say no word of reproach, for that would be of no benefit to them, it would estrange them from the church, and it might cause open hostilities between them and the officers of Major Laperrine. . . ."

But as he climbed aboard his leggy Mehari next day, Charles de Foucauld was a little less Father de Foucauld than he was the descendant of a long line of soldiers and martyrs whose device had been *Jamais Arrière*. Much as he admired and understood Major Laperrine's decision, the ex-lieutenant of the Fourth Chasseurs d'Afrique would have liked to push on to Timbuctoo. He hated turning back.

VII

It was a gypsy year for Foucauld. He accompanied Laperrine for the next few months of his "tour of domestication." He was again engaged in those journeys for which he had developed "the greatest horror."

He wrote in his diary: "I am not in the slightest interested in geography or exploration. Neither am I interested in evangelization as such. Of this I am neither worthy nor capable; and the time for it has not yet come. My work should be the preliminaries for evangelization, the cultivation of trust and friendship, for gentling, you might say, and for fraternization with the Hoggar and the Taïtok Tuareg. . . ."

Despite his disclaimer, Foucauld's notebooks bore close resemblance to the log of his Moroccan exploration. He logged latitude and longitude, weather, atmospheric conditions, character of the soil and what crops it might produce, the friendliness of the people and their chiefs—in a word, all the circumstances which might indicate whether or not this or that oasis would be a proper site for planting a branch of the Little Brothers of the Sacred Heart of Jesus. . . .

It was a dry year, Foucauld noted. At the wells of Tinghaor it took sixty hours to water the 150 camels and fill 150 goatskins.

At Silet the wells were in good supply, and the wheat grew well. At Abalessa there were many date palms and the crossroads of many caravans. Both spots would be favorable for the Little Brothers. They stayed five days at Abalessa and Father de Foucauld celebrated Mass there for Pentecost (May 22), in the presence of Major Laperrine and his staff. During their stay, several Tuareg chiefs rode in to pay their respects, bearing greeting from their tribal Amenokals.

On May 26 he said Mass at Tit, the scene of the decisive battle just two years earlier when the victory of Lieutenant Cottonest convinced the chiefs of three Tuareg tribes that they should make peace with the French. Tit was on the edge of the great Hoggar plateau, that gigantic upthrust of blackened crags, diabolic ravines, and stony wastes of incredible shapes and colors, the whole fantastic landscape dominated by peaks 10,000 feet high. At Tit Foucauld was sure he had found the site to settle down, establish his mission to the Tuareg, and begin building his fraternity of the humble imitators of Christ. Laperrine, however, was not yet quite sure. He was not certain that his friend had been sufficiently exposed to the land and the people he would have to live with.

"Not yet," he said. "It is too early to tell."

They pushed on. On June 7 the major introduced the priest to the Taïtok woman he had taken to heart from afar—Tarishat Oult Ibdakan, the Tuareg lady who had saved the survivors of the Flatters expedition of 1881—because her example of Christian charity had convinced Foucauld that the Tuareg were amenable to receiving the Gospel. He found her living in a series of tents with her retinue, a nomad like most Tuareg. He described her as "distinguished, simple and modest of manner, not talkative, quite prepossessing in all ways. She speaks fairly good Arabic. . . ."

Tarishat asked Father de Foucauld to write to a rifleman named Amer, one of those she had saved and repatriated. "He had promised her his weight in silver," Foucauld records, "but sent her nothing. She is in debt and 50 or 100 duros would make her very happy."

A week later Foucauld and Laperrine parted company. The

major returned to his headquarters at In-Salah, leaving his friend in the charge of Lieutenant Roussel who was assigned to patrol the Hoggar plateau for the next few months to establish a "French presence" among the Tuareg. Laperrine gave special instructions to Roussel to obtain permission from the Ameno-kal, if possible, for Father de Foucauld to establish himself "immediately and permanently" in the Hoggar. On Laperrine's departure, the priest wrote:

"After five months during which he showered me with kindness for which I shall never be sufficiently grateful, he left me saying that he hopes the next time he sees me it will be in the Hoggar."

Foucauld and the Roussel mission moved from spring to spring, making camp for several days whenever a spot of grazing land seemed peopled by the nomads. Besides saying Mass, his prayers, keeping up his detailed log, mingling with the Tuareg and perfecting his study of the language, Brother Charles worked incessantly at his translation of the Gospel into Tamashek. He made his own ink from charcoal mixed with camel urine.

"The natives are friendly," he wrote, "but they are not sincere. They bow to necessity. How long will it take before they really feel the sentiments they simulate? Perhaps never. If they should some day become sincere, that will be the day they become Christians. Will they ever be able to distinguish between soldier and priest, see us as servants of God, ministers of peace and charity, universal brothers? I do not know. If I do my duty, Jesus will lavish His mercies upon them, and they will understand."

For three months he traveled through the Hoggar, and the oases of Twat and Tidikelt, visiting some three hundred walled *ksour*, some merely a dozen mud huts, others fair-sized towns. In each Father de Foucauld fraternized with the Tuareg, prayed, left medicines and alms. His contributions for the poor were methodically calibrated according to the size of the *ksour*. A small or middle-sized village got seven francs—about $1.40 at contemporary exchange. A town got fourteen francs and a big town got twenty-one, a little over $4, a token display of Christian charity for which his sister and cousin footed the bill.

At In-Salah Lieutenant Roussel and the military convoy returned to garrison, leaving Father de Foucauld to proceed alone, with only one native Meharist as guide. He refused more. Instead of heading due north to El Goléa and Ghardaïa where he was to join Monseigneur Guérin, Foucauld swung to the west, plodding hundred of miles out of his way in order to keep to his resolve of visiting all possible *ksour* of Twat and Gurura as well as Tidikelt. He showed the Cross and left his token in tiny clusters of mud-plastered beehive *gourbi* and he stayed a day or two to rest in such oases as Aulef, Adrar, and Timmimun, "a rich populated center used to Europeans." He hurried through El Goléa, although three White Fathers welcomed him there. He was anxious to reach Ghardaïa and the Prefect Apostolic.

He had written Monseigneur Guérin weeks before, calculating with his usual geographer's methodical foresight, that he would reach Ghardaïa on September 20. When the word reached Ghardaïa by Meharist camel-borne courier, the Prefect Apostolic accepted the estimated time of arrival as though it had been plotted by sextant and chronometer. And on September 19 he rode out to meet his friend and intercepted him one-day's march from Ghardaïa. The two men embraced warmly—but Monseigneur Guérin was shocked by the appearance of the roving apostle.

Eight months and several thousands of miles, mostly on foot and mostly at a time when the pitiless sun of the Sahara was most cruel, had taken their toll. The most pious resolve, the most charitable soul, the most humble, self-effacing servant of God, the most completely unselfish imitator of Christ could not match the burning vindictiveness of the hostile desert. The handful of dates and bowlful of barley that Father de Foucauld considered proper provender for anyone worthy of becoming a Little Brother of the Sacred Heart of Jesus, were not sufficient fuel to carry a man thirty to fifty desert miles a day. The four or five hours of sleep a night—how could a dedicated soul spare more, with all the traveling, fraternizing, writing, translating, studying, and merely coping with the complicated business of living in a strange and barren land?—were not enough to restore the tissues burned up daily in the service of God and man.

When Monseigneur Guérin saw the ragged, emaciated, foot-sore, bent and limping figure coming toward him, leading the camel he should have been riding, he was on the verge of tears. The sunken eyes in the thin, deeply-lined face were those of an exhausted stranger. But the smile was that of a dear and saintly friend.

"You must be tired, Father," said the Prefect Apostolic. "You will rest at Ghardaïa."

"Perhaps, perhaps later," said Father de Foucauld. "But first there are so many important things to talk about."

Ghardaïa was indeed a place to rest. The curious white pyramid of a town arising from the green expanse of date gardens, the slanting rays of the evening November sun glinting on the palm fronds and gilding the minarets of the M'zabite mosques, the characteristic creak of the myriad pulleys of the ancient irrigation system—all carried Brother Charles back nearly twenty years, when he had first seen Ghardaïa in company of the learned Captain Motylinski. Yes, Ghardaïa was a good place to rest. The solicitous kindness of the White Fathers touched Foucauld deeply.

"You will eat with us at the refectory," said Monseigneur Guérin. "No nonsense now. We must put some meat on your bones."

"Yes, yes," Father de Foucauld agreed. "But first—."

And he dug into his saddle-bags to produce the complete manuscript of his Tamashek translation of the Four Gospels! It was a monumental job accomplished on the fly, often at night after a hard day's march, by the flickering light of an oil lamp under a tree or in his tent. The fact that in a few months he had mastered a new language, complete with the written Tifinagh characters, he brushed off modestly although he found Tifinagh "not very handy."

Tamashek, he wrote, "is an excellent language, very easy, and we can gradually introduce the words necessary to express religious ideas and the Christian virtues. We can also improve the system of writing without changing it. . . ."

On September 6, the day on which he completed his Tamashek translation, he wrote to Marie de Bondy: "Until now there has not been a single book written in this language. It is a great comfort to me that their first book should be the Holy Gospels."

During his five months as a nomad, Father de Foucauld had also written a long monograph which he called "Observations on Missionary Travel in the Sahara" which he gave to Monseigneur Guérin for its possible value to the White Fathers. It included detailed suggestions on dealing with native soldiers, slaves (he found the Tuareg treated theirs better than did the Arabs), travel, and the difference in approach between the Tuareg and Arab-speaking Berbers. Regarding religious instruction, he gave directions on how to use his translation of the Gospel which, he advised, should be read to the Tuareg.

"They should hear passages touching on natural religion or ethics, such as the parable of the Prodigal Son, the Good Samaritan, and the Last Judgment which should be compared to a shepherd separating the sheep from the goats, etc. It goes without saying that as soon as conversions begin, we will need a catechism in Tamashek."

Father de Foucauld remained in Ghardaïa from November 12 until the day after Christmas. During this time, in addition to rebuilding his strength, he made his annual retreat and had long conferences with Monseigneur Guérin.

On December 26 he set off on foot for El Goléa 200 miles away. Accompanied by two White Fathers, he walked beside his camel some fifty yards ahead of the others so that his silent prayers and meditation be not disturbed by idle chatter. He arrived in El Goléa on January 1, 1905, in time to wish Major Laperrine a Happy New Year and to congratulate him on his promotion to the rank of lieutenant-colonel.

Two days later he accompanied Laperrine to Adrar, then left him to turn north to Beni-Abbès where he arrived on January 24.

The fatigue of the last three weeks on desert trails vanished at the sight of the glaring white battlements of the *bordj* perched on the hill above the green date palms and fruit trees of the oasis; of the rose-tinged dunes of the Great Western Erg, the sea of sand stretching away to his right; of the rocky hollow in which lay the sun-baked brick walls of his hermitage, its scrawny palms and its rude crosses planted in heaped stones.

There were changes at the *bordj*. Captain Regnault had gone, replaced by Captain Doury, but the officers and men he had known over a year before cheered his return. They had had no news of him.

Blind old Marie, whom he had baptized when he thought she was dying, was still living in the hermitage compound, drawing the weekly pittance he had arranged for the Arab Bureau to pay her. A few of his indigent wards were still in his hostel. They had neglected his kitchen-garden, although he had left specific written instructions for its care: the date palms were to be watered daily with two *guénine* (about eight gallons); carrots every four days, barley every five days, cabbage and turnips every second day, broad beans every five days. The palms had survived fairly well, and the barley had reseeded itself in a ragged way, but his vegetables would have to be started all over again.

Father de Foucauld was nevertheless overjoyed to be home. Beni-Abbès, he had decided, was indeed his home, with peace and calm at the foot of the altar of his poor, makeshift chapel. He had traveled more than three thousand miles in the year he had been away.

"I come back," he said, "with no intention of going away again. My great wish is that the White Fathers should in the future undertake what I have undertaken this past year. My greatest wish is to remain in this cherished Fraternity where there is only one thing lacking—brothers in whose midst I may disappear. Our earthly afflictions are designed to make us feel our exile, to make us sigh for our homeland. Jesus chooses for each of us the kind of suffering He deems most appropriate to sanctify, and often the cross which He imposes is that which among all others we would refuse if we dared. That which He gives us is that which we least understand. He leads into bitter pastures which He alone knows are sweet. Poor sheep, we are so blind!"

The old Sahara hands in the garrison on the hill did not take too seriously Father de Foucauld's vow to stay put in Beni-Abbès forevermore. They knew his fervor, his burning restlessness to serve God, his soldier-like obedience to the orders of his ecclesiastical superiors. But those who served in the late watches, the officers and men who stood guard in the glittering star-lit silence of the desert night, were glad to hear again the quavering metallic treble of Marie de Bondy's bell at midnight and the small hours, proclaiming that Father de Foucauld had arisen from his uncushioned couch for Matins and the Lauds, and to chant the *Veni Creator* in his thin, uncertain tenor.

It was comforting to know that the saintly old ex-cavalryman was back in his hermitage once more.

TWELVE

APOSTLE TO THE HOGGAR

*Je suis le plus heureux des hommes. Rien
ne me manque.*

I am the happiest of men. I lack nothing.
—Charles de Foucauld, written in the
wastes of the Sahara.

I

Father de Foucauld was not well. He complained (to his
diary only) of bad headaches, fever, and a general combination
of vague ills. His infirmities were not enough, however, to keep
him off his feet or to prevent his celebration of Mass. Moreover,
the old procession of ailing and indigent Africans had again
resumed their way to the Fraternity to take advantage of the
Father's dates and barley, and his sympathetic ear for their
troubles.

Three weeks after his return he welcomed an important
visitor to Beni-Abbès—his fellow Saint-Cyrien who had also become a devotee of Africa, General Louis Lyautey, a future
Marshal of France, at that time regional commander at Ain-
Sefra. The general, who had developed into a *bon vivant* after
he began to collect the gold stripes around his kepi, now always traveled with his own cook. He insisted that the cadet-
epicure-become-ascetic should dine with him at the officers'
mess at the *bordj*. Father de Foucauld who could hardly refuse
an old schoolmate, particularly since he was now a general, ate
sparingly of everything and even sipped a little wine.

After dinner General Lyautey brought out a portable phonograph, put on some of the latest recordings of rather gamey ditties from Montmartre, and twisted his magnificent handlebar mustachios as he slyly watched the priest's reaction. The ex-lieutenant, however, merely joined heartily in the general chorus of laughter, although he did insist that the general and his staff attend seven-o'clock Mass next day (which was Sunday) at the hermitage.

"A ramshackle shanty, this hermitage!" General Lyautey recalled later. "His chapel was a miserable hallway between columns covered with reeds. His altar, a plank. His altar piece, a picture of the Christ on a calico panel. His candlesticks were of tin! [They were actually a gift from Mother Elisabeth of the Clarist Convent in Jerusalem.] We sat with our feet in the sand. And yet I have never heard Mass celebrated as it was by Father de Foucauld that Sunday morning. I could imagine myself in the Theban desert with the early Christian hermits. It was one of the lasting impressions of my life."

After General Lyautey had gone, Father de Foucauld settled down to his routine of washing the festering sores of his poor and feeding the hungry. He did not think seriously again of the Hoggar until April 1, when he received a letter from Lieutenant-colonel Laperrine informing him (without actually putting it in the form of an order) that there would be a company of the Camel Corps, commanded by Captain Dinaux, leaving In-Salah for the Hoggar by way of Ahenet, and the Iforas Adrar (*Adrar* is a Berber word meaning "mountain"). This would be an excellent opportunity for Father de Foucauld to get to the Hoggar for the summer.

Foucauld replied that he could not possibly leave Beni-Abbès before autumn, at which time he would decide whether he should remain cloistered at Beni-Abbès definitely, or whether he should devote part of his life to roaming through the spiritual wastelands of the Sahara.

A week later Laperrine wrote again, more insistently.

Foucauld wrote a frantic letter to Abbé Huvelin, making another appeal for some rugged soul to share his life in Beni-Abbès so that he might at last have a nucleus of his Little Brothers of the Sacred Heart of Jesus. He also cabled for advice to Monseigneur Guérin who by chance happened to be in Paris.

On April 22 the two ecclesiastics sent a joint cable: "Disposed to favor your accepting invitation."

So on May 3 Father de Foucauld loaded his portable altar on a camel and set off again with Paul Embarek for a desert rendezvous with Captain Dinaux. Charles de Foucauld had no qualms about venturing into the Sahara alone. Or practically alone. He did not count on Paul Embarek, who he knew from experience would run like a rabbit at the first sign of danger. He did count on his own experience as a man of the desert; he was not afraid of the trackless vastness of Tropical Africa. And he had perfect trust in God. If he had any misgivings at all, it was only that he was not yet worthy to die a martyr.

The sweltering heat of the Sahara was rising rapidly to its mid-summer torture point. When he found a friendly well or oasis, he would stop for a few hours when the blazing sun became unbearable—the *gaïla*. After all, he was in his forty-seventh year. For three weeks he penetrated deep into the Tidikelt and was well into the Twat region when he began to receive warnings from the friendly cadis of sympathetic *ksour* he had visited before. Aziwel, pretender to the post of Amenokal of the Taïtok Tuareg, was roaming the region. Aziwel was not friendly to the French.

Father de Foucauld knew that the Amenokal-to-be was not friendly. He had met his hostility at close range while traveling with Laperrine. Aziwel was one of those who did not come to pay his respects, although his tents were pitched a stone's throw from those of the Commander-in-chief of the Oases.

"You should go back to Adrar, Marabout," said the Cadi. "You cannot be sure of meeting Captain Dinaux at Akabli. And Aziwel is a violent man. He does not like Christians. You are alone, Marabout, and you are unarmed—."

"I am a man of peace," said Father de Foucauld. "I should like very much to meet Aziwel. I shall be living among his people."

A few days later, on June 5, Brother Charles found the camp of Aziwel near a desert well. Alone he strode up to the blue-and-gold tent of the future Amenokal, brushed past the two blue-veiled giants who guarded the entrance flap with buckskin shields and long two-edged swords, and stood in the presence of the Tuareg chief.

Aziwel stared at the priest for a long moment of solemn, silent surprise. He remained sitting cross-legged upon his rugs.

"El riras," said Father de Foucauld at last. "I come in peace." Aziwel smiled. He got up to greet his visitor.

Brother Charles found him "altogether changed since the previous year, quite self-assured and completely tamed." Considering his earlier comments on the sincerity of the Tuareg, he may easily have remembered the Tuareg proverb: "Kiss the hand you cannot cut off."

Brother Charles made contact with the Dinaux expedition at another desert well three days distant, and found four French civilians traveling with the captain: E. F. Gautier, a distinguished explorer and geographer; Pierre Mille, an author in search of exotic local color; a geologist named Chudeau, and a fat engineer from the Ministry of Posts, Telephones and Telegraphs, a man named Etiennot, supposedly making a preliminary survey for a trans-Saharan telegraph line.

Brother Charles was assigned to travel with Etiennot and his convoy of fifteen camels, some of which were burdened with the bureaucrat's bottled provisions. It was an unhappy combination. While Foucauld prayed, Etiennot drank and bellowed ribald songs. When Foucauld arose at two in the morning to say Mass, Etiennot complained of being awakened. Usually Foucauld managed to walk ahead of the group beside his camel so that his meditations would not be interrupted. He thoroughly disapproved of the route Etiennot had chosen for his telegraph line, and wrote to his friend Major Lacroix in Algiers explaining why it showed ignorance of desert conditions and would be almost impossible to maintain properly.

On the western approaches to the Hoggar highlands the expedition was joined by Moussa-ag-Amastane, Amenokal of the Hoggar Tuareg, the man Foucauld had been wanting to meet since the previous autumn. The young Amenokal (he was about ten years Foucauld's junior) and the grizzled priest took an instant liking to one another. Brother Charles described him as "very handsome, very intelligent, very candid, a very pious Moslem with all the good intentions of a liberal Mohammedan, and yet ambitious with a strong liking for money, pleasure, and honor—as was Mohammed, who was his idea of perfection. . . ."

Moussa's Moslem piety was a fairly recent acquisition, so the two men had the additional bond of having become religious when well along in adulthood. In his youth Moussa was not only a rakehell but a convinced and practicing brigand, devoted to cutting throats and pillaging caravans of unbelievers, particularly the rare French or other Christian unbelievers. He looked upon Foucauld's early sins as picayune—in fact, he still clung to some of the carnal errors which Foucauld had given up—yet he recognized sincerity in a holy man with the unerring instinct of a reformed sinner. Foucauld likewise recognized the sincerity of Moussa as a reformed pirate, although perhaps he had some reserves at the outset. In any event, the Amenokal willingly gave the priest permission to set up a permanent mission in the Hoggar.

Moussa traveled with the French caravan for two weeks, then took off on some nomadic mission of his own. Captain Dinaux's four civilians also left the caravan for points south. The captain and Brother Charles pushed on into the highlands, and on August 7, 1905, they reached Tamanrasset—a name which was underlined three times in the priest's diary and which was to be underlined many times more in the years to come.

II

The Tuareg and the Hoggar highlands belonged to another world. The people and their land were equally weird; both might have come from the pages of Jules Verne, the French writer of fantasy who died that year.

The landscape had been torn from the heart of the Sahara by some great volcanic convulsion and piled in monstrous confusion into a mile-high plateau, like a lunar nightmare. Grotesque towers rose into the sky another mile above the jagged rims of long-dead craters. Cleaver-like fissures split sheer cliffs of black and gray and dusty-pink granite. Dry stream beds threaded their sandy way through boulder-strewn fields and gray acres of broken basalt and lava.

The Tuareg had their own legendary story of the origin of their land. God, it would seem, carefully constructed the world

of proper proportions of earth and rock—no water figured in the
Tuareg version of the Creation, of course, because there was no
sea in the Tuareg world and what water there was came down
from extra-terrestrial space at rare intervals—and when He was
finished, He had a lot of large and odd-shaped rocks left over,
so He dumped them on Africa, and that's how the Hoggar was
born!

The people who tell this story were just as outlandish as the
land they lived in. A relatively small ethnic group—there were
few more than 100,000 at the time of Father de Foucauld,
scattered over an area nearly half the extent of the United
States—the Tuareg were of Berber origin. They were fair
skinned with straight brown hair sometimes fair and once in a
while red. They had brown eyes, although gray eyes were not
uncommon and blue eyes not unknown. Their features were
regular and neither Semitic nor Negroid. The men were big,
tough, and in a measure sentimental.

The Tuareg male—incidentally, *Tuareg* is the plural form of
the term; the singular is *Targui*—was a handsome creature,
averaging six feet tall or more, well built, equally at home in
the saddle of mare or Mehari or in the arms of a belle of his
matriarchal society. He was fearless and cruel in battle, sensitive
and even romantic in love. And in dress he was an eerie equal to
the bizarre grandeur of the Hoggar landscape.

The male Tuareg wore white hoods or hemispheric turbans
of deep indigo, roughly resembling a head bandage starting
just below the eyebrows. Around the face was wrapped a deep
blue veil—the *litsam*—drawn tight across the bridge of the nose
to hang below the chin, so that the entire face was covered except for a narrow slit for the eyes. The loose, knee-length shirt
and the trousers to the calf could be blue or white or striped,
but the voluminous cape enveloping the complete man was almost invariably indigo. So a troop of Tuareg nomads trotting
up to a water hole, mantles fluttering, gave the startling impression of a covey of blue specters.

The Tuareg were Moslems but not orthodox Moslems. They
prayed in Arabic, just as Jews in many lands still pray in
Hebrew and Catholics in Latin, but they were proud of their

own language, Tamashek, of Hamitic origin. They did not observe all Moslem holidays or all Moslem customs.

Where the Arab Moslem might have four wives and as many concubines as he could support, the Tuareg were essentially monogamous. The Arab women wore veils and were forced to lead secondary lives in seclusion. Tuareg women went unveiled —it was their men who wore veils, reputedly to protect the face against the dry, sand-laden winds of the desert—and were as emancipated as were women in many European countries. They led social lives, gave concerts, and were allowed to initiate divorce. They were, incidentally, physically attractive and quite feminine by nature, with all the coquetry and love of adornment the term implies.

The nomadic life was restricted to the upper strata of Tuareg society. The Tuareg lords roamed the Hoggar plateau seeking pasturage and water for their goats and camels, collecting tribute from vassal clans, trading with the peoples of the lowlands, and occasionally indulging in a razzia to plunder too-opulent and not-too-friendly caravans. The red sheepskin tent of the nomad was a status symbol of the nobility.

The middle-class Tuareg were the sedentary type peopling villages, living in huts of reeds or mud and straw, often without roofs, scratching a bare living from the hostile soil and engaging in petty trade.

A third class was the Harratin (singular: Hartani), of mixed Tuareg and Sudanese blood, often freed slaves or the descendants of freed slaves. They, too, eked out a bare subsistence from farming.

The slaves were exclusively Sudanese Negros.

This was Father de Foucauld's parish and these were his parishioners, although they did not know it. Nor did he intend to preach to them. His method was example, not precept. He would teach them Christianity by living humbly and in poverty in imitation of Christ.

III

On arriving in Tamanrasset Father de Foucauld wrote:

"By grace of Divine Well-beloved Jesus, I am able to settle in Tamanrasset or wherever else I like in the Hoggar, to have a house and garden there and to put down roots forever. I choose Tamanrasset, a mountain village of some twenty firesides in the heart of the Hoggar, the seat of the principal Dag-Rali tribe, far from any important center. I doubt if it shall ever see a garrison, the telegraph, or another European resident. There will be no mission here for a long time. So I have picked this forsaken place to settle."

Before Captain Dinaux left, he had his men build Brother Charles a rough shelter of branches and palm leaves. Left alone with Paul Embarek, Brother Charles recruited a few Harratin to help him build a more solid structure which would serve as both residence and chapel—a corridor-like edifice of mud and stones, twenty feet long by six feet wide, with one door and window, a roof of thatch, and a curtain separating the chapel and sacristy from the library and living quarters.

Here he celebrated his first Mass in Tamanrasset on Sept. 7, 1905, with Paul Embarek as server and no communicants.

The chief drawback of Tamanrasset as a residence was that it was sixty days of desert travel away from the nearest priest. However, wrote Foucauld, "I do not believe that the precept of confession is obligatory under these conditions. Despite my poverty, I live here in great peace and tranquility."

Brother Charles was certainly in a tranquil setting. The broad sandy wadi on the left bank of which he had erected his shanty and his chapel, was a river only every two or three years. The lusty Tuareg warriors were away much of every year. The Harratin were much too busy scratching for a bare existence to raise a fuss. And the landscape was exactly what Brother Charles had described as "peace and tranquility."

The stark beauty of the country around Tamanrasset was breath-taking. The village itself was drab and dreary—mud huts and straw shanties, surrounded by the dismal stony hammada and circumscribed by a bowl of suddenly dramatic mountains. To the north, the massif of Kudiat pushed its curiously-shaped shoulders upward until they reached the bare, rocky summit of two-mile-high Ilaman. To the East the relatively minor chain of the Hageran seemed overpowering because it was relatively close. To the West were the narrow, squirming ravines which seemed designed for the sole purpose of confusing the prospective traveler to In-Salah. To the South was the granite wall of Mount Hadrian, passable only by a cleft struck through the stone barrier by a stroke of the two-edged sword of the Tuareg's legendary giant Elias. And always on the horizon high, virile peaks.

At sunrise and sunset the whole landscape became drenched in a rainbow of unbelievable color. The dusty trees, the drab hovels, the gray prospect of the rocky valley, the warped and twisted prelude to the celestial heights—all were tinted with unrecognizable reds and blues, with misty purples and flaming golds and incredible greens . . . all visible through the desert transparency of a crystal-clear atmosphere unsullied by the dust and gaseous polution of civilization.

Only God could create such splendor from nothing.

Once he had oriented himself, Father de Foucauld—or Brother Charles (there was nobody to reprimand him for his failure to observe ecclesiastical protocol in the lonely lunar uplands of the Hoggar) methodically divided his time into set tasks. First of all was his duty to God and Jesus Christ—Mass, adoration, prayers, meditation, and imitation. Then there was the unusual business of being parish priest to people who had no idea they were his parishioners. For this he had to give up his beloved "hidden life"—the obscurity he had sought and won in Nazareth. He had to venture beyond the limits of his cloister—which incidentally were not yet established—to make friends with the Tuareg. And to make better friends with the Tuareg he had to perfect his Tamashek by study and by contact. A by-product of this necessity was his contribution to the sum of human knowledge, a better understanding of the Tuareg language and people. To this end he had immediately begun work on a French-Tamashek dictionary, a better Tamashek grammar than the out-dated monograph which Major Lacroix had slipped into his baggage when he left Algiers for the unknown south in 1901, and a collection of Tuareg folklore— proverbs, poetry, and legends.

In his spare time—nobody with Father de Foucauld's schedule could possibly store up any spare time unless he gave up sleeping to the extent of the ex-Hussar-become-ascetic—he collected an amazing amount of information about the people and the

country, carefully logging it in the manner of the young explorer who had written *Reconnaissance au Maroc* twenty years
earlier. He described the flora of Tamanrasset in great detail.
The only tree worthy of the name which grew within sight of
his hermitage, for instance, was the *éthel*—the atlee or salt
tamarisk—which grew in the dry bed of the wadi and from the
branches of which he hung his meteorological instruments.
Tufts of dusty gray shrubs dotted the rocky countryside. There
was quite a bit of barilla, the Algerian salt-wort which the
Tuareg called *guettaf*, a source of soda ash, and which grew into
a pale bush three or four feet tall. And there was lots of
diss, a reed-like grass used for making baskets, mats, and other
domestic impedimenta.

Brother Charles visited all the Tuareg he had met the year
before, bringing them small gifts such as simple household
remedies for common ills, colored religious pictures, and
needles. His gifts of steel needles were particularly popular
among people used to sewing with thorns to which string had
been attached, and Tuareg women would ride miles donkey-
back to the hermitage to ask the white marabout for some of his
marvelous needles.

Brother Charles wrote to Monseigneur Guérin suggesting
that a few White Sisters be sent to Tamanrasset to set up sewing
classes for the Tuareg women and to teach them such rudiments
of hygiene as washing themselves. No White Sister ever came,
and the Tuareg women continued "to work little and talk
much."

There were much more serious things to correct than idle
gossip, however. Brother Charles was shocked to discover infanticide was widely practiced by the Tuareg; girl babies particularly were considered undesirable. The ease of divorce also
disturbed him. And as for the famous—or infamous—*ahal*, the
Tuareg love séance, Brother Charles figuratively threw up his
hands.

The *ahal* was an immensely popular institution among the
Tuareg. *Ahals* of purely local interest were frequent and well
attended. An *ahal* scheduled for the tent of a beauty widely
known throughout the Hoggar would bring young men trotting

on their fine blond mehari camels from a hundred miles around. The *ahal* was a heterosexual gathering to be sure, and it was not devoid of sexuality. Yet it was not a true orgy in the sense that most Europeans have come to regard an orgy. It had strong romantic, and subtly sentimental overtones.

First of all, the *ahal* during fine weather was frequently held out of doors—perhaps under a tree, if there was one of suitable size in the neighborhood. Second, the putative themes of an *ahal* were music and poetry, at both of which the Tuareg excelled. The blue-veiled young buck who had urged his beige camel over the stony wastes to the *ahal* would have to woo the idol of his heart, soul, and libido with specially-composed verse and the incidental music of the *amzad*, the one-string fiddle of the Tuareg. There were no rules against the use of hands, lips, and noses in the *ahal* courtships; in fact, a physical obbligato was almost *de rigueur* while the love-lorn were sighing their romantic verses to music. Brother Charles was disturbed by the whole ritual, but he did not attempt to interfere with it.

As an old and reformed Lothario himself, Brother Charles had a peculiar insight into the relationship between the flesh and the spirit. He knew from personal experience that nonchalant dalliance need not necessarily leave scars upon the soul. He did not, therefore, make a capital issue of trying to interfere with what he called "the traditional distractions" of the Tuareg. He would much rather concentrate on fighting what he considered the major evils of slavery and the light-hearted murder, mayhem and pillage which the Tuareg razzia considered a legitimate form of livelihood.

"In regard to the local populations," he wrote, "I see no other duty than that of praying for them, winning their affection, giving them good advice occasionally and discreetly. . . . I strive to prepare the way for my successors, praying to Jesus that He may send them to me. It seems to me that the two most imperative current needs in the Hoggar are education and the restoration of the family. The ignorance of the Tuareg is such that they cannot distinguish the true from the false; and the degeneration of family life, as a result of loose morals and multiple divorces, leaves the children to grow up haphazardly, without proper training."

Brother Charles had been in Tamanrasset about three months when Moussa-ag-Amastane rode into the village with his herds, his camels, his slaves and his warriors to make camp on the banks of the wadi. He had heard reports of the works of the white marabout among his people and had decided it was time he investigated. The man after all was a *roumi*, an unbeliever and a blood brother of the French conquerors.

He had scarcely pitched his tents when Brother Charles came to call and present his respects. His second thoughts on the Amenokal were not greatly different from his first impressions as he communicated them to Monseigneur Livinhac:

"He is quite an intelligent man, guided by good intentions, broadminded. . . . He has consecrated his life to establishing peace among the Tuareg and to protecting the weak among them from the violence of the strong, and thus acquiring from In-Salah to Timbuctoo universal veneration for his liberality, his friendliness and his courage. . . . If God grants him long life, his influence will increase and endure. It is extremely interesting to observe this mixture of great natural talents and profound ignorance in a man who is a savage from certain points of view but from others deserves our esteem and consideration; for his justice, his courage, the loftiness and generosity of his character have given him a status without peer from the Twat to the Niger."

Brother Charles could not help adding the reservation with which he qualified the sincerity of all Tuareg.

"Do his fine qualities," he asked, "exclude ambition, sensuality, and a residue of hate and disdain deep in his heart for all non-Moslems? I think not, yet he seems to have enough true piety so that his concern for the general welfare will outweigh any special interest in determining his course of conduct. . . ."

In time perhaps Brother Charles could persuade the Amenokal to settle down in Tamanrasset, make it his true capital and dispense justice and wise counsel to his people the year round, instead of gadding about the countryside whenever the spirit moved him.

IV

Although the village of Tamanrasset sat astride the Tropic of Cancer in the very heart of the Sahara, its mile-high situation provided seasonal changes of temperature. The desert sun might blaze down mercilessly at noon all year, but when December came around the nights grew sharp and even downright cold. Wood was scarce in the Hoggar and camel dung was not the most satisfactory of fuels, so fires were scarce. Chilly nomads in transient Tuareg camps would burrow into the dry bed of the wadi with their spears, wrap themselves in their burnouses, and snuggle into the still-warm sand at sundown. The tall peaks along the horizon were spattered with snow, and the night wind smelled of winter and approaching Christmas.

This was not the first Christmas Brother Charles had spent alone. At least he now had the solace of the Blessed Sacrament and he still had Paul Embarek to serve the Mass, both lacking during his lonely Christmas in the Shotts of Tunisia and as a virtual prisoner of Sidi Abd Allah in Morocco. Still Brother Charles had a few weeks of depression during which he wrote sentimental letters to his sister, recalling their childhood Christmases in Alsace, and of course to Marie de Bondy. He wrote again to Monseigneur Guérin, repeating his perennial plea for someone to be his first novice in the fraternity of the Little Brothers of the Sacred Heart of Jesus. He knew Monseigneur Guérin would understand, for the White Fathers never staffed an outpost mission with a single priest. It was not the loneliness he minded. In fact, loneliness was part of the abnegation, mortification, and obscurity that he had so passionately sought. But as another year drew to its close, he began to despair of ever recruiting a kindred soul for his fraternity. He was already in his forty-eighth year. Would there be no one to carry on for him, to nurture the seed that he was planting?

Spring came at last, bringing a whiff of rain that caused the desert to sparkle with thousands of tiny wildflowers. Spring also caused vague stirrings in Paul Embarek's baser nature. He was homesick. He was unhappy among these strange nomads and the wretched Harratin. He yearned for women of his own kind and for food other than the eternal barley and dates of the hermitage. He was a materialist and he was inarticulate. The only way he could express himself was to act. On May 17, 1906, he departed from Tamanrasset.

Only a month before, Father de Foucauld had been complaining of the ex-slave in a letter to Monseigneur Guérin. "Paul has been going from bad to worse," he wrote. "I keep him only because it is impossible to say Mass without him."

When Paul left, Father de Foucauld prayed: "O God! May it be Thy will that I continue to celebrate the Holy Sacrifice! May this soul not be lost! Save it, I pray Thee."

His prayer was soon answered. He was without Mass for scarcely more than a fortnight. On June 3, which was Pentecost, his old friend Captain Calassanti-Motylinski arrived at the hermitage. The former language officer of the Fourth Chasseurs d'Afrique, now a professor of Oriental languages and Arabic studies in Constantine, had come to spend the summer in Tamanrasset. He wanted to brush up on his Tamashek.

Needless to say, Father de Foucauld was delighted. Not only was he overjoyed and relieved to have someone to serve Mass, but he was pleased to have such a distinguished lexicographer to work with him on the numerous linguistic projects he had under way. Not only was he writing a new Tamashek grammar and compiling a Tamashek-French and French-Tamashek dictionary, but he was translating into Tamashek extracts from the Bible which would be "at once an abridged version of the Holy Writ and a collection of the most useful passages from the poetic, sapiential, and prophetic books."

Father de Foucauld optimistically thought the two of them could clear up most of his ambitious schedule before the summer was over. He soon found out that it would be a matter of years, not months. But even his over-optimistic time-table would have been cut short by an unexpected calamity toward the end of the summer.

The two old comrades-in-arms were strolling through the twilight in the outskirts of the drab little village, absorbed in putting Tamashek names on the common nouns that came within their view. There was one noun for which neither of them could furnish a Tamashek equivalent because neither of them saw the handsome, lithe, reptilian length with the ditto marks gleaming along its scaly back, slithering out from between the rocks that bordered their path. It was not until Father de Foucauld stepped on the snake that Captain Motylinski recognized the ugly head with the protuberances behind the eyes as that of the cerastes—the venomous horned viper.

The viper sank its fangs into the priest's bare ankle above his open sandals. The venom apparently struck a vein, for the reaction was almost instantaneous. Brother Charles suddenly sat down on a boulder, his lips tight and white to hide the pain. At once his foot and leg began to swell and turn dark. He closed his eyes a moment to shut out the vertigo, then opened them in time to see the viper squirm away into the rocks. He smiled foolishly, waved vaguely in the direction of the retreating reptile, and, trying to remember what Saint Francis of Assisi might have said in similar circumstances, murmured, "Dear Brother Snake, I did not mean to—."

Then he vomited.

Captain Motylinski, who knew that the sting of the horned viper could well be fatal, tore a strip of cloth from his jacket and made a tourniquet above the fang marks. The swelling was ballooning and spreading at an alarming rate. Brother Charles was gasping for breath, and slipping into unconsciousness. He muttered several incomprehensible phrases, tried to gesture with his hands, then fell silent.

Motylinski picked up the scrawny, under-nourished hermit in his arms and started toward the village.

V

Father de Foucauld came to with the smell of burned steak in his nostrils. He was lying on a pile of rugs in a nomad's sheepskin tent. He blinked at the Tuareg and Harratin crowding into the entrance. He saw the worried look on the bearded face of his friend Motylinski. He recognized a Hartani farmer named El Madani, a man to whom he had once given some boric acid for an inflamed eye, who was fanning a brazier of glowing coals. He noted a blue-veiled Targui lifting an iron bar from the coals and advancing the red-hot tip toward him. He felt a searing pain in his foot and realized that the scorched flesh he smelled was his own. The pain rose excruciatingly in his leg and again he lost consciousness.

The drastic Tuareg method of treating the bite of the horned viper by cauterization proved successful. Motylinski's tourniquet had prevented the venom from doing fatal damage to the vasomotor and respiratory centers, while the cauterization had destroyed the poison in the region of the wound. The badly-burned foot, however, took weeks to heal completely.

Father de Foucauld reveled in his suffering. He felt he had been remiss in his religious life that summer. In July he had written to Abbé Huvelin accusing himself of being lukewarm in his prayers, lacking in courage, and without mortification. "Brother Snake" had been God's answer.

On September 15 his foot was sufficiently healed for him to leave Tamanrasset with Motylinski who was returning to the coast.

The two men reached El Goléa, via In-Salah, by mid-October. Here Motylinski went on to Constantine, and Foucauld, after a brief rest in El Goléa during which the White Sisters mended his clothing and his primitive sandals, headed for Beni-Abbès.

He was surprised, as he modestly records, by the warmth of his welcome. That of the French at the garrison was "perfect . . . beyond words." That of the natives at his beloved fraternity "beyond anything I had the right to hope." He stayed at Beni-Abbès only a few days, however. He was anxious to reach Algiers and make his annual retreat with the White Fathers at Maison Carrée.

The railway had been extended some 130 miles from Ain Sefra to Colomb-Béchar, at which point on November 24, Father de Foucauld boarded a train for the north.

THIRTEEN

THE LITTLE BROTHER WHO FAILED

Je suis le frère universel.

I am the universal brother.

—Charles de Foucauld

I

Brother Charles could scarcely believe his ears. The news was little short of miraculous. The first thing that Monseigneur Guérin told him on his arrival at Maison Carrée was that he had at last found an acolyte who was anxious to follow the rule of the Little Brothers of the Sacred Heart of Jesus and journey into the desert with Foucauld.

Brother Charles was overjoyed. His fraternity would finally become more than a name. He would at last have someone to share his lonely hermitage and carry on his work after his death.

The acolyte was a Breton lad, the son of a fisherman, who had grown up on the sea, accompanying his father in the family schooner for the cod catch off the Grand Banks of Newfoundland. When conscripted, he donned the brilliant uniform of the Zouaves—baggy red trousers, gaiters, short blue jacket and tasseled fez. He served three years in Africa and, like so many before and after him, fell in love with the continent. When the time came for his return to civilian life, he decided to remain in Algeria. So he offered his services to the White Fathers and became a novice under the name of Brother Michel.

During his three years as a neophyte at Maison Carrée, he had heard of the saintly reputation of Father de Foucauld and asked permission to join him. His superiors warned him that the rule of Father de Foucauld was twenty times more severe than that of the White Fathers and even twice as strict as that of the Trappists. Brother Michel, however, was not discouraged. So Brother Charles welcomed him with open arms and thanks to God.

After Brother Charles had completed his retreat, he and Brother Michel entrained for Oran on December 10. They changed trains at Oran and headed south, Brother Michel wearing the modified Arab raiment of the White Fathers, Brother Charles still clad in his own uniform—the white gandurah with the front insignia of Marie de Bondy's red Sacred Heart and Cross, the wide leather belt and the outsize rosary.

When the train stopped at Ain Sefra, former rail head and still army divisional headquarters, Brother Charles was surprised to find the station platform crowded with military brass: General Lyautey himself and fifteen staff officers. The general insisted that the old Hussar break his journey at Ain-Sefra, and Foucauld complied, introducing the surprised and awed ex-private of Zouaves with great pride as the first Little Brother of Jesus.

General Lyautey insisted that the ex-lieutenant dine at his mess which as usual was an epicure's dream. Foucauld tasted of everything to be polite—even taking a token sip of the wines and champagne—but still ate sparingly. And when the coffee was brought on and Lyautey insisted that Foucauld drink a glass of "our good old Lorraine kirsch in honored memory of our dear Saint-Cyr," the priest complied by swallowing the cherry spirit at one gulp so that he could not accuse himself of enjoying it.

General Lyautey later made no secret of the fact that he was shocked by what he considered the decline of the old cavalry officer into a ragged itinerant priest. "Nothing remained of the old Foucauld," he is quoted as saying, "except one thing: his fine, luminous eyes." Lyautey also admitted that his officers adored the saintly hermit, and that they admired his horsemanship, even though he rode barefoot.

And all that night the future Marshal of France paid oblique tribute to the intelligence of the old Saint-Cyrien by keeping him up until the small hours, poring over maps, and picking the brains of the first European to have made an intelligent, comprehensive, and accurate geographical survey of Morocco. The general gave no hint that he was then organizing the campaign that was to make Morocco a French protectorate for nearly fifty years.

Next day Foucauld and Brother Michel went on to Colomb-Béchar where Foucauld acquired two camels for the desert trek and a groom to look after them. The groom was a former slave from Timbuctoo whom Brother Michel later described as "bibulous, stubborn, conceited, untruthful, lazy, and a repulsively uncouth glutton with no religion whatsoever. He had gladly accepted service with the Father, whom he believed rich, in the expectation of little work and an abundant and epicurean diet."

He was soon disillusioned by Father de Foucauld's chopped dates and barley gruel and immediately set his sights on greener fields.

Brother Michel was also somewhat disillusioned by Father de Foucauld's "fraternity" at Beni-Abbès of which he had heard so much. His own description deserves quotation: "The seven or eight cells designed for future monks were so low that an average man could easily touch the ceiling with his hand, so narrow that he could touch opposite walls with outstretched arms. No bed, no chairs, no table, no *prie-Dieu* to kneel upon. A man had to sleep in his clothes stretched out on a palm-leaf mat on the ground. The sacristy was fairly large and served the Father as library, store room, bedroom, and study. . . . During the long offices and pious practices all day and night, we had to stand or kneel or squat on mats. Next to the sacristy there was a large empty room which the Father reserved for visiting dignitaries such as the Apostolic Prefect, high Army officers, or other persons of rank who might wish to stay at the hermitage. . . .

"We spent Christmas [1906] at the hermitage. At midnight Mass a hundred officers, non-coms and soldiers filled both the chapel and the sacristy."

There was only one woman present at midnight Mass that Christmas eve—blind old Marie, who was still living on the few francs a month Foucauld had arranged to pay her. "A beautiful soul in an ugly body," as Brother Michel described her. "She devoted all her days to prayer and never failed to take communion every time the Holy Sacrifice was offered at Beni-Abbès. Upon the departure of her benefactor, she wept hot tears and uttered cries of sorrow."

Brother Michel recorded the hour-by-hour schedule of prayer and ritual, noted that in off hours Father de Foucauld retired to the sacristy to work on his Tamashek dictionary or write letters while he withdrew to his cell, "the only one with a fireplace," where he read the Holy Writ, ground wheat between two stones in the manner of the country, crushed dates in a mortar, or cooked barley cakes in the ashes.

At meal time, after Father de Foucauld had read a few passages from *The Imitation of Christ,* they squatted on mats around a pot, just taken from the fire, "eating in the most profound silence, fishing for food with a spoon, drinking water from the same jug. The menu seldom varied. It was sometimes a plate of rice boiled in water or rarely with condensed milk, sometimes mixed with desert-grown carrots or turnips, sometimes a kind of marmalade of dates mixed with wheat flour and water, which was rather pleasant tasting. No napkins, no tablecloth, no knives or forks. We arose after fifteen or twenty minutes, and after prayers and thanksgiving we went into the chapel, chanting the *Miserere,* to visit the Very Blessed Sacrament and for joint spiritual reading."

The day after Christmas, Brother Charles and Michel left Beni-Abbès. They had a military escort for two days. When they parted company, Brother Charles handed over the keys of his hermitage to the captain of the garrison saying: "Take good care of the House of the Good Lord. I am leaving it in your trust."

Brother Michel found that life on the desert was more rugged than life either as a Zouave private or a Breton fisherman. He noted that the desert winter temperatures varied from 70 Fahrenheit at noon to 5 or 6 degrees of frost at night. He recalled how they burrowed into the sand at night, Tuareg fashion, in a vain attempt to keep warm.

"In the heart of silent nature, in this dead land where no human being has ever settled, it was quite easy to lead a life of solitude and contemplation," wrote Brother Michel. "The Father never once missed celebrating the Holy Mysteries on his portable altar at daybreak, usually in the open air but three or four times during wind squalls under a tent which we had pitched the evening before."

Brother Michel was also aware of Father de Foucauld's yearning for martyrdom. "He would have liked to give to Jesus Christ the greatest proof of love and devotion that a friend could give to a friend, to die for Him as He died for us. . . . The beauty and grandeur of the prospect of immolation elated his generous faith and transformed his words, always firm and warm, into veritable paeans of joy. 'If only I could be killed by pagans some day,' he would say. 'What a beautiful death! My very dear brother, what an honor and what happiness if only God could grant my wish!' "

From the first days of their common life in the desert, however, Father de Foucauld seemed to have misgivings about the fitness of Brother Michel for a career of hermit. His diary contains reference to the young Breton's mental and physical limitations as early as the Christmas sojourn at Beni-Abbès. Nevertheless he was determined to give the acolyte at least a year's trial, and when the two men reached In-Salah in February 1907, Foucauld bought a house of sorts in which Brother Michel could rest and which would serve as a relay station for the fraternity between Tamanrasset and Beni-Abbès.

The dwelling, if it could be called that, cost less than one hundred francs and the repairs came to almost as much. Foucauld wrote to his beloved cousin Marie de Bondy asking her to underwrite the expense and also to send him 200 francs to purchase a third camel for Brother Michel who did not seem up to walking the thirty miles a day that were normal for Brother Charles.

The military doctor at the In-Salah garrison, however, declared that Brother Michel was in no physical condition to travel and would only become a burden to Foucauld should he go on to Tamanrasset with him.

"Like Moses, I was destined to see the promised land only from afar," wrote Brother Michel.

With mingled feelings of regret and relief, Brother Charles

provided Brother Michel with money and supplies, secured two reliable guides for him, helped him mount his camel, and early in March bade him farewell as he rode off to the north. From Maison Carrée Brother Michel later became a Carthusian monk at Tarragona in Spain, where the Carthusians were distilling their delightful green and yellow Chartreuse during their exile from France.

Brother Charles was once more alone—as usual. His fraternity of the Little Brothers of Jesus seemed destined never to have a disciple.

II

Brother Charles of Jesus—he clung to that name despite Abbé Huvelin's original objection that since ordination he must accept the more dignified title of Father de Foucauld—was not idle during his indecisive weeks at In-Salah. Here the business of furnishing the new "relay station" was quickly taken care of. A few packing crates for tables, chairs, and altar. A few palm-leaf mats for sitting and sleeping. An empty sardine can as a stoup, empty liqueur bottles as cruets, an original panel of Jesus (by Charles de Foucauld) as an altarpiece. . . .

He was also working hard at his Tamashek dictionaries. In fact, he found a new and valued tutor—M'Ahmed ben Messis, a man after his own heart in more ways than one. Messis was the son of a Tuareg mother and a Chaambi father. Because his mother was of the Tuareg nobility and because of the matri-archal tendencies of the Tuareg tribes, he was considered as a Targui. And he was extremely loyal to France. In fact, he was the man who had delivered the murderers of Foucauld's room-mate Vallombrosa-Morès to the authorities. As proof of the fact, he showed Brother Charles his roommate's pistol which had been given him as a token of appreciation by Mme. Val-lombrosa. He had also served as a guide to Lieutenant Cottonest whose handful of troops had defeated the Tuareg at Tit and brought about the submission to France of the three most im-portant Tuareg tribes, including that of the Amenokal of the Hoggar, Brother Charles' friend.

What was even more important for his contemporary chores, Brother Charles found Messis an intelligent and learned man who was an authority not only in Tamashek and the written language of Tifinagh, but knew the lore of the Tuareg.

Brother Charles was deep in his philological work when Colonel Laperrine appeared in In-Salah. The priest was delighted to embrace his old fellow Saint-Cyrien—until the colonel gave him the bad news. Captain Motylinski was dead. He had died in Constantine on March 2 of a disease vaguely diagnosed as "desert fever." Foucauld, convinced that the fatal malady was something Motylinski had contracted during his summer sojourn at Tamanrasset, was doubly crushed. Not only had he lost an old and dear friend and valued collaborator in his linguistic project, but he felt a sense of guilt that he may have somehow contributed to the demise of this brilliant scholar.

Characteristically, his diary gave no indication of the deep sorrow Motylinski's death produced in Brother Charles. Even more characteristically, his actions of the succeeding months gave evidence of his sentiment. In a letter to Monseigneur Guérin in May he wrote:

"I have begged Laperrine to have published by whomever he might choose as Commander-in-chief of the Oases the Tuareg grammar and the French-Tuareg lexicon which are finished. I want him or his command to be the copyright owners of these works as well as the Taureg-French lexicon which is still in work, and the Tuareg poetry which I am collecting. My sole condition is that my name be not connected with the publication, that it be unknown completely. Next year I should like to devote my entire attention to the revision of the Holy Gospel and the translation of the extracts from the Bible which I have been working on previously. After that, I should like nothing better than to live a life of prayer and manual labor as an example to the Tuareg who are in dire need of the example."

Foucauld went on to explain that his linguistic work was undertaken not for personal glory or even for the advance of human knowledge. His grammar, his Tamashek dictionaries and his translations of the Scriptures were exclusively for the use of the missionaries who might follow him to work among the Tuareg and cultivate the ground that he had plowed and seeded.

He insisted that all his philological studies be published under the name of the late Captain Calassanti-Motylinski.

III

When he learned that a detachment of eighty men commanded by his old desert friend Captain Dinaux was leaving In-Salah for the Hoggar in March and that M'Ahmed ben Messis was to accompany the expedition, Brother Charles quickly applied for permission to go along. This way he could combine linguistic research with sowing the seed for others to harvest. . . .

With Messis he would sit up for hours at night, bent over a flickering candle while discussing word meanings in his low-ceilinged tent. By day he would collect Tuareg poetry, proverbs and traditional folklore. Foucauld had already remarked the curious fact that while the Tuareg had their own written language, they had no books, no written history, no recorded folk lore. There was, however, a great body of folk poetry dealing largely with love and deeds of derring-do. It was entirely oral lore, passed on from mouth to mouth, and was being augmented almost weekly through the *ahals* and the exultant versification of some nomad returning from successful brigandry. With the help of Messis, Foucauld was recording hundreds of verses.

When Brother Charles began offering one sou a verse for Tuareg poetry, the response was overwhelming, "enough to fill my tent for a month," he recorded. "Neighboring douars [nomad camps] also sent word that if I could pass by, their women would give me more poetry. So I visited several douars spending hours in a tent or under a tree, surrounded by women and their children, writing down their verses and giving them small gifts. I am very happy that this friendly interchange is developing in importance. It is only a first step, very small, very humble, but it has to be taken to sweep aside so much prejudice, aversion, and mistrust."

Brother Charles remained in the field with the Dinaux expedition until early July, when Captain Dinaux turned back to return to In-Salah, taking M'Ahmed ben Messis with him. Brother Charles, after some hesitation, decided to go on to

Tamanrasset. He had not missed one day of saying Mass since leaving In-Salah, as there was always a Frenchman of the expedition to act as server. But—. "What will I do when I get back to Tamanrasset?" he wrote to Father Guérin. "It is for our Divine Master to arrange things."

IV

The black Hartani farmer squatted in the doorway of his reed shanty and yawned. He scarcely heard what the Christian Marabout was saying.

"I have brought you these seeds to help you diversify your crops," said Father de Foucauld. "The vegetables are well suited for desert soil, El Madani. The cucumbers and squash grow quickly in warm sandy soil. The Chantenay carrots are short and fleshy and don't need deep topsoil. . . ."

El Madani yawned again. Foucauld knew what he was thinking: all this would mean more work. Didn't he have enough trouble as it was, scratching the ground to plant his barley and millet? And who cares about all these strange new foods anyhow? The colored pictures that the Marabout showed him were pretty enough, but why should a man break his back trying to grow something which probably would not even taste good?

"I will help you plant," said Father de Foucauld. "I will help you dig. I will show you how to make hills for the cucumbers."

Of course, if the Christian Marabout was going to do the work himself. . . . El Madani stretched out his hand for the seed packets. He did not say "thank you." He did not smile. His eyes were dull and suspicious. Father de Foucauld again could read his thoughts.

What causes the Christian Marabout to do these kindnesses for me? Why does he bring steel needles and a pair of scissors for my wife? Why does he give me medicines for my sore eyes? I cannot understand such behavior. I have done nothing for him except perhaps fan the coals to heat the iron that cauterized his snake bite. What does he expect to get in return for his good deeds? He must want something. . . .

El Madani's own code was simple. He was lazy. He did nothing for his fellow Harratin that did not have a reason, and nothing for himself that was not absolutely essential. He believed firmly in the local proverb: "Begging is more honorable than working." Foucauld also suspected that he had added a phrase of his own to the proverb: "Stealing is more honorable than begging and much more profitable." Even among Harratin, El Madani was considered pretty much of a rogue who lived as much by his deftly larcenous fingers as by his meager gardening. That was why Father de Foucauld loved to do things for him. Anybody could be kind to someone who appreciated kindness; there was no merit in that. But being kind to someone who was always looking for ulterior motives, who was suspicious because he was himself constantly doing suspicious things, was a challenge and a lesson in the moralities. Being good to a confirmed scoundrel was an example of Christian living more eloquent than a thousand sermons.

Beside the seeds Foucauld had brought from Algeria, he had sent to Paris for more. He would make Tamanrasset a garden spot. Moreover, he would make Tamanrasset a village worthy of the name, not a drab collection of miserable shanties. He helped the Harratin build little houses of stone and sun-dried bricks to replace their hovels of straw and reeds. He would give Tamanrasset an air of permanence to off-set the transient character of the fly-by-night camps of the Tuareg nomads.

Even the Amenokal was impressed. In the fall of 1907 when he returned from his summer wanderings, Moussa-ag-Amastane studied the building activity which Brother Charles had stimulated during his absence, and summoned the Christian Marabout into his blue-veiled presence.

"Sidi Marabout," the Amenokal announced, "you have given me a sound idea. I shall make Tamanrasset my permanent capital. I shall have a palace built here and it shall become the seat of justice for all the Hoggar."

Brother Charles was delighted, for Moslem piety had made a righteous man of Moussa. Moreover, he was an able administrator. In two years, as Foucauld wrote to Father Guérin in July, 1907, he had brought order out of anarchy, secured obedience from his underlings, organized his warriors into a disciplined armed force, appointed a cadi to administer justice according to Koranic law, and established severe penalties for murder, looting, and robbery. Creation of a permanent seat of government at Tamanrasset was a logical consequence.

However, one phase of Moussa's building projects alarmed Foucauld. A proposal to build a market with stalls for individual farmers was fine. But Moussa's plan to erect a mosque, with an attendant *zawaïa* (an Islamic religious fraternity) was a horse of another color. Moussa talked of levying a Hoggar-wide tithe to build and support the mosque and the *zawaïa*, and of importing Koranic professors from Tidikelt and Twat to teach religion and Arabic to the Tuareg youth.

"This Islamization of the Hoggar," wrote Foucauld, "would be extremely grave. At present the Tuareg, who are only lukewarm Mohammedans, come to know us quite easily and become friendly and frank. The people of Tidikelt and Twat, however, are bigoted, close-lipped and secretive; they hold us in abomination. If through their Koranic teachers they can impose their evil influence on our children here, the people of the Hoggar will, I fear, become much more hostile to us during the next few years. Today they are defiant, fearful, and unsocial. Tomorrow, if the Moslem influence of the Twat prevails, they will develop a profound and lasting enmity."

Brother Charles found solace in prostration before the Blessed Sacrament, happiness in his solitude, and in obeying the will of God.

"In the face of such moral bankruptcy," he wrote, "human means are obviously powerless, and only God can bring about the great transformation necessary. Prayer and penitence! The further I go, the clearer I see the principal means of action on these poor souls. What am I doing in their midst? The greatest good that I do is merely being here. My presence here insures that of the Blessed Sacrament. Yes, there is at least one soul between Timbuctoo and El Goléa who adores Jesus and prays to Him. My presence among the natives makes them familiar with Christians and particularly priests. Those who will follow me will find friendlier and less defiant spirits. This is indeed little, but it is all that is possible at present. Wanting to do more would compromise the whole future."

Foucauld suspected that the *éminence grise* responsible for the Amenokal's great burst of religiosity was his khoja, a combined secretary and Koranic adviser, named Ba Hammou. The khoja was a tall, lean, dark Moslem from the Fezzan in South-western Tripolitania, but he dressed in the Tuareg manner with the multiple robes, mantles and overskirts and the mummy-like head wrappings. In fact, he had been in the service of Tuareg chiefs for more than a score of years, a fact which did not particularly dispose Father de Foucauld in his favor, inasmuch as he had also served Attisi-ag-Amellal, one of the architects of the Flatters massacre, whom the French had deposed as Amenokal of the Hoggar Tuareg in favor of Moussa.

Ba Hammou was the son of an Arab chieftain of Ghat (spelled *Rhat* on some maps because the Arabic sound of *gh* approximates the throaty French *r*), was learned in Arabic and the Koran, and an expert in Tamashek. He was also steeped in Tuareg lore, for he was older than Moussa—almost as old as Foucauld, in fact. And while Foucauld distrusted his crafty eyes and hard, sharp features, and suspected he had no scruples, he found the khoja "very intelligent, with a marvelous memory." Therefore he hired him at the daily rate of a little more than three francs (sixty cents) to work from sunrise to sunset (except Sundays) at the job of editing, revising, and adding to the French-Tamashek and Tamashek-French dictionary which Foucauld considered of "primary importance to my successors."

Foucauld was convinced that it was God's will that he remain in the Hoggar until the dictionary was finished. He also made sure that his relationship with Ba Hammou was a two-way street.

"I am learning much," he wrote to Monseigneur Guérin at Christmas time in 1907, "but I also have the opportunity of teaching *him* much. I am thus able to correct many false ideas, not only Ba Hammou's but of others, for in Africa words have wings."

Foucauld did not need Ba Hammou to carry his messages back to the Amenokal, for Moussa spoke very freely to "Sidi Marabout," as he called Brother Charles, and Brother Charles was just as free with his advice to Moussa about mending his personal behavior and administering justice to his people. The Amenokal, in fact, took the priest very seriously and often bemoaned the fact, perhaps half in jest, that all his saintliness was wasted inasmuch as he was not a Moslem and could therefore not expect to enter paradise.

Ba Hammou not only edited the Foucauld-Motylinski dictionary, but he also furnished the Christian Marabout with sheafs of Tuareg lore in prose and in verse. The verse, however, was not his forte.

"For poetry," he told Foucauld, "you must go to the fountainhead. I will take you to my cousin Dassine. She has often asked to meet you."

Brother Charles needed no urging.

V

Dassine was more than just the most beautiful, the most famous, and the most talented woman of the Hoggar. Dassine was an experience.

Brother Charles knew of course that Dassine was a poetess of renown, a virtuoso of the *amzad,* a sort of one-string fiddle; a glamorous, romantic figure whose *ahals* brought love-sick swains riding to her tent from a hundred miles around; a woman of means, stature and influence; the only woman in the Hoggar who could say "no" to the Amenokal, even when he proposed marriage. Knowing all this, Brother Charles still caught his breath when he entered her tent.

Dassine was an imposing presence, combining grace and dignity. She was in her thirties, tall and solidly built and probably well proportioned, although the outlines of her figure were only suggested beneath the voluminous, flowing draperies of her Tuareg attire. She was unveiled, of course. She was fair skinned with fine, regular features: high forehead; long, dark questioning eyes under sweeping lashes; straight nose; full lips that were both sensitive and sensuous; strong, rounded chin and graceful throat. She parted her dark hair in the middle and plaited it in a score of tight, narrow braids which flowed from under her loose head-cloth as far as her small, high breasts. She radiated warm charm and great strength.

She gave off tinkling sounds with every movement, for she dripped with barbaric jewelry. Her earrings were great silver disks as big as saucers. From her necklace of glittering metal triangles there hung a huge triangular stomacher of copper and silver from which dangled dozens of smaller triangles.

She heightened the color of her cheeks with red ocher, outlined her arching eyebrows with kohl, tinted her hands with indigo and her fingernails with henna.

When Dassine took her *amzad* into her lap to accompany herself as she recited poetry, Brother Charles made sketches of the strange instrument which are still in existence. It could be described as a small kettledrum with a short, narrow neck. The taut, banjo-like head was stretched over a bowl-like frame, nearly three feet in diameter. The bridge was a St. Andrews' cross holding the single string several inches above the membrane. Dassine played it with a small U-shaped bow.

She sang poems of war and love, cowards and heroes, camels and gazelles. She recited a poem Amenokal Moussa had written to her when he vainly sought her hand:

> Dassine is like the moon.
> Her throat is fairer than a sleek young colt's
> Tethered in a field of April grain. . . .
> God has given her much to boast of;
> She walks head high, proudly among men,
> While men who come to see Dassine walk lamely
> With head down, their veins drained dry of blood.
> They dream all night of her when she is far,
> She who gives them not the slightest thought.

Having spurned the love of Moussa-ag-Amastane, Dassine married one of the hundred blue-veiled Tuareg warriors who paid her court, a man named Aflan who had the foresight to kill his most likely rival, Suri-ag-Shikkat.

She still had a long repertoire of poems about Moussa, however, and since they were still the best of friends, she gave them all to Brother Charles. There was one, for instance, upbraiding the *imrad*, the sedentary middle-class Tuareg, for not joining Moussa on one of his pre-reformation feats of brigandry:

> You have no more honor, O evil *imrad*!
> You have rejected Moussa, sending him alone to Ahenet,
> Land of the violins, to recruit his comrades.
> Look you, even the lame and the one-armed follow Moussa,
> But not you!

The white-footed camel of Akamadou the Lame One pressed on
Close beside the camel of Moussa.
One-armed Kaimi rides along with Moussa and his men.
Beside the well of In-Belren we have left our women. . . .

Then there were the love songs addressed (indirectly) to a
favorite camel:

> O my light-beige mehari,
> Why do you look longingly at Mount Tufrick?
> You know that at the peak
> Resides the cure for my poor eyes.
>
> The sun is sinking, my white mehari,
> And I am sick with love.
> Where lies the remedy?

The remedy, of course, was "she who is as graceful as a lovely
antelope, as fair as a date palm heavy with plump ripe
fruit. . . ."

Dassine also added to Foucauld's growing list of Tuareg
proverbs such nuggets of wisdom as: "Take not for guide a
man who drinks only from a jug. . . . Logic and argument are
the fetters of a coward. . . . Better the night spent in anger
than in repentance. . . . The palm of the hand cannot eclipse
the sun. . . . To its mother a beetle is fairer than a ga-
zelle. . . ."

A curious relationship immediately developed between
beauteous, glamorous Dassine and the tattered, scrawny, aging
priest who was losing his hair and his teeth, and whose appearance reflected the fact that he cut his own hair and trimmed his
own beard without benefit of mirror. Dassine could see into the
saintly soul of this ascetic and was fascinated by the burning
zeal in his eyes. Foucauld, on the other hand, could look beyond the coquetry and gaudy externals of the free-wheeling
specimen of emancipated womanhood to the warm humanity
of a generous spirit.

Dassine was on the surface far different from the other
women who had been most influential in his life—such mother-
substitutes as Aunt Inès, his beloved cousin Marie de Bondy,
and Mother Superior Elisabeth of the Clarist convent in Jerusalem. Aunt Inès and Marie de Bondy were of Foucauld blood

and the same social and family background. They were handy, welcome, and sympathetic donors of the mother love Charles de Foucauld had lost at the age of six. Mother Elisabeth, too, was of similar social background and the same ancestral roots in Périgord. Dassine could hardly come from stock farther removed—a primitive, nomadic people with naturalistic instincts and Moslem training against the pious, Catholic sophistication of the French aristocracy. Yet the woman who had never before seen a Christian had much in common with Aunt Inès, Cousin Marie, and Mother Elisabeth: they were all born matriarchs who delighted in running other people's lives.

Brother Charles certainly sensed this as he and Dassine became closer and closer friends. It did not take him long to realize the power Dassine possessed over Moussa, and the determination with which she exercised it. Furthermore, the Amenokal seemed to have perfect confidence in her judgment. During Moussa's frequent absences, "there is no doubt about who makes the decisions," wrote Father de Foucauld. "It is Dassine. She commands without seeming to. She is extremely intelligent and knows exactly what is going on."

During the years of their close association, the gay young matriarch and the aging hermit became in effect joint rulers of the Hoggar for at least six months of every year. Because she was anxious to learn European ways and apply them where possible to Tuareg life, Dassine was eager for Foucauld's counsel. And Brother Charles did not fail to take advantage of the fact by slipping in morsels of Christian morality whenever possible.

Dassine's influence, combined with the reluctance of the Tuareg nobles to pay the tithe and the corruption of the cadi who absconded with the funds collected for the proposed Koranic school, canceled Moussa's plans for building a mosque and zawïa.

It was a minor triumph for Brother Charles, but there was so much more to be done. He had discovered, for instance, while working on his dictionary with Dassine and her cousin Ba Hammou, that in the Tamashek language there was no word for "virgin."

FOURTEEN

STARVATION

Mon Dieu, faites que tous les humains aillent au ciel.

God grant that all human beings may go to heaven.

—Charles de Foucauld

I

The gaunt specter of starvation stalked the fantastic peaks and craggy valleys of the Hoggar during the winter of 1907–8. There had been no rain in nearly two years; even the wildflowers had not come up the previous spring. The seeds which Father de Foucauld had carried across more than a thousand miles of desert sprouted feebly then died. The goats which were one of the Tuareg's chief sources of food were either away seeking green pastures or so rail-thin that they gave no milk. The last of the meager barley crop was gone.

When the hungry women began to congregate wistfully outside the hermitage of the Christian Marabout—the veiled men were far too proud—Brother Charles began to share his own supply of grain and sent a request for help by the next monthly courier. But it would take the courier weeks to reach In-Salah, and more weeks for the camels, which Colonel Laperrine would load with wheat, to make the return trip across the desert. Meanwhile, as he looked at the sunken cheeks, the spindly legs and bloated bellies of the starving children, Brother Charles cut down on his already austere diet so that he could give a little more to the famished.

Brother Charles prayed to the Virgin Mary and recorded the prayer in his diary: "Well-beloved Mother, have pity on these people for whom your Son died. Give them your help. Your poor priest appeals to you on their behalf."

When the camels finally arrived with Laperrine's wheat, Brother Charles ground it himself in his primitive stone mill. He filled the empty bowls the women brought him. He gathered in the children of Tamanrasset and those within a day's ride for a daily opportunity to eat their fill—even though he might go to his hard bed hungry that night, a phenomenon to which he had long become accustomed.

The Tuareg, particularly the women, were amazed and somewhat distressed by this generous performance by a non-Moslem. They knew of course that the *roumi*, the outlander and unbeliever, was a holy man in his own sphere. But they deplored the fact that the Christian Marabout, for all his goodness, would not go to heaven. One of the women, as reported by Dassine, prayed every day that the White Marabout might become a Moslem so that his charity could be properly rewarded in the hereafter.

Brother Charles, happy as he was to alleviate to some small degree the sufferings of a hungry people, particularly to dispel the hopeless hunger in the eyes of the Tuareg children, was still wretched for he could not celebrate Mass. On the second anniversary of his first Mass celebrated at Tamanrasset in the ramshackle structure which he called "the Frigate" because of its queer shape, he prayed to Jesus:

"Two years ago today Thou has deigned to give Thy Presence to this poor chapel. Do Thou, to Whom no one has ever appealed in vain, convert these people, visit them and sanctify them, for they are Thine. No Mass, for I am alone."

Later he wrote: "I have never believed that I had the right to Communion alone outside the Mass. If I am wrong," he appealed to Monseigneur Guérin, "please write me immediately. Your word would make an infinite change in my situation, for I am here involved with the Infinite."

And on December 25: "Christmas Day. No Mass for the first time in 21 years, for I am alone."

January 1, 1908: "May I be joined to every Sacrifice offered this New Year's Day. No Mass, for I am alone."

Alone!

It was not only the loneliness of the European in an alien desert that affected Brother Charles. Nor was it only the loneliness of the only Christian in a Moslem world which had never before seen a Christian. The complete despair of a sinner come to the ecstasy of faith, to the bright light of Christian truth and the love of Jesus, only to have the solace of the Sacrifice denied him—only a brother zealot could understand such suffering. Monseigneur Guérin understood.

Monseigneur Guérin, as Prefect Apostolic, had sent an appeal to Rome on behalf of the lonely priest of the Hoggar:

"For six years this very saintly priest has unceasingly led a most admirable and heroic life in the apostolic prefecture of Ghardaïa. He is currently alone among the savage tribes of the Tuareg whom he has succeeded in pacifying and to whom he has offered the fine example of a life of extreme poverty, inexhaustible charity, and continuous prayer. For many years to come he will doubtless be the only priest able to penetrate into the heart of the Tuareg country. Therefore the Prefect Apostolic of Ghardaïa very humbly begs Your Holiness, in consideration of the outstanding virtues of this servant of God and of the very great good that he has accomplished, to deign to grant him the great favor. . . ."

But the petition of Monseigneur Guérin apparently lost its way somewhere in the devious channels of Vatican bureaucracy or was submerged under a pile of papers on some Cardinal's desk. In any event, it took another needle from Father Guérin and a final nudge by Father Burtin, procurator of the White Fathers in Rome, to get Vatican approval for Father de Foucauld to celebrate Mass without a server.

The news finally reached Tamanrasset via the Apostolic Prefecture at Ghardaïa, ecclesiastical courier to El Goléa, military courier to In-Salah, and special Meharist messenger, mounted on the fastest camel in the Sahara Camel Corps, to carry Colonel Laperrine's relay of the Pope's word to ex-Lieutenant de Foucauld.

"*Deo gratias!*" Father de Foucauld exclaimed to his diary

when the Papal dispensation reached him on January 31, 1908.
"Deo gratias! Deo gratias! How good is my God! Tomorrow I
shall be able to celebrate the Mass. Thank you, O Lord!"

The blessed relief at being permitted the Sacrament once
more produced a sinister relaxation in Brother Charles. For
months he had been living on his nerves, far beyond his normal
limits of endurance. His linguistic work, his social mission
among the Tuareg, his frantic efforts to alleviate the suffering
caused by the drought and famine, with no let-up in his long
routine of prayers, meditation, and adoration of the Eucharist,
had lifted him to a frenzied plane of inspired activity where
sleep, food, and self had ceased to exist. Curiously, when he
was again admitted to the realm of spiritual transport that the
Mass produced in him, his corporeal body reasserted itself. He
fell seriously ill.

His great energy deserted him. He was so weak he was forced
to lie completely motionless for hours. He no longer had the
appetite even for the miserable handful of dates and barley that
he allowed himself daily. To Father Guérin, he wrote that he
had "something wrong with the chest, or rather the heart, which
makes me so short of breath that the slightest movement makes
me think the end is near."

"At our age," he wrote to France, "there is always something
that doesn't work. It's a fatherly warning from Above. I have
lost my teeth and my hair. My eyes are still good at a distance,
but are becoming weaker and weaker for reading. . . ."

He was obviously suffering from an acute vitamin deficiency
due to his self-restricted diet. The symptoms were those of
scurvy. Instinctively he knew that he had carried his program
of self-mortification beyond the saturation point. Between spells
of vertigo and nausea he managed to get off a message to
Laperrine asking for some condensed milk, some dried and
tinned vegetables, and, of all things, some wine.

The letter alarmed Colonel Laperrine who immediately
wrote to Monseigneur Guérin, saying that "for him to admit
that he is tired and to ask me for condensed milk means that he
must be really sick. . . . I may make the trip to the Hoggar or
perhaps send a doctor there. . . . I am going to tell him a few
things and I will take it upon myself to speak for you when I

say that penance leading to progressive suicide is not permitted."

A week later (February 11, 1908) Laperrine wrote again to the Prefect Apostolic, "a few lines on the run to give you the latest news of de Foucauld. . . . He was more seriously ill than he admits. He had fainting spells and the Tuareg who have taken very good care of him were badly worried. I have lectured him, for I am sure that his exaggerated penance accounts for much of his weakness and that overwork on his dictionary does the rest. As my lecture will not suffice, I have added three camels loaded with supplies. . . . Next time he comes north you must get your hooks into him and keep him for a month or two at Ghardaïa or Maison Carrée so he can rebuild his hump, if you will excuse the old Saharan expression."

Pending the arrival of Laperrine's camels, the worried Tuareg did their best to restore the White Marabout to health. The unexpected warmth and devotion of his "parishioners" did almost as much for the priest's convalescence as the local herb remedies and vegetables they brought him. The lovely Dassine herself came to the cramped quarters of the hermitage to nurse the Marabout. She sent for one of her herds of goats that was miles away seeking grass and brought it to stricken Tamanrasset so that Foucauld might have milk.

By the time Colonel Laperrine, accompanied by Captain Nieger and a company of the Saharan Camel Corps, reached the Hoggar late in June of 1908, Brother Charles was sufficiently recovered to ride out twenty miles to meet him.

"He radiates health and good cheer," Laperrine reported to Monseigneur Guérin. "On June 29 he arrived at my camp galloping like a second lieutenant at the head of a troop of Tuareg horsemen. He is more popular than ever among them and appreciates them more and more."

The colonel added an aside that the old second lieutenant was somewhat less appreciative of the Harratin whom he considered lazy and of base instincts.

Laperrine remained at Tamanrasset until July 22. During their more than three weeks together, the two old soldiers talked of matters mundane and military, as well as of Father de Foucauld's concern for the Tuareg soul. With the same eye for detailed observation that made his *Reconnaissance au Maroc* a textbook for the French Army, the ex-cavalryman had drawn up a worried report on the political situation in the Hoggar for presentation to Laperrine. He believed that Moussa-ag-Amastane, as a loyal ally, deserved protection against Attisi-ag-Amellal whom the French had deposed as Amenokal in favor of Moussa. Attisi had taken refuge in southern Libya and was still harassing Moussa with frequent raids across the border into his former domain. Father de Foucauld recommended two steps to which Laperrine immediately agreed.

First, the colonel rode into Moussa's camp some two miles from Tamanrasset completely unarmed, thereby showing his utter confidence in Moussa's loyalty. The Amenokal was delighted.

Second, he picked a site for a fort to be garrisoned by a company of Meharists with a handful of French officers and noncoms some forty miles east of Tamanrasset. This fort, which would command the approaches from southern Libya, Laperrine proposed to name for the man who had suggested it—Fort de Foucauld. Brother Charles threw up his hands in horror. He forbade absolutely the use of his name. His was the hidden life. He must remain obscure.

"You would do me a great favor," he said, "if you named the fort in memory of the man who first interested me in Africa, the Africans, and the African languages."

Laperrine agreed that the new post should be called Fort Motylinski.

II

There is no doubt that Henry Laperrine's long-standing affection for Charles de Foucauld was deep and sincere. Neither is there any doubt that Laperrine considered his friend as one of his most valuable assets in keeping peace in the Sahara. Not only was the universal love and respect inspired by Brother Charles a great advantage for French prestige among the Tuareg, but his letters by the monthly courier were more informative than the reports of most intelligence officers. Therefore, like a good friend as well as a wise commander who conserves his resources, Laperrine was determined to do his best to keep Charles in good health. He conspired with Monseigneur Guérin to get the hermit out of the desert for a much-needed rest and he wrote to the family in France to urge Charles to come home for a vacation.

Consequently Charles was bombarded by letters from his sister and his dear cousin Marie de Bondy insisting that he owed it to his family to show himself for a while.

He had been gone for seven years, Marie de Blic pointed out. Was it right that brother and sister should be separated for so long? Besides, he had nieces and nephews whom he scarcely knew. Charles argued that he was a monk and did not travel for pleasure. Furthermore, he was no treat to look at. "At a distance," he wrote, "I seem much better than I am."

To Marie de Bondy's plea that he was now fifty years old and owed it to himself as well as his family to breathe again however briefly the air of his homeland, he suggested that she consult Abbé Huvelin "who is my interpreter of God's will."

Abbé Huvelin approved of the trip. Meanwhile Brother Charles had thought of a plausible reason for going to Paris, a reason which had nothing to do with his own pleasure or his family's. He would try to establish a Union of the Little Brothers of Jesus. This would be an organization of laymen and would have nothing to do with his fraternity, which he still hoped to see in being on African soil. The Union would consist of Catholic businessmen, scientists, and scholars whose work took them to Africa, and who would agree to spread the truth among the Africans by simply living like Christians in a non-Christian land.

With this aim in mind he agreed to make the trip, and on Christmas Day 1908 left Tamanrasset for the long journey across the desert. With brief stops at El Goléa and Ghardaïa, he reached Maison Carrée on February 13, 1909. He did not tarry with the White Fathers and sailed from Algiers a few days later as a deck passenger.

When he landed at Marseilles, he had planned his itinerary almost to the hour, for he did not want to remain in France more than three weeks and intended to make full use of his time. The cold mistral sweeping down the Rhône valley reminded him that he was no longer in the desert and had better adapt his attire accordingly. He temporarily discarded his sandals for a pair of second-hand shoes, and replaced his white headgear with sun flaps by a conventional black ecclesiastical hat shaped like a scalloped squash.

Brother Charles spent his first night in Paris in Montmartre—in adoration before the Holy Eucharist in the basilica of the Sacred Heart.

Next day he paid his respects to Abbé Huvelin at Saint-Augustin. He found his spiritual guide greatly aged since he had last seen him. The old priest was past seventy, quite feeble, and moved his twisted limbs with painful difficulty. Foucauld felt that this was to be their last meeting and was deeply moved. The old priest's mind, however, was as keen as ever. Foucauld sought his advice in the matter of his proposed secular third order of the Union of the Little Brothers of the Sacred Heart. Abbé Huvelin smiled wistfully, as though recalling his earliest advice to Foucauld when as a Trappist novice he first thought of founding his congregation of Little Brothers: "You are not in the least fitted to be a leader of men." Then with a gesture of resignation he said:

"No matter what I say you will persist. And if it be God's will, you will ultimately succeed."

And he stretched out his trembling hands to bless the man to whom he had given faith, the gay young rakehell who in twenty years had become a scrawny, bronzed, half-bald ascetic.

For the few days he remained in Paris, Foucauld stayed at Marie de Bondy's town house in the Avenue Percier, a stone's-throw from his old bachelor apartment and a few blocks from the Saint-Augustin church. Cousin Marie, too, had aged considerably. She wore black dresses continuously, with high neck-bands. She was a grandmother, too. Although one of her sons had disappointed her by pursuing pleasure and pulchritude in a manner he believed appropriate for a young viscount of the Foucauld line (to such an extent that she had thrown him out of her house), one of her daughters had married a Marquis de Forbin, just as grandmother Inès would have wished, and had produced two fine children.

To Brother Charles of Jesus his Cousin Marie was still the most beautiful woman, physically and spiritually, that he had ever known. The few days he spent in her company after a separation of so many years was going to accent his loneliness even more when he returned to the desert. That, however, was part of his life of abnegation.

Brother Charles secured one member for his projected third order while in Paris—Professor Louis Massignon, brilliant young Orientalist who was making a name for himself as an Arabic scholar. Massignon suggested that Foucauld secure the blessing of the Cardinal Archbishop of Paris for his Union of Little Brothers.

An interview with the Cardinal was arranged. His Eminence listened quietly while the hermit explained his project of propagating the faith by example, rather than by precept, by having decent Europeans live a true Christian life among Africans. When Foucauld had finished, there was a moment of silence. Then the Cardinal Archbishop said:

"I understand that you were once a Trappist."

"For seven years, Your Eminence."

"I suggest you re-enter the order," said the Cardinal, and the interview was over.

Father de Foucauld did go into the Trappist monastery of Our Lady of the Snows next day, but he had no intention of re-entering the order. The old stubbornness of the Foucauld motto was still deeply ingrained in him. *Jamais Arrière!* How did His Eminence expect to provide for someone to carry on the work now being done by the only priest in the Hoggar? Who was to nurture the seeds now being planted? Who would harvest the grain? . . .

Foucauld went to see Dom Martin, prior of Our Lady of the Snows, who had welcomed him into the silent world of the Cistercian Order nearly twenty years before, and who had prepared him for his ordination. They prayed together. Dom Martin approved of what his former novice was trying to do.

So did Monseigneur Bonnet, the Bishop of Viviers, whom Foucauld also consulted. Technically, Foucauld was still attached to the diocese of Viviers, even though he had not been there since his ordination, so his bishop's blessing was most gratifying.

From Viviers he traveled to the Mediterranean. He made a

stop at Toulon to see his sister's second son, whose godfather he was. Young Charles de Blic was now a naval cadet. After checking on the future admiral's use of the sextant, an operation accompanied by recollections of how difficult it was to fix latitude and longitude in Morocco while disguised as a Jewish rabbi, Brother Charles moved along the Riviera to his sister's winter villa at Grasse, and to renew ties after eight years.

It was Carnival time on the Riviera, and the fragrance of mimosa was flecked with confetti and shaken by the street sounds of revelry from Cannes to Menton. Father de Foucauld, however, spent his time urging his sister to invite friends to Viscount de Blic's villa for knitting bees.

Father de Foucauld—or Brother Charles of Jesus—or Viscount de Foucauld—sister Mimi was completely confused during her happy week of welcoming the bizarre sibling she had not seen in so long—insisted that during his week at Grasse he must learn to knit. And because his time was limited, he put in long hours of overtime learning the intricate stitches of socks, scarves, and sweaters. The business of turning the heel of a sock was more of a problem than getting a potable drink from a desert water hole. He listened carefully and tried to follow the instructions of the sombre-clad beldames from nearby Cannes, Nice, Vence, and Beaulieu as they called out "knit one, purl one. . . ." He thought he had finally mastered the trick, and when he left from Marseilles less than three weeks after his arrival in France, his baggage included wool and knitting needles.

III

Brother Charles of Jesus was anxious to get back to work. He stayed in Algiers just long enough to get the White Fathers' final approval of his Union of the Brothers and Sisters of the Sacred Heart of Jesus. (He had included the sisters so that couples, even couples coming from France to settle in Africa as farmers or small shop-keepers, could join in the enterprise of decent people demonstrating to non-Christians that true Christian living was the way of God.)

He picked up a few supplies, including a copy of the *Short Study of Tamashek Grammar* which had just been published under the name of Calassanti-Motylinski, and took off for the

desert by rail as far as Colomb-Béchar. He arrived in Beni-
Abbès just in time to celebrate Mass for Easter Sunday (he had
cut short his stay with his family in France in order to be able
to celebrate the Eucharist for the officers and men of the French
garrison during Passion Week). He allowed poor old blind
Marie to weep on his shoulder (she was still living on the few
francs per month he had arranged for the Bureau of Native
Affairs to pay to his only adult convert). He chased the bugs
out of his chapel, patted the heads of a few lepers, received a
welcome which always astonished him, and was on his way
again. Hundreds of miles across the Sahara, walking painfully
on aging feet, leading his pack camels, lost in prayer and meditation as he walked, was becoming a routine for Brother
Charles.

Even on his long desert treks, far from an oasis, he would try
to comfort others. A French corporal, for instance, woke him
during his heat-of-day siesta, to ask advice. The corporal had
been living with a Sudanese woman, an escaped slave, of whom
he was terribly fond. She had even accepted his religion. She
wanted to become a Christian. But he had been ordered back
to France. The army would certainly not sanction his taking
an escaped slave back to France. He could certainly not do it
himself on a corporal's pay—coppers per day. He could not
make a living in the desert, if he stayed. What was the corporal
to do?

"Leave it to me," said Brother Charles of Jesus. And he arranged to send the woman north to the White Fathers where
she would learn a trade and not be forced to return to slavery
as a result of her love, however unholy, for a French conscript.

"Please accept this woman for your workroom in Ghardaïa,"
wrote Brother Charles to Monseigneur Guérin. "Let us save a
soul."

Early in April Charles of Jesus was back in the Hoggar. He
was delighted to note that the construction of Fort Motylinski
was progressing well. It was a crenelated bastion, something out
of a stage play about the Foreign Legion. He was surprised to
find that Colonel Laperrine had sent some of his masons down
from Motylinski to enlarge the hermitage—"The Frigate" as
the colonel called the long and narrow structure—into a man-

size building. More than four or five people could stand erect in the chapel now.

Brother Charles was also delighted to find a faint blush of green here and there on the Hoggar plateau. At last there had been a little rain. He sank to his knees to thank God.

When he arose the first of the Tuareg who had heard of his return swarmed around him to greet the Christian Marabout, the universal brother, the man who fed the hungry and who asked nothing for himself. It was an effusive welcome. Brother Charles wept.

When at last he entered that end of the hermitage which had been his bedroom, he found an army cot had been set up. Dear old Laperrine! This was obviously an order. For once he did not protest the gift of his absent friend. He stretched out on the cot. For the first time in many years, he did not spurn a bed. He was very tired.

FIFTEEN

SENTIMENTAL JOURNEY

Fame is the sum of all misconceptions circulating about one individual.
—Rainer Maria Rilke

I

"Nonsense," said Colonel Laperrine. "This is a formal parade. This is a review of the potential allies of France. I'm talking to you as one old Saint-Cyrien to another. Let's have no raggedy-assed mendicant priest walking barefoot alongside his fellow Frenchmen. You'll ride the best mehari in the Saharan Camel Corps and you'll take the salutes right beside me. After all, this is quid pro quo. Granted, you're viceroy for Jesus Christ and the Kingdom of God. But unofficially you're also envoy extraordinary for me and the French Republic. The prestige of France allows you to operate here in the Hoggar, to make friends for Christ without getting your throat cut by the Ajjer Tuareg or some Senusis from the Fezzan. And you in turn enhance the prestige of France by being the only true Christian within a thousand miles. We need each other. Get on that camel."

"On one condition, *mon colonel*," said Foucauld. "That you leave your medical officer with me now, without waiting for the fort to be garrisoned. And that he take the salutes with you, too, for I have much work for him and his prestige must be equal to yours."

So Dr. Robert Hérisson sat camelback at Colonel Laperrine's left, with Father de Foucauld at the right while the war drums thundered and five hundred veiled Tuareg, the Amenokal in the van, rode past in a mist of dust raised by the camels' hoofs. The sun glinted on their long swords and lances, and the huge curiously-shaped buckskin shields seemed to flutter like great leaves with the rolling gait of the meharis.

After the review, Colonel Laperrine held court for the Amenokal and his chieftains, with Foucauld acting as interpreter. At one point the hermit hesitated, and a ripple of laughter ran through the gathering.

"The Amenokal's cousin," Brother Charles interpreted at last, "wants to know if it is true, as he had heard, that the French government disapproves of those Tuareg soirees devoted to love, music and poetry—the *ahals*."

Laperrine chuckled as he said: "My reply may not meet with your canonical favor, but please tell our friends that the Republic of France approves of love in all forms."

Foucauld's straight-faced translation was greeted with hearty laughter.

Dr. Hérisson was based on the hermitage until Fort Motylinski was finished. He did not enjoy it greatly, although he wrote a long and detailed account of his life with the Christian Marabout, whom he admired even though he did not admire his cuisine. He described Foucauld's preparation for lunch. With coarse-ground wheat he made a flat, round, unleavened cake which he cooked under the coals. In an iron pot he boiled some unappetizing dates "full of sand and goat hairs." Lunch was ready.

"Have you ever eaten *khéfis?*" Foucauld asked. "It's my regular diet. I don't know if you'll like it, but that's all I can offer you. *Khéfis* seems to me to be a complete food. It is easy to prepare and is kind to my poor teeth."

"Here's the recipe," wrote Dr. Hérisson. "You take the wheat cake still smoking hot, you break it into pieces in your tin plate, you pit the dates and pour the date jam over the bits of wheat cake. Then you take some old Arab butter, liquefied, and pour it over the rest. Then you knead the whole mess with your hands until it is about the consistency of putty. The taste is sweetly insipid, but not bad."

"Tonight," said Foucauld, "we will have *couscous* without meat. It's my usual dinner. You'll like it better."

Dr. Hérisson didn't think much of it.

The hermit gave the doctor specific instructions about dealing with the Tuareg: "Be simple, affable, love them and make them feel that they are loved. . . . Don't act your rank; don't even act like a doctor. Don't be vexed by their familiarity and informality. Be human, charitable, and always gay. Laugh always. As you see, I always laugh, even though I show my bad teeth. Treat their ills patiently and well, for they respect our science, our kindness, and our power. And don't be annoyed if they ask you to treat a goat."

Foucauld thought the doctor might be able to teach the people of the Hoggar a little elementary hygiene. Although water was too often scarce in the Sahara, the Tuareg did not seem kindly disposed toward it even when it was plentiful. And the effluvia emanating from beneath all the robes, cloaks and draperies they wore became positively hair-raising in summer. The hermit had brought some soap from France but had awakened little interest in his proposition that cleanliness was next to godliness. And he was completely baffled by the problem of approaching the women. He had repeatedly asked Monseigneur Guérin to send him some White Sisters, but to no avail.

Dr. Hérisson, however, needed no White Sisters. He used the indirect approach to the ladies of the Tuareg matriarchy. Dr. Hérisson was a musician, as well as a physician. He was a cellist. Along with his little black bag and medicine chest he had brought his cello into the desert. And when he started on a campaign of vaccination against small pox, he decided that the women, as well as the men, should be vaccinated. He began by carrying his cello into the tent of the lovely and dominating Dassine, and playing a few snatches of French folk songs.

Dassine was delighted. The *roumi* doctor's cello was even larger than her one-string fiddle. "The grandfather of all the *amzads*," she called it. Would the *roumi* doctor play the songs of his country if she invited some of her women friends to hear him?

The *roumi* doctor would be delighted—if the ladies would allow themselves to be vaccinated against small pox.

Dassine agreed. She was an adventuresome person, she believed in progress, and she was curious about western ideas.

Moreover, any friend of the Christian Marabout was a friend of hers. She would be the first to be vaccinated.

Dr. Hérisson gave his concert and vaccinated twelve Tuareg ladies in one afternoon.

In some ways, however, the doctor was a disappointment to Brother Charles. First of all he was a Protestant and did not attend Mass. Second, he was not a very religious man at all. When Father de Foucauld gave him a Bible and recommended that he read it now and then, the doctor put it in his trunk and forgot about it. Furthermore, the doctor made no effort to learn either Arabic or Tamashek while he was in the Hoggar. But what really miffed the good father was the fact that Dr. Hérisson, during his year at Fort Motylinski, failed to carry out certain anthropological research that Foucauld had suggested.

There were a number of ancient tombs in the area and Father de Foucauld suspected they belonged to a pagan race which lived in the desert before the Tuareg. He wanted the doctor to dig up the bones, examine them, and see if there was not some relationship between the Tuareg and their predecessors.

"The only time I saw Father de Foucauld really vexed," Dr. Hérisson recorded, "was the day shortly before my final departure from the Hoggar when I confessed to him that I had exhumed no ancient bones for seven or eight months."

When Dr. Hérisson left, Laperrine replaced him immediately. Brother Charles had won his point. The Hoggar would not be left without a medical man.

The year 1910 was a sad one for Brother Charles. In Spring Monseigneur Guérin died at the age of thirty-seven. Although a much younger man than the hermit of the Hoggar, his physique was apparently less able to withstand the rigors of life in the desert.

In July Abbé Huvelin passed away in Paris. His death was indeed a loss to Brother Charles. "He has been my father for twenty-four years," he wrote. "I cannot express what he has been for me and how much I owe to him."

He found his consolation in the Saviour. "Yes, Jesus suffices," he wrote. "Wherever He is, there is no lack. However precious are those who shine by His reflection, it is He who remains All. He is the All in time and in eternity."

Foucauld's friend and classmate at Saint-Cyr, Major Lacroix of the Bureau of Native Affairs, also died that year in Algiers.

In November Brother Charles lost another dear friend, although not by an act of God. Henry Laperrine, after nine years as commander-in-chief of the Saharan Oases, was promoted to be full colonel and recalled to France to command the Eighteenth Chasseurs. He would never return to Africa during Foucauld's lifetime.

Father Voillard, who was Monseigneur Guérin's successor in the White Fathers' Saharan hierarchy, soon received a renewed plea from Brother Charles for a priest "to continue the very small work begun here. He could live beside me, either as I live or not. I do not ask to be his superior, but his friend. . . .

"As early as 1905 Captain Dinaux, then chief of the Arab Bureau at In-Salah, asked that White Sisters be sent to the Hoggar. Now that there is a permanent garrison here, with a French officer, a doctor, and several French noncommissioned officers, mail service twice a month, greater security and living comfort, perhaps the time has come to think again of the possibility? . . ."

No White Sisters were forthcoming, and Brother Charles was again left to deal with the Tuareg women as best he could by himself. He did quite well, in fact. He gave tea parties and held knitting bees.

Led always by Dassine, groups of the elite of the Tuareg matriarchy would gather under the gray-green *éthel* tree that grew beside the wadi not far from the hermitage. From the branches of the tree, which looked for all the world like a great dusty willow, hung the instruments of Foucauld's weather bureau—his thermometers and the recording barograph that the Meteorological Institute of Algiers had lent him—which swayed gently in the breeze above the heads of the noble ladies.

Brother Charles, the only male among the voluminously draped females, squatted on the ground Arab style, poured mint-scented tea, distributed sugar, told Bible stories in Tamashek, and asked questions. He never ceased adding to his collection of Tuareg proverbs, poems and folklore. Part of his uniform for his tea parties was a note pad (made of old envelopes and whatever scrap paper he could salvage) and a stub of a pencil hanging from his belt beside his rosary.

The knitting needles and wool he had brought back from France stood him in good stead. Even though he himself still had trouble turning the heel of a sock, he taught the beldames to knit. There were of course no Tamashek words for *knit* and *purl* so the Tuareg equivalents came out quite similar to *tricoter* and *broder*.

While he told his stories, explained life in France, dropped in a few plugs for the Christian virtues and added a hint as to the value and use of soap, the good ladies giggled, chatted in undertones, and smoked their pipes. The man who used to have his own Havana cigars made to order and would smoke no other, now smoked not at all.

As Brother Charles continued to record his Tuareg lore and lexicography, he also continued to dispense his Christian homilies, his household hints, and his little gifts from the legendary land beyond the seas. He passed out his packets of steel needles, which had become one of his secret weapons. He added darning needles, with instructions on mending worn textiles. Occasionally he gave out bits of cloth. And hair dye (black, of course, since the Tuareg beldames were mostly all grandmothers or about to be—the girls married early in the Hoggar) which Cousin Marie de Bondy had sent on Brother Charles' request.

The dolls which Marie de Bondy had sent because Brother (or Cousin) Charles had asked her to help the children, did not exactly advance the cause of God and Jesus Christ in the Hoggar. They were beautiful dolls, the best obtainable in the Galleries Lafayette in Paris—their eyes closed (with real eyelashes) and some of them made sounds which were close to the Tamashek for Mama or Papa when squeezed. Unfortunately, few of them got to the children. These life-like figures, although their dress was completely alien, were perfect for the performance of some of the pagan and animistic rites which had stubbornly survived the advent of Islam among the Tuareg. Some of the dolls, stylishly attired with the leg-of-mutton sleeves and bustles of the time, ended as objects of fetishism (with gouged eyes, and with thorns inserted into appropriate parts) or as participants in the ceremonies of fecundity.

Brother Charles was always the charmer (toothless and hairless though he might be) to the female artistocracy of the Hoggar. And they loved him. What a pity that such a good man was not a Moslem! One woman whose five children he had saved from starvation during the famine of 1907 told him that she prayed to Allah every night that the Marabout would see the light and accept Islam.

Brother Charles, on the other hand, encouraged the ladies to practice their own religion. He taught them to make rosaries— without a cross—from olive seeds and date pits. They were long ones, because each pit called for a prayer. As they told their beads, the ladies were supposed to say "I love Thee, O God," for every small seed and "I love Thee with all my heart, O God," for the big ones. There was only one God, wasn't there?

II

One of Abbé Huvelin's last acts was to send Foucauld 200 francs toward the building of a new hermitage. Brother Charles was expanding his "parish." Despite all his efforts, the Tuareg remained a nomadic people. When summer dried up the grass on the Hoggar plateau, the Tuareg moved their tents and their flocks to higher ground where the valleys were still green. So Brother Charles decided to follow his "parishioners."

He chose a spot called Asekrem about 40 miles from Tamanrasset at an altitude of nearly 10,000 feet. Although the place was almost inaccessible—it was three days' travel from Tamanrasset over trails that were often little more than goat runs—it was the center of many Tuareg camps in summer. In this aerie Brother Charles built a hermitage of stone and mud mortar. It was a long, narrow affair; there was scarcely room for two men to stand abreast. The single door was built with a high sill to keep out snakes. The hermitage contained a chapel, with an altar sent by Abbé Huvelin before his death, and a library in which the hermit worked. He had transported many boxes of books and crates of provisions over steep tracks that camels negotiated with difficulty. His spring was an hour's walk from the hermitage.

The view from Asekrem was wildly beautiful—breath-taking distances speared by fantastic peaks and obelisks—"a beautiful place in which to worship the Creator," he wrote. The scenic beauty was not appreciated by Dassine's cousin Ba Hammou whom Brother Charles brought along to work on the dictionary. The Targui linguist groaned over the Marabout's dawn-to-dark work schedule. He complained of being awakened by the priest's nocturnal religious rites. He grumbled over the long haul for the water supply. But Brother Charles kept him working and the pages of the dictionary began to pile up by the hundreds.

Brother Charles would always take time off, however, to receive visits from his "parishioners." When they learned that he was installed at Asekrem, whole families of Tuareg would come up to pay their respects to the Christian Marabout, to eat with him, to camp for the night beside the hermitage. They often came from a day or two away, and Foucauld was delighted to improve relationships. "Some of these families are quite good people," he wrote to Father Voillard, "as good as they can be without Christianity. Their souls are guided by natural instincts. Although Mohammedan by faith, they are quite ignorant of Islam and so have not been spoiled by its influence."

One regular visitor to Asekrem was a lad from the Tuareg aristocracy named Ouksem-ag-Shikkat, son of a tribal chief. Ouksem took a great liking to the Christian Marabout and often volunteered to lug water and do other chores.

With the approach of winter, Asekrem became an eerie, dreary place. Bitter winds shrieked down from the jagged peaks, howled across the rocky plateau and besieged the hermitage with shrill, mournful voices. The cold at night was biting. Ba Hammou at last revolted. He would no longer work on the dictionary if Brother Charles insisted on staying at Asekrem.

Reluctantly Brother Charles returned to Tamanrasset.

The Amenokal had been absent that summer and fall. Before the death of Major Lacroix and the transfer of Colonel Laperrine to Europe, Foucauld had convinced them both that an official visit of Moussa-ag-Amastane to France was imperative. A grand tour was therefore arranged.

Accompanied by two Tuareg nobles, Moussa saw everything. In Paris he did the *tournée des grands ducs* which included all the night spots of Montmartre and onion soup in the Central Markets district at dawn. He reviewed the troops and was decorated with the Legion of Honor. He visited the Creusot arms factory. He saw the races at Longchamp and the stud farms in the provinces. Apparently he was greatly impressed by the outward trappings of French civilization and the evident opulence of the Foucauld family. On the way home he wrote to Foucauld in Arabic, using the Arabic form of his name—"Sultan Moussa-ben-Mastane"—and addressing Foucauld as "Honorable Excellency, Our Dearest of Friends, Monsieur the Marabout Abd-Aïssa (Servant of Jesus)."

"I saw your sister," wrote Moussa. "I spent two days at her home. I also saw your brother-in-law. I visited their splendid houses and gardens. And *you* live in Tamanrasset like a wretched pauper!"

Dassine as usual made all the important decisions while Moussa was away. Working with her, Foucauld drew up a plan to present to the Amenokal upon his return.

"I will try to make him understand that three things are necessary to the eternal salvation of his people," Foucauld wrote. "First, insure training and discipline in childhood and youth, now left to themselves like animals. Second, secure some degree of education. Third, work toward transforming his Tuareg from nomads to a sedentary people, all in allowing them to remain a pastoral people.

"The third point depends upon the first two, for discipline and education are incompatible with the nomadic life. . . . Three years of peace due to French authority have already given the people here a sense of permanence. When I first came to Tamanrasset there was only one house; the other dwellings were nothing more than huts. Today there are fifteen or twenty houses and more are being built. The huts will have soon disappeared. . . . Farming is on the increase. Unfortunately the Tuareg do not farm themselves, but get the Harratin or the negroes to do the work. The Tuareg supervise the planting and harvest the crops, but they do not deign to put hand to hoe. It would be a great benefit to this country if monks would settle here and work the land with their own hands."

It was the old refrain—alone! Always alone! Nobody to share his hermitage—four hermitages now, including Beni-Abbès, the relay chapel at In-Salah that was so far little more than a memory of Brother Michel, Tamanrasset of course, and now the new eagle's nest which allowed him to take the Blessed Sacrament two miles high to Asekrem. A lesser man would have long ago given up his idea of the Little Brothers of the Sacred Heart of Jesus, but never a Foucauld. *Jamais Arrière!*

Early in 1911 Father de Foucauld took off on another recruiting trip to France—three months of weary desert miles to spend three weeks in metropolitan France. Passing through Maison Carrée, he formally chose Father Voillard as his spiritual guide to take the place of the late Abbé Huvelin. He also asked for volunteers from the White Sisters and got a unanimous response in the affirmative—meaningless, because the rules of the order prevented White Sisters being sent to any spot in the desert where there were no White Fathers. And no White Fathers were as yet assigned to the Hoggar.

As usual, Father de Foucauld's itinerary was laid out almost to the hour. At Marseilles he shared a meal with his old comrade-in-arms the Duc de FitzJames. He sought religious counsel at Notre-Dames des Neiges, at Viviers, and in Paris. He made special trips to Nîmes, Angoulême, and Bergerac, where he had heard there might be material for the Little Brothers. He found none. He spent time with Cousin Marie in Paris and Sister Marie in Burgundy. He made a sentimental pilgrimage to Alsace-Lorraine to see distant relatives at Saverne and Luneville, and Grandfather Morlet's old apartment at Nancy.

On his way home he spent three days at Beni-Abbès, his first desert parish, to be greeted by blind old Marie, a few veterans of the garrison, a few faithful of the original Universal Fraternity, and, of all people, by Paul Embarek.

The ex-slave had at last run out of wild oats. He swore he was ready to settle down. He recognized his past sins and asked forgiveness. He knew there was no better man in all the world than Father de Foucauld. He wanted to serve him for the rest of his life.

Father de Foucauld didn't believe a word of it, but it was his Christian duty to forgive. He took Paul back to Tamanrasset with him.

SIXTEEN

EDUCATION OF A TARGUI

*For whom the Lord loveth, He correcteth,
and He scourgeth every son whom He ac-
cepteth.*

—Hebrews, 12

I

The Hoggar was again in a sorry state. Not only had there
been another year and a half of drought, but whatever crops had
survived the lack of rain were destroyed by a plague of aphids
in 1911. The plant lice had eaten both the Spring wheat and
the Autumn millet. There was not a quart of wheat barley, or
millet to be bought in Tamanrasset. Since there was no feed
for the goats, there was no milk, butter or meat either. And inasmuch as butter and meat were media of exchange, neither
could the people clothe themselves.

"Many eat nothing but roots," Father de Foucauld wrote. "I
can't feed the people, but I have given away much more clothing than I usually do. The cold weather is here."

He spent the Christmas season in prayer, in adoration of the
Infant Jesus (there was of course a *crèche* in the hermitage),
and in receiving the visits of Tuareg he had not seen since his
return from France.

"I must see all my poor neighbors who begin to be my old
friends," he wrote, "for I am now in my seventh year of residence at Tamanrasset."

He had brought them all small gifts from France—needles,
safety pins, matches, scissors and knives.

He also saw the officers from Fort Motylinski who dropped in on him occasionally. He was especially pleased by the new commandant, "a charming and very distinguished" officer, Lieutenant Depommier. With his fellow countrymen he discussed the disquieting situation in adjoining Libya that winter.

The Italo-Turkish War was already several months old. Since the differences leading to hostilities were of African origin, the brunt of the fighting had been in Africa. On Oct. 5, 1911, Italian naval guns had shelled Tripoli and shortly thereafter Italian marines landed at Benghazi. The Turks, more worried about being driven out of Europe by the rising Balkan League, fought only a rear-guard action in Libya. They did, however, try to incite their fellow Moslems to *jihad*—a holy war against the Italian Christians. Killing foreigners had long been a favorite pastime of that fanatical Moslem sect called the Senusis, as Brother Charles well knew from his experience chasing Bou Amama when he was Lieutenant de Foucauld. There were plenty of wild-eyed, blood-thirsty Senusis in Libya, among both the Arabs and Berbers. And they were spilling over across the Fezzan border into Tuareg country, technically loyal to France.

It was true, of course, that not all Tuareg were pro-French. The Amenokal of the Ajjer Tuareg, whom the French had chased into exile, was venting his spleen across the frontier by encouraging and arming Senusi bands, recruited among both Arabs and Ajjer Tuareg, to attack the Hoggar. Several French-led patrols had been jumped and cut to pieces. Some had been able to fight their way out of the desert traps. It was not a pretty picture.

Yet in answer to alarmed queries from his Sister Marie and his Cousin Marie, who were obviously better informed in France than were the nomads of the Hoggar, Brother Charles sent only reassurance.

"Don't worry," he wrote. "There will be no holy war. True, the Turks will do their best to preach *jihad* among the Arabs of Tripolitania, but that does not affect us. The Sahara is vast. The Tuareg are luke-warm Moslems and equally indifferent to the Italians, the Turks, and the Holy War. They are interested only in the harvest and pasture for their livestock."

Father de Foucauld, the old Chasseur d'Afrique, had his own theories about dealing with the Tuareg dissidents, however. He communicated his ideas not only to Amenokal Moussa, who was usually in the mountains, but to French officers in the area, up to and including the commander of the Saharan Oases—with copies to his old friend Colonel Laperrine.

The old soldier found it more pleasant to talk of more gratifying subjects with the youngsters now coming into positions of military responsibility in Africa. For instance, there was the heart-warming news that General Lyautey had completed his task of bringing Morocco under French influence. "Rabbi Josef Aleman" felt that he had in some way contributed to the event which many Moroccans had told him thirty years ago they had prayed for: French administration rather than local corruption. The former "Rabbi" felt a little hurt that the future Marshal Lyautey, great administrator, great civilizer, great empire builder, and great friend of the African (his will specified that he be buried erect, in Arab style), had not called him in for the final act. After all, Lyautey had repeatedly picked his brains about the great unknown spaces in Morocco and had certainly used his book and maps in his campaign. . . .

It was not pique, however—he admired his fellow Saint-Cyrien until his death—that prompted the saintly ex-Hussar to make the following prophetic declaration at this time.

"If we act according to our lights," he wrote, "if we civilize instead of exploiting, in fifty years Algeria, Tunis and Morocco will be an extension of France. If we do not live up to our duty, if we exploit rather than civilize, we will lose everything, and the union we have created from these diverse peoples will turn against us."

II

Brother Charles' theory of civilization was a simple one. If he could show the non-Christian how a good Christian family lives, he would have scored a triumph worth a thousand sermons. He himself, even though he lived as nearly as he could in the imitation of Christ, was only one voice crying in the Sahara. And since he could not entice other good Christians to join him in a life of abnegation, poverty, and charity, the next best thing would be to take one of his Tuareg "parishioners" to France, not to visit munitions works, the Montmartre flesh pots, and the art museums, as the French government had done with Moussa, but to show him how a decent French family lives, how good European Christians worship God and follow the teachings of Jesus Christ. By mid-1912 he had settled on his candidate—Ouksem-ag-Shikkat, the young tribal chieftain's son who helped carry wood and water to the high-perched hermitage at Asekrem.

Ouksem was at first delighted, then apparently afraid. After all, it was a great adventure for a Tuareg lad, a son of nomads, who had never left his mountains except to take his family camels and goats to pasture, or to trade hides against millet in Tidikelt. A boy who had never smelled salt water might well hesitate about crossing a sea. And what if all the things that were said about the infidel *roumi* were true? Would he ever come home?

Ouksem never actually resisted the plans of Brother Charles. First of all, he had to get married to his childhood sweetheart, a step-sister. She was now eighteen and he was almost twenty-two. And he could not marry her before he accompanied the family caravan to the region of the Diggera Tuareg in the Damerghu country some five hundred miles to the south on the border of Nigeria to bring back some scarce millet. When he returned, the Fall was well advanced and Brother Charles did not want to "expose a Saharan chest to the rigors of a European winter." So the expedition was postponed until the Spring of 1913.

It was really an expedition. Brother Charles sent out dozens of letters, most of them written on the backs of old envelopes, scraps of wrapping paper, whatever he could find, for he was hundreds of miles from the nearest stationer's. And yet on the back of every envelope he turned over to the courier to In-Salah, there was his hallmark—the Sacred Heart surmounted by the cross, and flanked by the words, "Jesus Caritas." The letters outlined a formidable itinerary, designed to show Ouksem the real France, and to warn his prospective hosts not to be alarmed by the arrival of a blue-veiled warrior.

Brother Charles and Ouksem finally got under way at dawn of April 28, 1913. To save the fee of a desert guide (100 francs), they traveled with the courier carrying dispatches from Fort

Motylinski to In-Salah. It took them six weeks to reach Maison Carrée and the White Fathers. They sailed for France on June 10—in first cabin. Brother Charles, who for twenty-three years had always crossed the Mediterranean as a deck passenger, wanted to show his young protégé the best of European life.

The best consisted of such personages as the Duc de Fitz-James (former Hussar at Pont-à-Mousson) who entertained them at Marseilles, and the Bishop of Viviers; a broad blue river flowing between steep cultivated slopes—the Rhône as it flowed all year round near Viviers; exotic food, like the fish which lived in the rivers and in the sea (and which Ouksem would not touch) and vegetables like asparagus or endives which he also eschewed.

Brother Charles took his young friend to the naval base at Toulon, where they lunched aboard a destroyer on which his godson Charles de Blic was now an officer. This was the beginning of a long lesson in the French family, including collateral branches which Charles himself had not seen in many years, although he wrote fairly regularly: the Marquis de Foucauld who lived at the Château de Bridoire in Périgord, and Count Louis de Foucauld, also one of the original Foucaulds of Périgord.

They visited Marie de Bondy who was summering with her grandchildren on the Atlantic beaches near Biarritz. The children were no doubt as much intrigued by the tight, well-buttered braids of the young man from Tamanrasset as Ouksem was fascinated by the gentle white-haired surf of the Bay of Biscay.

The main course in Brother Charles' curriculum of French civilization for young Ouksem was a sojourn with his sister Marie, her husband, the Viscount Raymond de Blic, and their children at the Château de Barbirey in Burgundy. Here the Targui lad was exposed to the warm pleasures of a large and closely-knit French family. He learned to ride a bicycle, an operation for which he had to tuck up the hem of his Tuareg gandurah with safety pins. He learned to knit, because Brother Charles wanted him to teach the art to the women of his tribe, and he became much more adept than his mentor; he could turn a heel much better than Brother Charles could ever hope to. And he learned a few words of French from Foucauld's nephew Edouard.

"If you teach him French," Foucauld had told his nephew, "when you come to see me in Africa he will teach you to ride a mehari, an art at which he is a past master."

Ouksem became adept at eating with a fork. In the evening he learned to play such French games as *Furet* and listened to the Blic girls sing. He received a hunting rifle as a gift and immediately shot a partridge, a hare, and a squirrel.

Brother Charles took his protégé to Lyons to see Henry Laperrine, now a brigadier general commanding the Sixth Dragoons. Laperrine thought that Ouksem should be able to compare his mountains of the Hoggar with the Alps. "Take him to Switzerland," said the general. "I'll go with you." So they went to Chamonix to admire Mont Blanc and the Sea of Ice glacier, crossed the Bernese Alps to Lucerne, and re-entered France through the Jura.

It was a real vacation for Brother Charles, and he was completely relaxed. While at his sister's in Burgundy, he even considered playing hooky from vespers one day but finally went to church anyhow because his absence might have caused talk among Marie de Blic's neighbors. He may have had a premonition that he would never see France again, that he was saying goodbye for the last time to his beloved Marie de Bondy, to his sister and her family, to his religious advisers, and to his old and dear friend General Laperrine.

He was of course not in the least afraid of death. In fact, he had for years felt that being alive indicated his unworthiness to enter into the Life Everlasting. During his last stay in the lofty hermitage of Asekrem, he had written a new will, specifying that he should be buried without shroud or coffin at the exact spot of his death, and that his grave should be marked by no monument except a simple wooden cross.

And as it had been for the past twenty years, his motto was still: "Live as though you were to die today as a martyr."

III

In September, 1913, Brother Charles of Jesus and Ouksem-ag-Shikkat sailed again from Marseilles. It was November 22 before they had crossed the desert to the Hoggar. Brother Charles insisted on camping on the outskirts of Tamanrasset so that he could make his entrance and unload his camels before dawn. Thus he would be able to get resettled in his long-abandoned hermitage before his "parishioners" were aware of his return.

Ouksem-ag-Shikkat was just as glad to get home as was Brother Charles. He was of course full of his sojourn among the *roumis,* although his reactions may not have been exactly those which the Christian Marabout expected. He was proud of the few words of French he had learned, and loved to show off before his friends and family, talking to the Marabout in his own language. He also strutted more than a little with his new rifle. But while he told funny stories about the strange vegetables and water-borne creatures the *roumis* used as food, he was not quite as eloquent a propagandist for French home life (and the Christian virtues) as Brother Charles had hoped. He did, however, delight in teaching the Tuareg women how to knit.

He had been home only a few weeks before Ouksem was off again with the family herd of camels, bound for some greener land (and trading area) six or seven hundred miles away, on the Sudanese border.

"Poor Ouksem," wrote Brother Charles to his brother-in-law the Viscount de Blic, "is off again for six months after only three weeks at home. . . . During his first year of marriage, he has spent only forty nights with his bride. When will his soul come to us altogether? His whole family are good people, but it is difficult for anyone to stop believing what he has always believed, what those around him have always believed, and what all those he has loved and respected believe."

During the early days of 1914, however, some of Ouksem's relatives came to the hermitage almost every day to exchange a few words with the fabulous Marabout who had taken their boy to Never-Never Land and brought him back alive!

Brother Charles was again busy with his dictionary and anthology of Tamashek poetry. And he never ceased to try to recruit a fellow hermit to take up his work, as well as a few White Sisters to work among the Tuareg women. When his efforts to secure White Sisters seemed indeed hopeless, he wrote to France in an effort to get Frenchwomen to volunteer their services. He drew up a list of eight points which French women must be ready to accept in order to come to the Hoggar highlands and help the Tuareg.

1. Willingness to learn the language, "which is not difficult."

2. Much patience and gentleness.

3. Elementary knowledge of medicine, especially of the diseases of young women and children.

4. Ability to vaccinate and the equipment to do so.

5. Ability to raise children abandoned by their mothers at birth. This was a major premise of Brother Charles. He could never swallow the fact that the Tuareg social code countenances infanticide or abandonment particularly in the case of children born out of wedlock. He wanted to establish some variation on the old *tour* of the French foundling home, whereby unwanted children could be left for community care without the mother revealing her identity.

6. Ability to teach the elements of hygiene.

7. Knowledge of simple laundry and ironing (but not starching) and a little cooking—enough to be able to teach others.

8. Ability to plant a kitchen garden, build a chicken coop, and a stable for a few goats. "There are plenty of goats here, but the Tuareg do not know how to feed them on alfalfa or other grasses. There are chickens, but of a small variety, and our people do not know how to shelter them from birds of prey. Nor do they raise the fruits and vegetables that the soil here could certainly produce. . . ."

As an after-thought, he added:

"One thing especially must be taught to the Tuareg women—personal cleanliness. They never wash themselves, wash their clothing scarcely more often, and smear their hair with butter. They have no fleas, for there are no fleas in this country, but they have plenty of other parasites. They say that washing makes them ill. This is partly true, because they wash in the open and never dry themselves. They must be taught to use towels and to perform their ablutions in a sheltered spot. A Frenchwoman in Tuareg country should have a good supply of Castile soap and plenty of ordinary towels to give the local women . . .

also thousands of sewing needles of all sizes and a few thousand safety pins a year."

Like the White Sisters who never came, like the Little Brothers of the Sacred Heart of Jesus who would not cross the desert, no women volunteers ever came from France to work with Brother Charles among the Tuareg.

SEVENTEEN

WAR IN EUROPE
—FERMENT IN THE SAHARA

*Donnes à qui demand et ouvres à qui
frappe.*
*Give to him who asks and open to him who
knocks.*

—Charles de Foucauld

I

In March of 1913, shortly before Brother Charles had left for
France with Ouksem, French General Bailloud had come to
Tamanrasset to test the possibility of establishing direct wireless communications between Paris and the Hoggar. The experiments were successful, and Brother Charles recorded with
great satisfaction that the signals from the transmitter atop the
Eiffel Tower could be received at Tamanrasset and Fort Motylinski with the greatest of ease. The general announced that he
would recommend a sufficiently powerful station be built in the
region to assure two-way communication with Paris. Then, after
offering a camel barbecue to the Tuareg and Harratin of
Tamanrasset to thank them for their cordial reception, General
Bailloud moved on with his experimental equipment to make
tests elsewhere in the Sahara.

Bureaucracy, even military bureaucracy, moves slowly, and
the Hoggar was certainly far down on the priority list. So
when the tragic August of 1914 came around, Tamanrasset and
Fort Motylinski were still isolated outposts. The nearest telegraph was at El Goléa, so that official dispatches intended for
Fort Motylinski still had to travel overland from El Goléa by

camel—a lapse of twenty-five days from Paris to Tamanrasset. Letters and newspapers took forty days. Thus when Germany declared war on France and struck through neutral Belgium, Father de Foucauld, unaware that the Europe he knew was going up in flames, went blissfully about his routine at the hermitage. He celebrated his solitary Mass, spent hours in adoration of the Blessed Sacrament, visited the sick and helped the poor as usual.

That Spring he had begun his final revision of his monumental Tamashek dictionary. By July 31, the day that a last minute British attempt to prevent World War broke down, his diary entry read: "This evening reached page 385 of the dictionary."

A month later, when the German armies under von Moltke had reached the Marne and were poised for an attack on Paris, Foucauld's diary entry read: "August 31.—I have reached page 550."

At five in the morning of Sept. 3, a courier from Fort Motylinski pounded on the door of the hermitage with the news that France was at war. Captain de la Roche, commandant of the fort, announced that he was taking most of his garrison to the Adrar, for purposes not disclosed, and was asking Foucauld to ask Moussa-ag-Amastane for twenty men, and several other tribes to contribute men for replacements.

Foucauld was immediately transformed into the old Chasseur d'Afrique. Moussa was far away on the Sudanese border, but a courier was sent after him. Moussa's stand-in, Afegzag, with some urging by Dassine, mobilized a camel patrol of fifty men from five tribes and left for Fort Motylinski the same evening.

Couriers from In-Salah who used to arrive only twice a month now trotted in every few days. Most of them brought bad news. The Germans were in Brussels. . . . The French Government had moved from Paris to Bordeaux. . . . One of them brought 1500 rounds of 1500 cartridges for Moussa. Another courier brought word from Captain de Saint-Léger, regional commander, ordering Captain de la Roche to return to Motylinski. Foucauld sent a Meharist into the desert to find the captain. . . .

Foucauld wrote to General Laperrine, asking him to arrange

things so he could serve in the front lines as stretcher-bearer or chaplain. It was two months before the general's reply came back: "Stay in the Hoggar. We need you there."

Even before the reply came, Foucauld realized that he would be of more use to his country by remaining in the Sahara. Despite the lack of communications, the news of French reverses was spreading through the desert, and some of the tribes whose allegiance to France had been pledged reluctantly, were ready to revolt. The Senusis in Libya needed no urging by agents of the Moslem Turks, now allies of the Germans, to cross the border into French Hoggar, picking up dissidents along the way. Even after Joffre's great victory in the first battle of the Marne (news of which did not reach Father de Foucauld until October 12), the wave of revolt continued to gain momentum.

In October a band of dissidents ambushed Moussa-ag-Amastane at Tin-Zouaten, 300 miles southwest of Tamanrasset. Moussa escaped with his life, but lost ten prisoners and 400 camels. He tracked the rebels across the Sahara for two months before he caught up with them. Attacking, he killed seven of the enemy, recaptured his own camels and took those of his enemies as well, leaving the surviving foes to die of thirst in the desert.

The ex-lieutenant in Father de Foucauld was greatly disturbed, but he was at great pains not to show it to his "parishioners," most of whom had never even heard the word "Germany."

"You must realize what it costs me to be so far from our soldiers and the front," he wrote to his family, "but my duty is quite obviously to remain here to help keep the local population quiet. I will not leave Tamanrasset until peace comes. . . . Nothing has changed in the outward aspects of my calm and regular life, for the natives must see nothing that may indicate that anything out of the ordinary has taken place."

Henri Laperrine was now a major-general commanding a division in action, yet he remained in constant touch with his old friend. Foucauld wrote to him with every courier, keeping him abreast of the current unrest among the Saharan peoples, and the general replied with meticulous promptness even though he was in the thick of battle.

"Although I go about my business with apparent calm," the hermit wrote to the general, "my spirit is with you at the front. After the abridged dictionary and the dictionary of proper names, I have finally finished the unabridged French-Tamashek dictionary, ready for the press. I am now getting final copy of my poetry ready for the printer. It seems very strange to me in these parlous times to be spending my days copying bits of verse. . . ."

To his family, too, his letters were prosaic. "I am well," he wrote to his sister's family. "Despite the drouth and the locusts, the gardens of Tamanrasset continue to grow. There are no more huts here, and some of the houses even have fireplaces. . . . I see Ouksem often. Marie asks if he still knits. He knits marvelously! Almost all the young folks in his camp and in the village are learning from him how to knit socks and sweaters, and now to crochet caps. . . ."

And on September 7, 1915, he wrote in his diary: "Tomorrow it will be ten years since I celebrated my first Mass in the newly-constructed hermitage. I owe many thanks and much gratitude to the Good Lord for all the favors he has granted me here."

He added a footnote to the effect that in all that time he had not made a single convert. It was not, however, an apology. He still looked upon himself as the man to plow the ground and plant the seed. The harvest of souls would be for those who came later.

In addition to his philological works and his worship of God, he continued his tea parties under the trees with the *grandes dames* of the Tuareg aristocracy. He was beginning to read to them—in Tamashek translation, of course—the *Fables of La Fontaine*: The Lion and the Mouse, the Ant and the Grasshopper, the Fox and the Crow. . . .

But his letters to Laperrine grew increasingly alarming. On Nov. 19, 1915 he wrote: "The courier from the Ajjer has not yet arrived, but I have learned from other sources that the Dehibat outpost on the Tunisian border has been attacked by Senusis under the command of officers in khaki uniforms, with field glasses and revolvers (German, no doubt). General Moinier has sent reinforcements. The situation is indeed dangerous all along the Tunisia-Tripolitanian border."

II

By April 1916 the situation had gone from bad to worse. The rebel tribesmen had taken a fort from the French. The Senusis, 1,000 strong, armed with artillery and machine guns, had besieged for three weeks the fort at Janet, fifty miles inside the frontier of the Fezzan. When their supplies and ammunition ran out, with their access to water cut off by the invaders, the little garrison of fifty men broke out into the desert but within three days they were surrounded and forced to surrender.

Not only was the defeat humiliating, but, as Father de Foucauld wrote to General Laperrine: "The road is now open for the Senusis to come here unopposed. By 'here' I do not mean only Tamanrasset, where I am alone, but Fort Motylinski. . . . I have advised retiring to an impregnable position in the mountains, with supplies and ammunition, where we can hold out indefinitely, even against artillery. There is water in the spot I have chosen. If my advice is not followed, only the Lord knows what will happen if we are attacked. But I think it will be followed. . . . Don't worry if you are without a letter for some time, for our couriers may be intercepted. I am in daily contact with Second-lieutenant Constant, commanding Fort Motylinski, and if necessary I shall make occasional brief visits. If he is attacked, I will of course join him. . . . The population here is behaving perfectly. We are all in the hands of God. He will decide what is to happen."

Father de Foucauld traveled to the fort a few days later to map his defensive plans. He knew the country better than the young shave-tail Constant, after all, and he already had four emergency redoubts picked out. With the narrow gorges and ravines of the Hoggar, it was merely a matter of having a strategic sense and of knowing where the water was. On his way to the fort he found a fifth possible site.

He went over the ground with Constant and picked a defensive site in a ravine, the mouth of which was blocked by dense reeds. He indicated where trenches should be dug among the reeds and which steep slopes should be fortified. At first sign of attack, Constant would move in with his garrison, which at that time consisted of four Frenchmen—two sergeants, a corporal of engineers, and one private—and thirty African soldiers and non-coms.

Foucauld reported these dispositions to Major Meynier, commander of the Oases, and also wrote the details to General Laperrine, adding: "With this number of rifles, the strong-point can be successfully defended against a superior force and even against artillery."

Forty-eight hours after his departure, Brother Charles was back in Tamanrasset, still disturbed by the threat from the northeast, but outwardly calm for the benefit of his African friends. He had refused all suggestions from the French army that he take refuge at Fort Motylinski. He would remain with his "parishioners" until the war was over. He agreed, however, to the erection of a *bordj*—a fortified structure in which he could live and hold religious services and which could house the civilians of Tamanrasset in case of Senusi attack.

The Marabout himself drew plans for the *bordj*. It was a square structure, fifty feet on a side, with a square crenelated bastion at each corner. The walls, made of stone, sun-dried brick, and mud mortar, were six feet thick at the base and seventeen feet high. In the square central courtyard was a poison-proof well, twenty feet deep. There were four large rooms: the chapel, a guest room, Father de Foucauld's living quarters and study, and a storeroom. A moat six feet deep surrounded the *bordj*. The only door had a high snake-proof sill and was so low that a man had to stoop to enter. He would then have to walk down a long corridor so narrow that there was not room for two men abreast. There was a second door at the end of the corridor. Both outer and inner doors were reinforced inside with steel plate. Outside the outer door stood an oblong of screening wall to protect the entrance against direct gunfire. On the parapet above the door there was a crude wooden cross made of branches from the atlee tree.

Father de Foucauld chose as site for his *bordj* a slight rise across the wadi from his hermitage. It was closer to the village in case of emergency. It was, in the words of an army officer who inspected it, "impregnable. Two men, even one man with grenades, could assure its defense."

The priest was quite pleased with his creation. He was sure

that even dear old Grandfather de Morlet, who had built the defenses of Strasbourg, would be proud of his military engineering.

On June 23, 1916, the chapel and the living quarters were near enough to completion for Brother Charles to move from the hermitage to the new *bordj*. The little fortress would not be completed until October, but the ex-officer was anxious to establish the security of his area. If France were to lose the Hoggar to the Senusi and the dissidents, all chance of bringing the Tuareg to Jesus Christ would be lost. His military activity was his battle for the right to bring God to the unbeliever.

On the fifteenth anniversary of his ordination, he wrote to Monseigneur Bonnet, bishop of Viviers, his gratitude "for having adopted me and made of me a priest of Jesus. With all my heart I pray for you who accepted me as your son more than fifteen years ago. I pray, too, for the dear diocese of Viviers. . . . At this time of the Pentecost, I am thinking more than ever of the fifty million unbelievers of the French dominions. May the Holy Spirit reign in their souls, and may France, which asks their help in defending their temporal mother country, help them in obtaining the eternal fatherland."

Foucauld anxiously awaited each courier with official dispatches from El Goléa—although the news was still three weeks late. He took a vicarious pride in the performance of his classmates of Saint-Cyr: Pétain, whose brilliant and gallant defense of Verdun was making history; d'Urbal, whose magnificent rear-guard action in Flanders had won universal acclaim; Mazel, who had won command of the Fifth Army. His diary also noted the exploits of his contemporaries who were a class or two ahead of him at Saint-Cyr: Maud'huy, who had beaten back the Germans in the Vosges; Sarail, who had helped Joffre stem the German advance on the Marne and was now fighting in the Balkans; Driant, who had fallen at Verdun. . . .

To General Mazel he wrote: "This corner of the Sahara from which I write you, my dear Mazel, is still peaceful. However, we are on a constant alert because of the growing agitation of the Senusis in Tripolitania. Our Tuareg here are loyal, but we may be attacked at any moment from across the border. I have transformed my hermitage into a fortress. There is nothing new under the sun. In looking at my crenelated parapets. I think of the fortified churches and monasteries of the tenth century. . . . I have been entrusted with six cases of ammunition and thirty Gras carbines, which remind me of our youth. [The Gras carbine was standard equipment in the French army of 1874.] I am pleased that our good Laperrine is serving under your orders. I hope you can keep him for a long time. The tranquillity of our Algerian Sahara is due to him, to the wisdom and vigor of his actions; and the loyalty of the so-called difficult peoples we owe to the incomparable memory he has left behind him in Africa."

Then, perhaps remembering his ancestor who stood beside Jeanne d'Arc during the coronation of Charles VII at the Cathedral of Rheims, he added:

"Here with the translation of a ninth century prayer which probably was often recited and chanted in the Rheims Cathedral: 'Eternal and All Powerful God who has established the Empire of the Franks to be the instrument of Thy Divine Will throughout the world, the glory and the bulwark of Thy Holy Church, herald with Thy Celestial Light forever and everywhere the suppliant sons of France, that they may see their duty to extend Thy reign throughout the world, and that they may become ever more charitable and more valiant to accomplish Thy truth as revealed to them."

III

"How kind is the Good Lord to conceal the future from us!" Brother Charles wrote in his diary. "What torture would life hold for us if we were to be granted a glimpse of the unknown! And how kind is God to reveal to us so clearly the celestial future which is to follow our earthly ordeal!"

Brother Charles did not fear the future, for in his breviary there was still the phrase he had written in the tool shed outside the Clarist convent in Nazareth: "Live as if today you were to die a martyr." He was however more and more worried over the bad news from the Libyan frontier. The fort at Janet had changed hands several times, and had finally been abandoned by the French. Other outposts had been abandoned. "This retreat before a few hundred rifles is deplorable," he wrote. "There is obviously some serious failure on the part of our command, although at what level I do not know. I do know, however, that even without a fight we are retiring and the Senusis are advancing. If our methods do not change promptly, the Senusis will soon be upon us."

The situation was naturally made to order for wild rumors. One of these false alarms was a source of great satisfaction for Brother Charles. After the report of an imminent attack had proved groundless, the Marabout wrote: "The alert only served to prove the loyalty of the people. Instead of showing the slightest sign of going over to the enemy, they rallied around the officer at the nearby fort, and around me, ready to defend the fort or my hermitage. This fidelity has been very sweet to me, and I am exceedingly grateful to these poor folk who could just as well have taken refuge in the mountains where they would have nothing to fear, but who preferred the haven of Fort Motylinski and my hermitage, even though they knew that the enemy had cannon and believed that a bombardment was certain."

The Amenokal also gave proof of his loyalty. Although Moussa-ag-Amastane was 400 miles away when he heard that the Senusis were preparing to attack Motylinski and the Marabout's *bordj*, he sent all the men he could spare—eighty camel-mounted warriors—by forced march to join in the common defense.

The Senusis, however, were busy farther north. Late in October Foucauld reported several actions in his letters to General Laperrine. A band of 300 Senusis commanded by a deserter from the Camel Corps of Tidikelt, jumped a French supply caravan traveling the 200 desert miles between Fort Flatters and Fort Polignac, well inside the frontier, with a number of casualties. Another razzia in the Ajjer Tuareg country rustled a hundred camels from the Inrar tribe and withdrew. To the south, in the Aïr Tuareg area, Senusi raiders were offering immunity to Tuareg who would follow them into the Fezzan and join the dissidents—or else. A patrol of Sudanese riflemen from Agadès drove off the Senusis.

The outlook was ominous. With Moussa away, the winds of unrest seemed to blow the stronger, fanning the faint spark of nationalism ignited by the Senusis. Dassine was still a friend of the Christian Marabout and of the French and she was still making decisions in the absence of the Amenokal. Her influence among the people, however, was not quite what it once was. In the eleven years since Foucauld had first come to Tamanrasset Dassine had grown rather heavy, her bloom had faded and her beauty had become coarse. She was still a *grande dame,* a noted poetess and musician, but the young men who used to ride dozens of miles to attend her *ahals* were advancing into middle age, and the new generation seemed more susceptible to other influences. Senusis from the Fezzan and the Ajjer Tuareg country trotted through the Hoggar on their camels, posing as traders, but quietly disseminating subversion. The French after all were not invincible, they said. It was obvious now. Had not the French been finally driven out of Janet? Were they not giving up Fort Polignac because they could not maintain supply lines? The young Tuareg of the Hoggar listened.

Father de Foucauld, seeing the outward calm of Tamanrasset and the evident loyalty of the Hoggar chiefs, was apparently unaware of the hidden ferment, of the slow disintegration of authority. He had finished the final revision of his French-Tamashek dictionary. On October 28, 1916, he recorded that his collection of Tuareg poetry was also complete and ready for the printer. He was pleased and encouraged that despite the war French civilization was advancing into the Sahara. The long-promised wireless station would be erected within the year. The automobile road from In-Salah to Tamanrasset was almost finished, and when the first car completed the 400-miles journey, the hermit would feel less alone; he would be only days, instead of weeks, from a center of population. After the war, he would really have a chance to recruit Little Brothers of the Sacred Heart. And now that his labors as lexicographer and folklorist had been completed, he could devote all his time and efforts to spreading The Word. In all his fifteen years in Africa, he had made not a single convert. He did not count baby Abd-Jesus or poor old blind Marie who had no idea of the meaning of her adopted religion, although he had baptized both. There was so much work to be done.

"The plight of the people around me is enough to make a man weep," he wrote in October 1916. "They are surrounded by so much evil and error, that it is difficult for those who are good by nature to lead a decent life. There are sound, honest characters among them, but in their ignorance and in such an environment, how will they save themselves?"

However much he might complain to his diary, Father de Foucauld was always the soul of patience and understanding with his benighted friends. The stores which he had accumulated in his new *bordj* against a possible siege—the sacks of grain and flour, the tins of condensed milk and other food, the bolts of cloth and the supplies of medicines and sundry household objects—were a great temptation to the poor Harratin the priest had engaged to help in constructing the building. These were vast riches to people who sometimes did not eat two meals a day. As the *bordj* was nearing completion, the temptation proved too great for El Madani, the black Hartani farmer of dubious honesty whom the hermit had befriended ever since he first came to Tamanrasset. The corporal of engineers who had come over from Fort Motylinski to superintend putting the finishing touches on the *bordj*, caught El Madani stealing a bolt of calico from the storeroom.

"What do you want done with the thief, Father?" asked the corporal as he haled El Madani before the priest. "Shall I have him whipped here or sent to Fort Motylinski for sixty days' hard labor?"

Father de Foucauld stared at the Hartani for a moment, then smiled wistfully. El Madani looked sullenly at his own bare toes.

"Let him go home," said the priest at last.

"But Father, I caught him red-handed—."

"I gave El Madani the cloth, Corporal."

"Then why was he sneaking off with it? Why did he try to hide it?"

"I promised it to his wife for a dress. He may have forgotten." He put his arm on the Hartani's shoulder. "Go, my friend," he said. "Tell your wife to make a beautiful dress. I hope she enjoys it."

When El Madani had gone, the corporal shook his head and said: "You're too good, Father. That man is a born thief and a no-good scoundrel. Everyone knows that he'll steal anything that's not nailed down. If you'll excuse the expression, Father, he's an ordure."

"He's a poor unfortunate wretch," said the priest. "He has been brought up in darkness. We don't love enough, Corporal."

"He won't give that calico to his wife. He'll sell it. He'd cut your throat for a silver duro. Why are you so good to him, Father?"

Father de Foucauld smiled sadly. "Didn't Jesus love Judas Iscariot?" he asked.

EIGHTEEN

BETRAYAL

*I have fought the good fight, I have ac-
complished the course, I have kept the faith.*
—II Timothy iv, 7

I

As December 1, 1916, fell on a Friday, Father de Foucauld
celebrated the Mass of the Sacred Heart, as he always did on the
first Friday of the month. Then he sat down to write letters, for
December 1 was also mail day.

Writing letters was a ritual in more ways than one. First of
all, there was the business of assembling materials. He was
400 miles from the nearest stationer, even if his self-imposed
poverty would have permitted the purchase of paper and envelopes. He saved odd bits of wrapping paper and blank pages
of incoming letters, on which he now wrote to General Laperrine, bringing him up to date on the strategic situation in the
Sahara. He wrote to another old Sahara hand, Major de Saint-
Léger, wishing him a happy new year and victory for France.

He wrote to his sister Marie, giving news of people she knew,
describing the beauties of winter in the Hoggar, and telling her
that when the new auto road was open, he expected her to visit
him—or at least one of her sons.

He wrote to Mother Marie de Saint-Michel, former Mother
Superior of the Clarist convent at Nazareth, who had fled the
Holy Land when the Turks became German allies, and who
had taken refuge in Malta.

"I am able to say Mass every day," he wrote, "and I have

another source of happiness: I have the Blessed Sacrament reserved in my little chapel. I am still alone. Now and then I see a Frenchman; every thirty or forty days one comes through.

"We live at a time when the soul feels the great need of prayer. In the storm that rages over Europe, we feel the emptiness of creation and we turn to the Creator. . . . And when all creatures seem obviously on the brink of nothingness, the presence of the Supreme Being in the Blessed Sacrament is a great comfort.

"Do pray, dear Reverend Mother, for the poor infidels who surround me, and for their very poor missioner. And together let us pray for France."

To his beloved cousin Marie de Bondy he wrote his seven hundred thirty-fourth letter since their temporal farewell in Paris on the eve of his becoming a Trappist, nearly twenty-seven years before.

"It seems we do not love enough," he wrote. "How true it is that we shall never love enough. But the good Lord Who knows from what mud He has fashioned us and Who loves us more than any mother can ever love her child, He Who never lies, has told us that none who comes to Him shall ever be rejected."

And finally he wrote a long letter to Louis Massignon, the brilliant young orientalist and Arabic scholar who had become the first member of Father de Foucauld's projected lay order of the Union of the Little Brothers of the Sacred Heart of Jesus—an organization that now had nearly fifty members, none of whom were in the Hoggar. Ex-professor Massignon was now a language officer attached to the French Army of the Orient in the Balkans, and had written to Father de Foucauld for advice regarding his desire to transfer to the "Porpoises"—the Marines —for actual combat.

"I am greatly moved by the thought that you are perhaps going to risk greater dangers, or perhaps are already risking them [Massignon's letter was nearly two months old]," Father de Foucauld wrote. "You have done well to ask for transfer to combat service. Never hesitate to ask for a post of greater danger, sacrifice, or devotion. Leave honor for those who want it, but let us always demand the difficult and the perilous for ourselves.

We Christians must give an example of sacrifice and devotion, a life-long principle to which we must be faithful without thought of pride. . . .

"Do not worry about your home. Trust your loved ones to God. . . . Have confidence that the destiny God reserves for you will be the best for His glory, for your soul, and for the souls of others, since you ask only that of Him, since His will is yours, fully and without reservation.

"Our corner of the Sahara is quiet. With all my heart I pray for you here and for your loved ones. . . ."

II

The two men dismounted from their kneeling, squealing camels and stood for a moment silhouetted against the eerie glow of the sunset. They were tall, almost spectral figures, shrouded in blue robes, their faces hidden by blue veils wrapped around their heads, the whole curious ensemble capped by white hoods. They were obviously Tuareg.

They walked with slow, stately stride as though to show their superiority to the motley crew of cut-throats gathered about the miserable fire of poor twigs and camel dung. The last rays of sunlight gleamed on gunmetal and burnished steel as the twenty-odd squatting bandits stirred restlessly. Most of them were bearded Moslems of the fanatical Senusi sect. Some were Ajjer Tuareg. A few were dissident Hoggar Tuareg won over by the Senusis. The rest were Harratin of mixed Sudanese and Berber blood. None was a man of good will.

"We have word for Si Mohammed Labed," said one of the new arrivals.

An Arab arose. "Labed has not left the Fezzan. I am Ebeh, his lieutenant. What is the word?"

"The Christian Marabout is in Tamanrasset," the Targui said.

"Alone?"

"The Marabout is always alone."

"I mean, does he have military protection?"

"There are no soldiers closer than Fort Motylinski, ten leagues away. There are only a few French officers there and not many Meharists. The French are having a bad time in Europe."

"Then what are we waiting for? Let us ride!"

"One moment!" The Targui smiled mysteriously. "The Christian Marabout is alone, but he is barricaded in his *bordj.*"

"So? We have good rifles. We took them from the Italians at Gnat with our own hands. They shoot five times without re-loading."

"But the walls of the Marabout's *bordj* are two metres thick. And his door is reinforced with steel. Your rifles will be useless."

The Senusi chieftain made a harsh noise in his throat. There was a sharp hiss as he spat into the dying fire.

"What nonsense are you talking?" he growled. "Come to the point. You sent word to Si Mohammed Labed that you could deliver the Marabout. Were you making empty boasts?"

"No, Ebeh. We will deliver the Marabout. But there are com-plications. There is a matter of money."

"You agreed to work on shares." Again the Senusi spat into the fire. "The Marabout is rich. You will get your share of the loot. You will also receive your part of the ransom. Do you now go back on your bargain?"

"No, Ebeh. We are satisfied. But we must use trickery to get into the *bordj.* We have found a man who knows the *bordj* like the palm of his hand. He is familiar with the Marabout's routine and his signals. He is a Hartani and he guarantees that he will gain entrance for us into the *bordj.* He demands payment in cash—in silver duros."

"Where is this Hartani?"

"Twenty minutes from here, if your camels are fresh."

"We will freshen them up. Come, Senusis, the lamps! Let us waste no more time. We must take the *roumi* tonight!"

There was a confusion of shouts, the bubbling squeal of camels being prodded to their feet, a smell of dust and men and animals. Soon another smell mingled with the others—the greasy stink of primitive lamps being lit with brands snatched from the campfire. The lamps were hung beneath the bellies of the camels to make them run faster. The animals screamed with pain as the razzia moved off.

From afar the flickering lamps made a snake of light squirming across the stony hammada toward the rendezvous with El Madani, the Hartani.

There is no record of how many pieces of silver El Madani received.

III

The wan December daylight faded with desert swiftness. The last glow caught on the peaks of Tahat and Ilamane slid into darkness. The temperature dropped with incredible rapidity. As there was no orgiastic *ahal* that night, the hamlet of Tamanrasset was already drowsing. The few smoky flares were going out, one by one. The crenelated walls of Father de Foucauld's chapel-fortress were outlined sharply against the blazing stars of the winter sky.

Inside the *bordj* Father de Foucauld was alone. Paul Embarek, now a family man, had served the priest's supper, then gone home to his wife and children who lived in a hut about half a mile from the *bordj*. Before he left, Paul had repeated the ominous rumors he had heard in the bazaar earlier in the day: that an armed band of Senusis had crossed the border from the Fezzan and were riding unopposed toward Tamanrasset, killing and pillaging along the way. There was even talk of a plot against the Father himself. The Marabout had better make doubly sure that the door was bolted after Paul had left.

Father de Foucauld smiled tolerantly. Poor Paul! He would never be able to distinguish fact from fancy. Of course the priest did indeed throw the bolt as he closed the massive door after the freed slave. That was a matter of routine, not for himself, for he would still gladly darken the soil of Africa with his own blood, but because the little *bordj* must be kept inviolate for the protection of his "parishioners" in case of attack. But an attack currently seemed more remote than ever.

When Paul had gone, Father de Foucauld sat down to write in his diary. Afterward he would spend some time in prayer and meditation at the foot of the Blessed Sacrament, then retire for the night. His journal entry for December 1, 1916, read:

"It seems to me that we are in no danger at this moment, as

far as Tripolitania and the Senusis are concerned. Our troops
have been heavily reinforced and I hope that they will drive
back the enemy beyond the frontier. We have had no serious
new alert since September. The country is very calm."

He had barely finished writing, when he was startled by an
insistent pounding at the only door of the *bordj*. He put down
his pen and stood up. The pounding continued. It seemed to
follow a pattern—a series of knocks grouped in double, triple,
and single raps—a pattern which he had instructed his "parishioners" to use in case of an emergency.

He crossed the courtyard and started down the long, dark,
narrow corridor that he had purposely designed as a bottleneck
that one man could hold against an important force of attackers.
The knocking grew louder.

He stopped a few feet from the door, listening, wondering.
At last he called: "Who's there?"

"Master!" came the reply, muffled by the thickness of oak and
steel. "It is I. I bring the mail."

Curious, thought Father de Foucauld, the voice is familiar.
He could have sworn that it was El Madani's voice. Well, perhaps it was not curious after all. Perhaps the courier, behind
schedule and in a hurry, had pushed on to Motylinski, leaving
letters for the *bordj* with someone he knew was a friend of the
Christian Marabout. El Madani was such a man. . . .

Perhaps there would at last be a reply from Father Voillaume
in response to his more and more insistent requests for a companion. Not that he minded solitude—he had always sought solitude—but he needed someone to carry on his work. He was getting on in years. He was now in his fifty-ninth year. . . .

The knocking resumed.

"One moment," said Father de Foucauld. He slid back the
bolt, twisted the heavy handle, and drew back the door a scant
foot. He held out one hand for the mail.

Instantly an iron grip was clamped about his wrist. He was
brutally dragged through the door with such sudden force that
he banged his head against the thick wall erected to protect the
entrance from artillery and rifle fire. As he sank to his knees in
an attitude of prayer, wild shrieks of victory made the night

shrilly horrible. The muzzle of a rifle was jammed against the back of his head.

A feeling of great elation welled up inside Charles de Foucauld's scrawny breast. The great desire of his African years, the wish to testify to his faith with his own life, seemed about to be fulfilled. Or was he again falling into deadly sin? Was he being prideful? Perhaps he was not yet worthy of martyrdom. . . .

He remembered suddenly his mother's dying words. "Father," she had said, quoting St. Luke, "not my will, but thine, be done." Did the Lord really wish the sacrifice he had always been eager to make? Or was he being again the selfish, wilful child of so long ago?

Strange that he should at this moment be thinking of his mother so long dead, or of his childhood that belonged to another century, another world. Was it true, then, that at the moment of death a man's whole life passed in review?

He turned his head abruptly, so that the spot of cold that was the muzzle of the rifle slid behind his ear. The corner of his eye caught the face of his guard, and he felt his heart sink. Why, it was only a boy, this African that held the rifle to his head—a Targui lad of thirteen, fourteen, perhaps only twelve. He had been a spindly-legged toddler when the priest had first come to Tamanrasset. His name was Sermi-ag-Thora. His mother used to come to the hermitage for a handful of rice or millet to feed the boy during the drought. . . .

When Charles had been a boy—. No, it could not be just a coincidence. The *bordj* behind him, the little chapel-fortress of sun-dried bricks plastered with mud that held the finger marks of its primitive masons, was almost an exact replica of a sand castle he had built one day when he was little younger than this Targui lad, and which he had destroyed in a fit of temper because some elderly relative had patronizingly suggested he put candles in the bastions and new potatoes in the courtyard in lieu of cannon balls. . . .

He was scarcely aware that someone had tied his hands and feet. He was watching the men tramping in and out of the open door of the *bordj*. They were carrying out the thirty Gras carbines and the six cases of 1874 ammunition, the sacks of wheat, the crates of canned goods, the bolts of cloth. He scanned the faces, hoping he would not recognize any of his friends. He did not see El Madani, although he was sure it was the Hartani's voice which had prompted him to open the door.

From the courtyard came shouts and profanity in Tamashek and Arabic, and the whack and crash of things being smashed.

A bearded Moslem swaggered up to Father de Foucauld, his eyes small with the arrogance of power, his right hand caressing the hilt of a long scimitar, his voice the savage rasp of the prosecutor as he hurled questions at the kneeling priest.

How many Meharists were there in the village? Who were they? When were they returning to Fort Motylinski? How many soldiers at Motylinski? When was the next supply caravan due from In-Salah? How many camels? What were they bringing?

Father de Foucauld said nothing. His lips moved, but no sound emerged. His eyes were closed. There had been indeed two Meharists in the village today—Bou Aisha and Boujema-ben-Brahim. He was praying that they had already gone back to Fort Motylinski. . . .

"And where have you hidden the gold?" screamed the Senusi chief. "And the silver? Everyone in the Sahara knows you are a rich man? Where have you hidden your treasure? Speak up, if you value your life!"

Father de Foucauld opened his eyes. He smiled sadly. He said aloud:

"I say to you, unless the grain of wheat fall into the ground and die, itself remaineth alone; but if it die, it bringeth forth much fruit. He that loveth his life doth lose it, and he that hateth his life in this world shall keep it into everlasting life."

The Senusi stared at the priest with a puzzled expression.

At last Father de Foucauld caught sight of El Madani. He was one of three men escorting a terrified Paul Embarek to the entrance of the *bordj*.

"You are the servant of the Christian Marabout?" demanded Ebeh, the Senusi chief.

Paul was too terrified to reply.

"We know you are the servant of the Marabout," repeated Ebeh. "Tell us where he has hidden the gold and silver."

Paul shook his head, still speechless.

"I suppose you want us to believe you do not even know the Marabout," Ebeh shouted.

Half-dead with fright, Paul Embarek could only shake his head. Then, "It is the will of God," he stammered at last.

Father de Foucauld thought he heard a cock crow somewhere in the village, but it was probably only his imagination.

Then he heard a sentry hail beyond the last bastion of the *bordj*, and this was not his imagination.

"The Arabs!" the sentry called. "The soldiers from the fort."

Father de Foucauld's heart-beat quickened. Was this a patrol from the fort, or was it merely the two Meharists stopping off at the *bordj* to pay their respects to the Marabout on their way back to Motylinski?

A sudden silence fell upon the Senusi raiders. Some of them dropped into the moat, others deployed across the camel tracks leading from the village, crouching, taking cover. The only sounds were the muffled tread of camels and the click of rifle bolts.

The silhouette of two camels loomed in the darkness. They came closer. A single rifle shot cracked. Then another. Then a volley. One Meharist rolled from his camel—Bou Aïsha. Bou-jema-ben-Brahim tried to turn his mehari around, but another fusilade felled him and his camel.

Instinctively Father de Foucauld stiffened, tried to rise to his feet.

The boy behind him was seized with panic. Perhaps there were other Meharists. Perhaps they would rescue the hostage he was guarding. He must not let the *roumi* escape. He pulled the trigger of his rifle.

The report was deadened because the muzzle was so close to the Marabout's head. Father de Foucauld sank back to his knees, slowly toppled to one side and rolled into the moat he had built to protect the poor Harratin of Tamanrasset in case of attack.

The Reverend Father Charles de Foucauld, Viscount de Foucauld de Pontbriand, ex-lieutenant of the Chasseurs d'Afrique, Brother Marie-Albéric of the Trappist Order, Brother Charles of Jesus, only member of the Fraternity of the Little Brothers of the Sacred Heart of Jesus, died as he had lived in the imitation of Christ.

A century and a quarter after the bloody Sunday in the garden of the Carmelite Monastery in Paris, when the Prince-Archbishop of Arles and his cousin and grand vicar, Armand de Foucauld de Pontbriand, had given their lives rather than renounce their faith, the last prayer of the grand vicar was at last granted.

Another Foucauld had died a martyr.

EPILOGUE

*Dieu voit tout, même la petite fourmi noire
dans la nuit noire sur la pierre noire.*

*God sees everything, even the little black
ant on a black rock in the blackness of the
night.*

—Arab proverb
translated by Louis Massignon

I

The Senusis spent the night eating and drinking. They cut up, barbecued and ate the camel of one of the Meharists. They argued for a long time about what to do with the body of the Christian Marabout. Should they carry it off and try to collect the ransom anyhow? Should they hang it from the tree in the wadi where the Marabout's strange instruments hung? Should they feed it to the dogs of the Shikkat Tuareg, the son of whose chief was such a good friend of the Marabout?

They also argued about whether or not to kill Paul Embarek. The Senusis were about equally divided, until the Harratin of the village, aroused at last by the shooting, came to plead for his life.

The Senusis took one more life, however. At daybreak the courier from Fort Motylinski rode up to the *bordj* to collect the Marabout's mail for In-Salah and was shot from his camel.

At noon the murderers trotted away with their loot.

Paul Embarek and some of the Harratin covered the bodies of the Marabout and the three Meharists. Then Paul set off on foot for Fort Motylinski.

Captain de La Roche immediately led a patrol into the desert in pursuit of the Senusis. He intercepted the raiders on December 17, and killed several before they escaped.

The captain returned to Tamanrasset on December 21 with a French sergeant and an Arab Meharist. They filled in the trench in which the four bodies lay, rendered military honors, and erected the plain wooden cross on the grave of Father de Foucauld as he had requested. Captain de La Roche then entered the *bordj*. He found the Father's last letters, sealed and stamped, lying on his camp table, but all the other papers were scattered in confusion about the room. Painstaking collation, however, determined that not a single page of the four volumes of the dictionary or the two volumes of Tuareg verse was missing.

Although the religious fixtures had been tossed about, they had not been damaged. Neither had the Stations of the Cross which Father de Foucauld himself had painted on panels from packing cases. Captain de La Roche found that the Monstrance had been knocked to the dirt floor, and, in his own words, "after puzzling over what to do with the Good Lord," he wrapped it in a white cloth and carried it reverently to Fort Motylinski.

At the fort he consulted a sergeant who had once studied at a seminary. The two Frenchmen then donned white gloves. The sergeant knelt in an act of contrition. Captain de La Roche opened the Monstrance, removed the last Host consecrated by Father de Foucauld, and placed it between the lips of the seminarian-sergeant—the last Communion of the Hermit of the Sahara.

II

When news of Father de Foucauld's death reached France, official Paris was shocked. The Minister of War happened to be General Lyautey, who was not only personally grieved by the murder of his fellow Saint-Cyrien but was the one man in the French War Cabinet who could foresee the long-range implications of the event. He summoned General Laperrine from the front lines for consultation in Paris.

Laperrine had been briefed so regularly and in such detail by his old friend's letters, that he could picture exactly what was going on in the area of his former command, the Sahara. He told Lyautey that Foucauld's estimate of the loyalty of the Hoggar Tuareg was probably correct, and that it was highly unlikely that any of Moussa-ag-Amastane's men had taken part in the assassination plot.

In fact, Moussa was far away in the south and did not learn of the priest's death until nearly two weeks after the murder. He immediately wrote a moving letter of condolence to Mme. de Blic. Dated the 20th day of the month of Safar, the year 1335 after the Hegira (Dec. 13, 1916), and couched in florid Arabic, the letter reached Fort Motylinski on Christmas Day and was translated into French for forwarding to Father de Foucauld's sister:

> The one God be praised.
>
> To her Ladyship Marie, our friend, sister of our Marabout Charles who was assassinated by the treacherous and deceitful people of Ajjer.
>
> From Tebeul Moussa-ag-Amastane, Amenokal of the Hoggar. May great welfare surround the aforesaid Marie.
>
> When I learned of the death of our friend, your brother Charles, my eyes closed and all grew dark for me. I wept many tears and I am in deep mourning. His death has caused me great sorrow.
>
> I am now far from the place where the thieving traitors and deceivers killed him. That is to say, they killed him in the Hoggar and I am in Adrar. But God willing, we will kill these people who killed the Marabout until our vengeance has been fulfilled.
>
> Greet your daughters, your husband, and all your friends on my behalf and tell them this: Charles the Marabout has not died for you alone; he has died for all of us. May God have mercy upon him and grant that we may meet him in Paradise.

Regardless of the loyalty of Moussa, the murder of Father de Foucauld indicated that French authority in the Sahara was in jeopardy. General Laperrine was returned to Africa.

Laperrine carried with him a little notebook in which he had listed all the members of the Senusi razzia that killed the Marabout of the Sahara. Although Father de Foucauld would undoubtedly have forgiven them, not so Laperrine. He sent copies of the list to every garrison and outpost in his command with orders to capture and execute the culprits. It was a long search. Laperrine had scratched out only half a dozen names before he died.

Sermi-ag-Thora, the lad who actually fired the fatal bullet, was caught and shot in 1922.

El Madani fled to Libya and was not apprehended until 1944. Old and blind, he was tried by a court martial of young officers who were still wearing diapers when Father de Foucauld was betrayed and killed. The Hartani swore on the Koran that he had done nothing except call to the Marabout through the door of the *bordj,* that he had done that only because his life was threatened, and that he was home in bed by the time the shot was fired. Possibly because he had not long to live anyhow, he was released.

When Laperrine came to Tamanrasset in December 1917, he had his old friend exhumed. He was surprised to find the body in a perfect state of preservation, and the face quite recognizable. On the other hand, the three Meharists who had been buried near him were in an advanced state of decomposition. Said a Targui who witnessed the exhumation: "It is not surprising, *mon général.* He was a great Marabout."

Laperrine reburied his friend a few hundred yards from the *bordj* and marked the grave with a plain wooden cross according to the hermit's wishes. The three Meharists were buried at his feet with markers at both ends of the graves in Arab fashion.

In 1920 Laperrine finally got permission to make the journey he had planned ever since he and Charles de Foucauld were second-lieutenants together: to cross the Sahara from north to south, to travel from the Mediterranean to Timbuctoo. Transportation methods had changed, however, since the days of the Fourth Chasseurs d'Afrique. This time he was going by air. Flying a biplane with a pilot and mechanic, he developed engine trouble and crashed during a sandstorm in the desolate wastes of Tanezruft, several hundred miles west of the Hoggar. Laperrine was badly hurt and died of thirst two weeks later, just before his companions were rescued. His body was taken to

Tamanrasset by camel and he was buried beside his old friend Charles de Foucauld.

III

The shock of her brother's death, augmented within days by the drowning of her favorite son, affected the mind of Marie de Blic, and she died in 1919 without recovering completely.

Marie de Bondy's château in the Indre Department was burned out in 1918 by a fire that started in her private chapel, destroying everything she owned, including souvenirs Charles de Foucauld had given one of her sons—relics of Saint-Cyr and. Saumur, the Chasseurs d'Afrique and Morocco. She did not long survive.

Ouksem-ag-Shikkat, the young Targui whom Father de Foucauld had taken to France for a lesson in French civilization, quickly unlearned everything the Marabout had hoped to teach him. The fanaticism of the Senusis had greater appeal to him than the family evenings of songs and games at the Blic château in Burgundy. He had apparently been aware of the plot to pillage the *bordj* and kidnap the Marabout but left Tamanrasset rather than take active part in the crime against the man who had befriended him. Thirty-five years later Europeans reported seeing Ouksem near the Sudanese border, a palsied old beggar in rags.

Among the sincere mourners at General Laperrine's funeral in March 1920 was Moussa-ag-Amastane, recently promoted to be officer of the Legion of Honor, and the once-lovely Dassine, now fat and wrinkled. Both died later that same year.

Tamanrasset is still a dreary village, but it now has a tourist hotel open during the winter months, a wireless station, and an airport. It is administrative headquarters for a handful of civil servants in transport and communications, and has a garrison which is called Fort Laperrine.

When I visited Tamanrasset ten years ago, Father de Foucauld's *bordj*-hermitage was being used as a temporary arsenal for Fort Laperrine. And Paul Embarek, a gangling slave of fifteen when the Father had bought his freedom, had only recently died. Until his death, the hardy old man had been acting as guide to winter tourists. For an extra fee, he would recite his eye-witness account of the murder of the Christian Marabout, and point out the spot where the fatal bullet, after passing through the Marabout's head, had lodged in the wall of the *bordj*.

IV

In 1927 proceedings were begun looking toward a possible beatification of Charles de Foucauld. The process of inquiry is an elaborate one, and its dozen or so stages take many years.

One of the first steps was a decision by Monseigneur Gustave Nouet, Apostolic Prefect of Ghardaïa, to move the hermit's lonely grave from Tamanrasset to consecrated ground near the White Fathers' mission at El Goléa. Although this was a direct violation of Foucauld's last will and testament, he was in life always obedient to the wishes of his religious superiors and no doubt would have acquiesced to the three reasons given by the Apostolic Prefect: 1. The Prefecture could more readily exercise effective watch over the venerated remains of Charles de Foucauld. 2. The cost of official authentication, verification, etc., during the process of inquiry would be considerably reduced. 3. The tomb would be more readily accessible to Christians on the Christian frontiers of the Saharan wastes.

On the afternoon of April 18, 1929, the body of Father de Foucauld was disinterred in the presence of Monseigneur Nouet, a delegation of White Fathers, and the military and civil authorities of Tamanrasset. The remains of his heart—only the pericardium had survived disintegration—were placed in a small casket and buried beneath the tall obelisk of Hoggar granite that marked the grave of General Laperrine. The body was wrapped in a new shroud bearing Foucauld's insignia—the Sacred Heart surmounted by the Cross in red, enclosed in a specially-built coffin, and transported to El Goléa by automobile. The hermit's last ride across the desert took only a few days to cover the distance that once took a month.

The tomb at El Goléa is an inclined, massive, six-ton slab of travertine erected by the Catholics of Nancy, city of his youth. Behind it stands an immense Crucifix.

Instead of the nameless grave he had ordered, the Foucauld monument bears a long inscription:

Here, awaiting the judgment of the Holy Church,
lie the remains of the
Servant of God

CHARLES OF JESUS—
VISCOUNT DE FOUCAULD
1858–1916

Died in the odor of Sanctity December 1, 1916,
at Tamanrasset

Victim of his own benevolence
and apostolic zeal.

In 1947 the preliminary process of inquiry into whether or not Father de Foucauld had attained the second degree of sanctity entitling him to public religious honors was terminated and the dossier formally turned over to the Vatican. It was a formidable mass of evidence, including nearly 20,000 documents and other exhibits. The physical labor of examining the evidence was alone an overwhelming job. And as for weighing the controversial matters involved. . . .

Was Father de Foucauld a martyr? Did he die because of his faith or because he was a political symbol of France? Did he die because he lived in abject poverty in imitation of Christ or was he murdered for gain by robbers and cutthroats? He was killed on consecrated ground, true, because the Blessed Eucharist was exposed within the confines of his chapel-*bordj*—but there were also rifles. True, the rifles and the walls of the *bordj* were for protection of his "parishioners" against the enemies of France, and without the protection of France no Christian missionary could hope to carry The Word to the Moslems.

Father de Foucauld had not made a single convert, true. As he had said so often, he was planting the seed. The harvest would follow. And though no Targui abandoned Islam for the Cross, he was universally respected for what he wanted to be—a universal brother. He led a saintly life. To the Moslems he was a holy man—a Marabout.

But in the eyes of the Catholic Church, was he a martyr? Or a saint?

As this book went to press in 1961, the Vatican had not yet spoken.

V

"Unless the grain of wheat fall into the ground and die, itself remaineth alone; but if it die, it bringeth forth much fruit. . . ."

Father de Foucauld had brought no convert to Christ.

Father de Foucauld had died alone. His pleas for someone to share his solitude and carry on his work had gone unanswered.

The grain of wheat had fallen to earth and died.

For nearly twenty years the prophecy according to Saint John remained unfulfilled. The grain of wheat had brought forth no fruit.

Then, in 1933, a group of five young Paris priests, scarcely out of the Saint-Sulpice Seminary, decided that they should go abroad and live among the natives in the tradition of poverty and of Nazareth. They were first drawn by the desert, as was Father de Foucauld, perhaps because it is in the desert that man most feels his insignificance; that in the desert the material things which separate him from God disappear most rapidly. They secured the aid of Monseigneur Nouet, apostolic vicar of Ghardaïa, who welcomed them because they carried with them mimeographed copies of Father de Foucauld's Rule for the Little Brothers of the Sacred Heart of Jesus—1899 version.

Monseigneur Nouet set them up in an abandoned military post at El Abiodh-Sidi-Sheikh in Southern Oran—the Africa of Father de Foucauld's youth. They were far from following the hermit's rule, however. At first they tried to strike a compromise between the Foucauld rule and that of the Carthusian monks. But they did not earn their own living, as prescribed by the Foucauld rule; they lived on remittances from their families. They studied Arabic only an hour a day. It took the ordeal of World War II to make them realize how far from the ideal of Father de Foucauld they were.

Since 1945, however, the Little Brothers of Jesus have indeed found the Sacred Heart of the founder who never lived to bless a follower. They formed workers' fraternities—small groups of men who lived and worked in the slums of Lyons, among the fishermen of Britanny, in the shanty towns of North Africa, and, later, among the miners of Peru and the metal workers of Damascus. They now have fraternities in a score of countries, from England to Japan, but their novices remain true to the desert; they spend their first months in Africa.

The Little Sisters of Jesus, who never materialized during the life of Father de Foucauld, came into being in 1939. Under the direction of Monseigneur Nouet, they began as Saharan nomads in emulation of Brother Charles of Jesus but in later years have also spread throughout the world—from South America to Alaska, from Africa to India and Australia.

Another feminine congregation, the Little Sisters of the Sacred Heart, founded in 1933, is perhaps closest to the ideals of Brother Charles of Jesus. They wear his insignia—the Sacred Heart with superimposed Cross in red—on their white robes. They work with their hands. They spend a third of their days in prayer and contemplation. They nurse the sick and help the poor and oppressed. And their parish stretches from Tamanrasset to Trivandrum, in Southern India.

When Father de Foucauld died, there were forty-nine members of the secular order which he called the Union of the Brothers and Sisters of the Sacred Heart. Only one of them—Member No. One—paid his dues. Member No. One, Professor Louis Massignon, revived the organization in 1928. In 1950 it was called the Pious Union, then the Charles de Foucauld Fraternity, and finally in 1955 the Secular Fraternity of Charles of Jesus. The membership is growing steadily.

In November 1951 Louis Massignon, addressing a meeting of the fraternity, said:

"Foucauld, like the Christ, has left us to complete his passion. It is for us to dream the great dream, to aspire to the great aspirations, that they may be perfected in us. Every day I find new depth in his letters in which he dreamed for me the dreams of which I was as yet unworthy, dreams which are already partially realized in a manner as incredible as it is incommunicable. The essential thing is to remember that our bond, beyond all foreseeable expectation, has been to remain at the disposition of

God, Who is both unforeseeable and imminent. God is absolutely new. He is Master of the Impossible, the Miracle of Miracles.

"Foucauld has left us much bold advice in this respect. 'Fear is the signpost to duty,' he said, by which he meant that we should run to meet danger head-on. Few spiritual guides would dare say as much. Foucauld whose own spiritual guide was thousands of miles away, wanted us to obey the disciplinary command of Saint Ignatius of Loyola, *Perinde ac cadaver.* He was a man of violent action who charged with such headlong momentum that he was alone when he reached the top. And in 1917 everyone insisted that he had failed completely.

"The day the news of his death reached me—I was in the front-line trenches—I understood how wrong they were. He was leading us when he died, and he was so far ahead, that I knew then we would have to work desperately to catch up with him. . . ."

Unless the grain of wheat fall into the ground and die. . . .

BIBLIOGRAPHY

BOOKS IN ENGLISH

BAZIN, RENÉ. *Charles de Foucauld: Hermit and Explorer.* Translated by
PETER KEELAN. London: Burns, Oates & Washbourne, Ltd., 1923.
BODLEY, RONALD V. C. *The Warrior Saint.* Boston: Little, Brown & Co.,
1953.
CAMPBELL, DUGALD. *On the Trail of the Veiled Twareg.* London: Seeley,
Service & Co., 1928.
CARROUGES, MICHEL. *Soldier of the Spirit.* Translation by MARIE-CHRISTINE
HELLIN. New York: Putnam, 1956.
FOUCAULD, CHARLES DE. *Meditations of a Hermit: The Spiritual Writings
of Charles de Foucauld.* Translated by CHARLOTTE BALFOUR. Preface
by RENE BAZIN. London: Burns, Oates & Washbourne, Ltd.
FREEMANTLE, ANNE. *Desert Calling.* New York: Holt, 1949.
GIBBONS, JOHN. *The Very Noble Viscount.* (*Great Catholics*, ed. by C. C.
WILLIAMSON.) London: Nicholson and Watson, 1938.
VOILLAUME, RENÉ. *Seeds of the Desert.* Translated by WILLARD HILL.
Chicago: Fides Publishers Assn., 1955.

BOOKS IN FRENCH

BÉJOT, LIEUT. LOUIS. *L'Assassinat du Père de Foucauld.* Avignon: Aubanel
Frères, 1929.
BERNEX, JULES. *Ceux de la Trappe.* Paris: Flammarion.
BOUCHER, MSGR. A. *La Vie Héroïque de Charles de Foucauld.* Paris: Bloud
et Gay, 1931.
BRÉMOND, JEAN. *Les Pères du Désert.* Paris: J. Gabalda.
BUFFET, EUGÉNIE. *Ma Vie, Mes Amours, Mes Aventures: Confidences
recueillies par Maurice Hamel.* Paris: Figuière, 1930.

CARROUGES, MICHEL. *Charles de Foucauld, explorateur mystique.* Paris, Éditions du Cerf, 1954.

CASTRIES, COMTE HENRY DE. *L'Islam.* Paris: Armand Colin.

CHARBONNEAU, GENERAL JEAN. *La Destinée Paradoxale de Charles de Foucauld.* Paris: Milieu du Monde, 1958.

DERVIL, GUY. *Trois Grands Africains—Lyautey, Laperrine, Foucauld.* Paris: J. Susse.

EYDOUX, HENRI-PAUL. *L'Exploration du Sahara.* Paris: Gallimard.

FOUCAULD, CHARLES DE. *Dictionnaire Touareg-Français (dialecte de l'Ahaggar).* 4 vols. Paris: Imprimerie Nationale, 1951–2.

——. *Dictionnaire Abrégé Touareg-Française.* 2 vols. Algiers: J. Carbonel, 1920.

——. *Évangile à l'Usage des Pauvres Nègres du Sahara.* Ed. by GEORGES GORRÉE. Paris: Arthaud, 1940.

——. *Lettres à Henry de Castries.* Introduction by JACQUES DE DAMPIERRE. Paris: B. Grasset, 1938.

——. *Lettres Inédites au Général Laperrine, Pacificateur du Sahara.* Paris: La Colombe, 1954.

——. *Notes pour servir à un essai de grammaire touarègue.* Ed. by RENÉ BASSET. Algiers: J. Carbonel, 1920.

——. *Père de Foucauld—Abbe Huvelin; correspondance inédite.* Preface by CARDINAL FELTIN. Ed. by JEAN FRANCOIS SIX. Tournai (Belgium): Desclée, 1957.

——. *Poésies Touarègues.* 2 vols. Paris: E. Leroux, 1925–30.

——. *Reconnaissance au Maroc 1883–4.* 2 vols. Paris: Challamel & Cie., 1888.

——. *Reconnaissance au Maroc; augmenté de fragments inédits redigés par l'auteur pour son cousin, François de Bondy.* Paris: Soc. d'Éditions Géographiques, Maritimes et Coloniales, 1939.

FRISON-ROCHE, ROGER. *L'Appel du Hoggar.* Paris: Flammarion.

GARRIC, ROBERT. *Le Message de Lyautey.* Paris: Les Éditions Spès.

GAUTIER, EMIL FELIX. *Trois Héros: Le Général Laperrine, le Père de Foucauld, Le Prince de la Paix.* Paris: Payot, 1931.

GERMAIN JOSÉ and FAYE, STÉPHANE. *Le Général Laperrine, Grand Saharien.* Paris: Plon, 1931.

GORRÉE, GEORGES. *Sur les Traces de Charles de Foucauld.* Paris: Éditions de la Plus Grande France, 1936.

——. *Au Service du Maroc: Charles de Foucauld.* Paris, Grasset, 1939.

——. *Les Amitiés Sahariennes du Père de Foucauld.* Paris, Arthaud, 1946.

——. *Charles de Foucauld, Intime.* Paris: La Colombe, 1952.

GRAULE, COMMANDANT E. *L'Insurrection de Bou-Amama.* Paris: Charles Lavauzelle, 1905.

HÉRISSON, ROBERT. *Avec le Père de Foucauld et le Général Laperrine.* Paris: Plon, 1937.

Howe, Sonia E. *Les Héros du Sahara*. Paris: Armand Colin.

Julia, Elisabeth. *Le Moine sans Clôture*. Paris: Bonne Presse, 1948.

Ladreit de Lacherièrre, Jacques. *Au Maroc en suivant Foucauld*. Paris: Soc. d'Éditions Géographiques, Maritimes et Coloniales, 1932.

Lefranc, Jean. *La Vie du Père de Foucauld*. Paris: Albin Michel, 1942.

Lehuraux, Leon. *Au Sahara avec le Père de Foucauld*. Paris: Éditions Saint-Paul, 1946.

Lesourd, Paul. *La Vraie Figure du Père de Foucauld*. Paris: Flammarion.

Lhote, Henri. *Aux Prises avec le Sahara*. Paris: Les Oeuvres Françaises.

Lyautey, Maréchal Louis Hubert. *Vers le Sud Marocain*. Paris: Armand Colin, 1937.

Maraval-Berthoin, Angèle. *Dassine, Sultane du Hoggar*. Paris: Fasquelle, 1951.

———. *Le Hoggar: Chants, Fables, et Légendes*. Paris: Fasquelle, 1954.

Massignon, Louis. "La Vicomtesse Olivier de Bondy et la Conversion de Charles de Foucauld." *Bulletin de l'Association des Amis du Père de Foucauld*. Paris.

———. "Les Images des Saints Dessinés par Charles de Foucauld en Terre Sainte." *Bulletin de l'Association des Amis du Père de Foucauld*. Paris.

Pichon, Charles. *Charles de Foucauld, le Houzard*. Paris: Éditions de la Nouvelle France, 1945.

Pottier, René. *Un Prince Saharien Méconnu: Henri Duveyrier*. Paris: Plon, 1938.

———. *La Vocation Saharienne du Père de Foucauld*. Paris: Plon, 1939.

Robert, Claude Maurice. *L'Ermite du Hoggar*. Algiers: Bacconier, 1938.

Roulers, Charles. *Le Marquis de Morès*. Paris: Plon.

Schneider, Edouard. *Le Petit Pauvre dans ses Ermitages*. Paris: Grasset.

Vaussard, M. *Charles de Foucauld, Maître de la Vie Intérieure*. Paris: Éditions du Cerf, 1947.

Verge, Gabriel. *Monographie du Domaine de la Trappe de Staouëli*. Algiers: Hentz.

Vermale, Dr. Paul. *Au Sahara Pendant la Guerre Européenne*. Paris: Larose, 1926.

Vignaud, Jean. *Frère Charles*. Paris: Albin Michel, 1943.

Voillaume, René. *Les Fraternités du Père de Foucauld*. Paris: Éditions du Cerf, 1947.

THE AUTHOR AND HER BOOK

MARION MILL PREMINGER'S *life strangely parallels that of her subject. Like Charles de Foucauld, she was born into a family of
moneyed European aristocrats. And as de Foucauld turned to God
and devoted his later life to primitive tribes, Marion Mill Preminger
turned to Africa to devote herself to the lepers of Dr. Albert Schweitzer's jungle hospital. She has served at the hospital in Gabon and
has worked on its behalf in the United States, founding the Albert
Schweitzer Hospital Fund. The author is a world traveler and an
expert on African women's rights. Her collection of primitive
African art is one of the finest in New York. She is also a prominent
lecturer, philanthropist, social worker, and foreign correspondent.
Her autobiography,* All I Want Is Everything, *has appeared in
several languages. Marion Mill Preminger and her work have been
the subject of a number of books. Her friends among the writers
of three continents include Thornton Wilder, who gave her what
she considers her greatest honor—the dedication of his latest play,*
The Alcestiad. *The author is a Chevalier of the French Legion of
Honor. She was also the first woman ever to receive the distinction
of being appointed a Grand Officer of the Etoile Equatoriale, the
highest African award. She is a recipient of the Republic of
Gabon's Grand Medal of Reconnaissance. All of the author's honors
are too numerous to mention. But among them are awards from
the General Federation of Women's Clubs, the New York Federation of Women's Clubs, The Federation of Jewish Women's Or-
ganizations, the American Women's Club, the Club of Printing
Women, of New York, and the Arab Feminist Union. She is also the
recipient of the Golden Heart Award for her hospital work performed "regardless of race, color or creed."*

279

NIHIL OBSTAT

WILLIAM F. HOGAN, s.t.d.
Censor Deputatus

IMPRIMATUR

✠ THOMAS A. BOLAND, s.t.d.
Archbishop of Newark

NEWARK, NEW JERSEY—September 7, 1961

Printed in the USA
CPSIA information can be obtained
at www.ICGtesting.com
JSHW082154140824
68134JS00014B/233